FRANCO CORELLI
AND A REVOLUTION IN SINGING
Fifty-Four Tenors Spanning 200 Years
VOLUME III

Corelli as Dick Johnson in La fanciulla del West, *La Scala, 1964*

Franco Corelli & a Revolution in Singing

Fifty-Four Tenors Spanning 200 Years

Volume 3

by Stefan Zucker

BEL CANTO SOCIETY 2018

© 2018 Bel Canto Society, Inc.

New York and Key Colony Beach

All rights reserved. No part of this book may be reproduced in any form or by any electronic or mechanical means, including storage or retrieval systems, without permission in writing from the publisher, except by a reviewer, who may quote brief passages in a review.

Design: Kate Binder, Abraham Brewster

Frontispiece:

Franco Corelli in *La fanciulla del West,* La Scala, 1964

Photographer:

The Metropolitan Opera Archives

Library of Congress Cataloging-in-Publication Data available on request

ISBN-13: 978-1-891456-01-5

ISBN-10: 1-891456-01-5

BelCantoSociety.org

TABLE OF CONTENTS

- 11 Photographs
- 18 Acknowledgments
- 19 Please Contribute
- 20 Foreword
- 23 An Evening in the Theater with Franco Corelli and Stefan Zucker, Merkin Concert Hall, June 5, 1991
- 43 From Del Monaco to Chris Merritt
- 57   From the March 3, 1990 broadcast
- 77 Booing: True confessions
- 77   Putting Franco's Position in Perspective: Some opera fanatics booed him
- 117 Conversations with Carlo Bergonzi (1924–2014)
- 143 Kraus (1927–99)
- 167 The Origins of Lowered-larynx Techniques
- 169 Jean de Reszke's Larynx-lowering
- 173 Did Caruso Use a Laryngeal Method?
- 175 Some Lessons with Melocchi (1879–1960)
- 177   The Lowered-larynx Mafia
- 179 Corelli's Real View of the Stanley Method
- 181 Some Mario Del Monaco Successors
- 187 My Lessons with Marcello and Mario Del Monaco   Emilio Moscoso
- 190 Del Monaco's Diaphragm

193	A Corelli Student
	Enrique Pina
201	Francisco Araiza (1950–): A Rossini tenor who lowers his larynx
203	Francisco Araiza
205	Aspiration
207	William Matteuzzi and Giuseppe Morino: Unaffected by Del Monaco and Corelli
208	Giuseppe Morino: A voice that stays in the ear
213	Olivero Attacks Del Monaco's Technique
217	Different Singing Techniques
223	The Rise and Fall of Elena Filipova
235	Roberto Alagna on Sometimes Using Mask Placement, Sometimes a Lowered-larynx Technique
249	Bill Schuman
262	Three of Schuman's most prominent tenor pupils
262	Marcello Giordani
264	An email from Stephen Costello
265	Michael Fabiano
270	James Valenti
276	Virginia Zeani
281	Four Lowered-larynx Tenors
281	Jonas Kaufmann: The new Corelli?
285	José Cura
286	Rolando Villazón
290	Walter Fraccaro
293	Mask-Larynx-Hybrid Tenors
293	Vladimir Galouzine
293	Piotr Beczala

295	Mask-Placement Tenors Who Don't Cover
295	Vittorio Grigolo
299	Giuseppe Filianoti
299	Juan Diego Flórez's strengths and weaknesses
304	Lawrence Brownlee and Barry Banks
308	Eric Cutler
311	José Bros
312	Joseph Calleja
317	Mask-Placement Tenors Who Do Cover
317	Álvarez: He now offers catharsis
321	Aleksandrs Antonenko
321	Ramón Vargas
327	Salvatore Licitra
328	Johan Botha
328	Summation
331	Source Notes
342	Some Other Titles from Bel Canto Society
350	Index

Franco Corelli as Don José, in Carmen, *La Scala, 1959*

PHOTOGRAPHS

ADO	=	Adolfo Perez Butron	ENR =	Enrique Pina
ARI	=	Arielle Doneson	JAM =	Courtesy James Valenti
BIL	=	Courtesy Bill Schumann	MET =	The Metropolitan Opera Archives
BCS	=	Bel Canto Society Archive	MIG =	Miguel Lerin
CLA	=	Courtesy Clarissa Lablache Cheer	REG =	Regina Kraft
DEC	=	Decca	SON =	Sony Music
DER	=	Derek Blanks	TAM =	Tamino Autographs
DGG	=	Deutche Grammophon	USJ =	Courtesy Universal Classics & Jazz
ELE	=	Elena Filipova		

4 Corelli in *La fanciulla del West*, La Scala, 1964

22 Franco Corelli in *Gli Ugonotti* at La Scala (TAM)

26 Corelli in 1953 (BCS)

30 Stefan presents Franco with a plaque in honor of his having won an "Opera Fanatic" radio contest for Favorite Tenor of the Century. The celebration took place at Merkin Concert Hall in New York City, June 5, 1991. (REG)

32 Miguel Fleta as Cavaradossi (MET)

34 Corelli as Ernani (MET)

38 Corelli as Roméo in *Roméo et Juliette* (MET)

40 Corelli as Don Alvaro in *La forza del destino* (TAM)

42 Franco Corelli as himself (BCS)

44 Del Monaco as Otello (TAM)
44 Pier Miranda Ferraro as Otello (TAM)
47 Beniamino Gigli as Andrea Chénier (BCS)
49 Aureliano Pertile as Nerone in the world premiere of Boito's *Nerone* (1924) (BCS)
50 Mario Del Monaco as il duca in *Rigoletto*. The part is associated with a light voice. Early in his career Del Monaco sang it. (MET)
51 Jaime Aragall as Roland in *Esclarmonde* (MET)
52 Miguel Fleta as Canio in *Pagliacci* (MET)
52 Francesco Merli as Otello (BCS)
54 Pavarotti as il duca in *Rigoletto* (MET)
54 Gigli as himself (BCS)
56 Caruso as Cavaradossi (MET)
59 Chris Merritt as Idreno in *Semiramide* (MET)
62 Corelli as Andrea Chénier (TAM)
64 Del Monaco as Otello (TAM)
65 Gianni Raimondi as Rodolfo in *La bohème* (MET)
66 Mario Filippeschi (TAM)
67 Björling in Manon *Lescaut* (MET)
67 Richard Tucker as il duca in *Rigoletto*. Although he was a heavy tenor, he sang il duca throughout his career. (MET)
68 McCracken as Otello (MET)
71 Vickers as Otello (MET)
74 Del Monaco as Otello (TAM)
76 Scotto's interpretation of Lady Macbeth was full of interesting inflections and unusual emphases. Adelaide Negri, who sang a couple of the performances, provided the temperament, vocal color and power one associates with the role. I applauded them both.—SZ (MET)
78 Peter Sellars (BCS)
82 I agree with Etienne: the Met should have reengaged Negri (top), Galvany (right) and Deutekom (bottom). (BCS/MET/BCS)
84 Callas as Tosca, March 19, 1965 (MET)
87 Dalis, Fernandi and Sereni (MET)
90 Corelli as Andrea Chénier (TAM)
92 Giuseppe Lugo in *Bohème* (BCS)
94 Tebaldi in *Tosca*'s title role (MET)

95	Gianna D'Angelo as Gilda in *Rigoletto*. I heard her sing a lovely Lucia in Hartford in '61. (MET)
97	Sherrill Milnes as Iago (MET)
97	Carlo Bini as Don Carlo (MET)
98	Giuliano Ciannella (BCS)
99	Morley Meredith as Dappertutto in *Les Contes d'Hoffmann* (MET)
99	Wolfgang Wagner (BCS)
101	Richard Woitach (BCS)
102	Gino Quilico as Belcore in *L'elisir d'amore* (MET)
102	Joanne Grillo as Maddalena in *Rigoletto* (MET)
103	Peter Dvorsky as Gustavo in *Un ballo in maschera* (MET)
104	Ermanno Mauro as Cavaradossi (MET)
104	Livia Budai (BCS)
105	Harry Theyard (BCS)
105	Jean-Pierre Ponnelle (MET)
106	Carol Neblett as Amelia in *Ballo* (MET)
107	Schuyler G. Chapin (MET)
108	McCracken as Gherman in *The Queen of Spades* (MET)
109	Herbert von Karajan (BCS)
113	Kurt Baum as Radamès, Mexico, 1950 (BCS)
115	Corelli in *Turandot* (BCS)
116	Carlo Bergonzi as Rodolfo in *Bohème* (MET)
121	Bergonzi as Turiddu, 1971 (MET)
126	Bergonzi as Riccardo in *Ballo* (MET)
133	Bergonzi and Antonietta Stella in rehearsal for joint Met debuts in *Aïda*, 1956 (MET)
136	Bergonzi as Canio, 1959 (MET)
138	Bergonzi as Chénier with George Cehanovsky as Fléville, 1959 (MET)
139	Bergonzi as Rodolfo in Luisa Miller, 1988 (MET)
140	Bergonzi as Riccardo in *Ballo* (MET)
142	Alfredo Kraus as Roméo, 1986 (MET)
145	Kraus as Tonio in *La Fille du régiment*. That his mouth is lopsided presumably is unintentional. (MET)
147	Kraus as il duca. Notice the position of his mouth and cheeks and his bared upper teeth. (MET)

149 Kraus as Werther (MET)
153 Kraus as Edgardo in *Lucia di Lammermoor*, 1982–83 (MET)
160 Alfredo as Alfredo in *Traviata* (MET)
163 Kraus as Tonio in *La Fille du régiment* (MET)
165 Kraus as Ernesto in *Don Pasquale* (MET)
166 Mario Del Monaco as Lohengrin, La Scala, 1957. By his account he was unsuccessful in the part because it was "too lyric." He performed Siegmund in *Die Walküre*, in Stuttgart in 1966, and contemplated singing Tristan but found that Wagner calls for "falsetto and mezza voce." In the end he forsook German repertory, apart from Siegmund's "Ein Schwert," which he often sang in concert. (BCS)
171 Jean de Reszke (MET)
172 Caruso in 1903 as il duca, in a costume from his Met debut. Many tenors preferred to debut in the role. In 1903 he hadn't yet come to sing at full volume most of the time. (MET)
174 Gastone Limarilli as Dick Johnson in *Fanciulla*. His teachers included Melocchi and Marcello and Mario Del Monaco. (BCS)
178 Franco Corelli and Simona Dall'Argine in *Tosca*, offstage (TAM)
180 Nicola Martinucci as Radamès, Met. He could be stolid onstage. To wake him up in *Manon Lescaut*, Act II, at the Rome Opera in 1994, Elena Filipova took his hands and put them atop her breasts (so she told me). (MET)
181 Elena Filipova in the *Manon Lescaut* in question (ELE)
183 Giuseppe Giacomini. Corelli admired his emission, but he makes me squirm when he is sharp. (MET)
184 Del Monaco as Canio. His upper teeth are covered, his lower teeth are bared, and his jaw is dropped. (MET)
185 Peter Lindroos (TOR)
186 Del Monaco as Don José in *Carmen*, Met, 1952 (MET)
189 Emilio Moscoso as Andrea Chénier (EMI)
190 Enrique Pina. One of the handful of students to study with Corelli for a number of years, he is able to describe his teaching. (ENR)
192 Corelli dropping his jaw in front and in back while covering his upper teeth and lowering his larynx in a 1963 Met *Tosca*. Yet in a photo of a 1964 Met *Bohème*, not shown, he is singing while smiling, with the corners of his lips raised, probably in imitation of Lauri-Volpi, with whom he was studying Rodolfo. (MET)

194 Here is an enlarged version of the photo on p. 192 with Corelli dropping his jaw in front and in back while covering his upper teeth and lowering his larynx in a 1963 Met *Tosca*. (MET)

198 William Matteuzzi (BCS)

200 Francisco Araiza (BCS)

203 Araiza as Belmonte in *Entführung* (MET)

209 Giuseppe Morino as Gualtiero in the Macerata *Pirata* (BCS)

210 Magda Olivero as Violetta in *Traviata* (BCS)

213 Conductor Vincenzo Bellezza and part of the cast of *Fanciulla,* including Olivero, Lauri-Volpi and Giangiacomo Guelfi. Teatro dell'Opera, Rome, 1957 (BCS)

213 Rehearsals for *Francesca da Rimini,* with Gianandrea Gavazzeni, Olivero and Del Monaco, La Scala, 1959 (BCS)

214 Corelli as Raul in *Gli Ugonotti* (TAM)

216 Luigi Lablache and Mario as Dr. Dulcamara and Nemorino in *L'elisir d'amore.* (Mario, a nobleman, was known by the one name only.) He was renowned above all for elegiac singing and for communicating romance. (CLA)

220 Elena Filipova as Elisabetta in *Don Carlos,* Vienna State Opera, 1994 (ELE)

225 Filipova and Martinucci in *Manon Lescaut,* Teatro dell'Opera di Roma, 1994 (ELE)

227 Filipova as Minnie in *Fanciulla,* Canadian Opera Company, Toronto, 2001 (ELE)

230 Elena Filipova in 2010 (ELE)

232 "When I performed blood clots came out of me! I felt the sound in my chest and teeth. But up high, where you need the mask, I couldn't find my sensations. Above high A I couldn't feel the sound at all, on account of the swelling…. Thank God I had the courage to continue to sing with an instrument that no longer was responding and to endure the nastiest and most malicious criticisms."—Roberto Alagna (UCJ)

237 "I'm an autodidact. I learned from listening, from asking myself, "What are they doing in the half second before the sound— 'How are they breathing and placing their voices?' I sing along with Gigli and record myself. That's how I learned to sing. (UCJ)

243 "Singing is my life. I don't sing for money, fame or glory but because it's something essential for me—my therapy. But I'm no prostitute—even if I do something stupid!"—Roberto Alagna (UCJ)

246 Bill Schuman (BIL)

253 Giordani and Schuman (BIL)

256 Voice teacher Giovanni Battista Lamperti. According to his assistant William Earl Brown, Lamperti, although married, was homosexual, so he moved from Milan to Dresden, where he felt more comfortable. His absence changed the course of singing in Italy. Among other things top-of-the-head placement fell by the wayside, and covering became nearly ubiquitous among men. (BCS)

263 Costello, Giordani and Schuman backstage at Carnegie Hall, November 9, 2005, after a performance of *Guillaume Tell* in which Giordani encored his fourth-act cabaletta and Costello made his professional debut. (BIL)

265 Michael Fabiano (ARI)

266 Schuman, Giordani and Valenti, backstage after the Richard Tucker Gala, November 14, 2010, in which Giordani and Valenti had sung. Valenti had won the Tucker award that year. (JAM)

267 James Valenti (JAM)

275 Zeani in her signature role, Violetta in *Traviata*. Although the photo may be posed, from the look of her face you can sense that she is placing well down in the mask, including the cheeks. Notice her bared teeth and hint of a smile. (MET)

278 Jonas Kaufmann: In German opera he feels the words. In Italian opera he doesn't and is gutteral. (MET)

281 Jonas Kaufman (SON)

283 José Cura as Turiddu in *Cavalleria rusticana*. He too lowers his larynx. (MET)

285 Rolando Villazón (DGG)

289 Walter Fraccaro (DGG)

290 Vladimir Galouzine: He switches back and forth between lowering his larynx and placing in the mask.

295 Vittoro Grigolo. He is evocative of Schipa. He places in the mask and seldom covers. (MET)

296 Juan Diego Flórez: He places in the mask and doesn't cover. But he simplifies and transposes *Sonnambula*. (DEC)

303 Lawrence Brownlee (DER)

307 Eric Cutler

309 José Bros (MIG)

313 Joseph Calleja: He too places in the mask and doesn't cover. But he simplifies and transposes "Son geloso." (DEC)

316 Marcel Álvarez: He places in the mask and abruptly covers in the *passaggio* and above. But today he sings with personality and passion. (DEC)

321 Ramón Vargas: He can be wonderful when he doesn't blunt the freshness and focus of his tone by covering heavily to try to sound more appropriate for heavy repertoire. (ADO)

324 Salvatore Licitra: He places in the mask and covers heavily not only in the *passaggio* and above but sometimes in the middle. His one feeling is pathos.

327 Duprez: He provided momentum for the trend to sing with a massive darkened tone. That trend was furthered by Caruso and Del Monaco. Their influence endures. (BCS)

ACKNOWLEDGMENTS

Without the kindness and generosity of a number of people this book could not have been published. To them I owe a debt that I acknowledge with pleasure.

For their generous contributions to Bel Canto Society toward the publication of vol. 3:

Susan Gulesian
C. C. Stavrou
Gary Giardina, opera mourner
Vinicio Romagnoli, Cremona, Italy
Bianca Maria Orlanda and The Marlot Foundation
John Borders
Jane DeRocco
Rita Gendelman and James Altman
Alexander Haas
Roland Hirsch
Phyllis Hirshleifer
Cynthia Hoffman
John Miller
Tobias Mostel
Howard Mounce
Glenn Purdy
Peter Rabinowitz
R. Victor Sulkowski
Karen Toepper
Colin Ungaro
Aleksandr Yufa
Jolee Zola

John Pennino of The Metropolitan Opera Archives for unstinting document and photo research, for supplying photos and documents

The late Robert Tuggle, formerly the Director of The Metropolitan Opera Archives, for enabling the research

Néstor Masckauchan and Tamino Autographs

Marian Tepper Stern, proofreader

Abraham Brewster and Kate Binder, for design and type

PLEASE CONTRIBUTE

The market for opera books has contracted. Commercial publishers have given up on them, and university presses are publishing very few and not spending much on them. In recent years the most active was Northeastern University Press. But they are selling off existing inventory for all their titles (not only opera ones) and are not printing anything. We are the only ones willing to publish large-scale opera books on high-quality paper, with a view toward keeping them in print over many years. Please see information about our forthcoming titles, beginning p. 342.

The University of California Press recently published *Grand Opera: The Story of the Met* by Charles Afron and Mirella Jona Affron, funded by the Ahmanson Foundation. The Metropolitan Opera Archives contributed documents and photographs to the book although not to the extent that it is doing with ours.

Why can't we obtain funding from the Ahmanson Foundation? Because it restricts itself to supporting only organizations based in Los Angeles. The point is that today opera books require subvention.

I work on our books day and night and have put six years of my life and $70,000 of my money into writing the Corelli books and nineteen years and many thousands of dollars into writing the Gigli book, and my resources are depleted. (Much of the money went into photo acquisition as well as type and design.) That is why I'm seeking funding from you.

Like The Metropolitan Opera, Bel Canto Society is a 501(c)(3) not-for-profit corporation incorporated in New York State. Contributions to it are tax deductible to the full extent of the law.

Please contribute generously.

Thank you,
Stefan Zucker
President
Bel Canto Society, Inc.
370 Third Street #424
Key Colony Beach, FL 33051

FOREWORD

What are the choices that caused singing to evolve?

As we have seen in vols. 1 and 2, Del Monaco by his account began his career as a Gigli imitator. But he and Corelli came to reject sweet-tenor singing. In Corelli's words, romantic tenors sounded like adolescent boys. He and Del Monaco made them sound like fifty-year-old men.

He and Del Monaco each tried to block the other's career. Corelli even said that if he saw Del Monaco he might sock him in the jaw.

Del Monaco rejected mask placement in favor of singing with his larynx held low. Corelli started out with that technique but then modified it so that his larynx "floated." Later he took up mask placement but then reverted to using the floating larynx.

Corelli said the music was paramount. Di Stefano said the words were more important.

Gigli sang open, closed and covered to achieve chiaroscuro.

But in this volume Bergonzi demonstrates that he used degrees of covering to sound more dramatic. Kraus rejects covered singing altogether. Bergonzi insists that true Verdi singing is covered. But Tamagno, who was coached by Verdi and created Otello, never covered.

Today's tenors trace their approaches to Del Monaco, Corelli, Bergonzi or Kraus.

Ordinarily singers study with a teacher because a friend recommends him or because a school assigns him. In essence the technique a singer ends up with is determined by a role of the dice. These volumes make clear the choices singers have with regard to interpretation and technique.

As we have seen, across the years singers interpreted and sounded very different from those of today. For example, they made rubatos where today's singers wouldn't. Their interpretations were far freer with regard to tempo, rhythm and the notes performed. Their vibratos were different.

They sang passages in head tones where today's singers use chest tones. They used a great amount of variety of dynamics, whereas most today sing as loud as they can most of the time. Many of them sang with bright tones, whereas many today sing with dark or rounded tones. They imbued words with feeling, whereas many today instead concentrate not only on darkened sonorities but also on volume. To monitor their voice productions for the most part they relied on sensations, whereas many today instead manipulate their organs of phonation—the position of the larynx, the soft palate, the tongue, the cheeks, the head, the nostrils, the lips, the sternum, the buttocks, the rib cage and more.

The volumes also show singers and public the depth of reflection that such superstar singers as Corelli, Bergonzi, Kraus and Alagna engage in to accomplish their goals. In this vol. today's most prominent voice teacher, Bill Schuman, who teachers a huge number of Met singers, sets forward his teaching and the reasons why he makes certain choices.

This vol. provides singers with a choice of models. Singers perform the way they do because of their studies. When fans cheer one singer or boo another, they are approving or condemning a singer's underlying philosophy of how to sing.

Across the decades Bel Canto Society has developed a worldwide following of people interested in the history of singing. These three vols. attempt to deepen their understanding of the subject by discussing the choices and tradeoffs that caused tenor singing to evolve, from the late eighteenth century until today.

Franco Corelli in Gli Ugonotti *at La Scala*

AN EVENING IN THE THEATER WITH FRANCO CORELLI AND STEFAN ZUCKER, MERKIN CONCERT HALL, JUNE 5, 1991 (THE FIRST OF FIVE SUCH EVENINGS IN VARIOUS THEATERS)

Stefan Zucker: On Saturday's "Opera Fanatic" broadcast [on the Columbia University radio station, WKCR-FM, New York] we played a recording with you of *Adriana* from the San Carlo in 1959. Your middle voice struck me as fuller, as more baritonal, than it became in the early 70s. Do you agree this was so?

Franco Corelli: Yes. The repertory I was singing wasn't as high as it later became. The theaters came to believe in me more and gave me more difficult operas beginning with *Il pirata* by Bellini to the point that we made some transpositions because for spinto tenor it's very difficult to sing some D-flats and maybe one D-natural. Not that one or two are difficult, but because there were four, five or six we had to transpose it. The tessitura is very high in *Pirata*.

SZ: Some have viewed the climax of your career as *Gli Ugonotti* at La Scala in '62. How did the performances of *Ugonotti* come to pass, and how did you feel about the part of Raul?

FC: *Ugonotti* was my finest moment, my most beautiful success, for never did I see the public standing and applauding for so long as after the gran duo with Simionato. They applauded for more than twenty minutes. This means something very good and important. It was the most beautiful answer I ever received from the public and the crowning of my studies. I had been very nervous about accepting the assignment. When I looked at the score, I thought this is almost two operas in one. But Maestro Gavazzeni, a musicologist, made some cuts and the night was unforgettable. La Scala found Sutherland, Simionato, Cossotto, Ghiaurov. Even the comprimarios [the singers of supporting roles] were of the first category. Not only were the performances sold out, but thousands were turned away, for the work is very interesting. Even if the music isn't really important—a music that goes directly to the heart—Meyerbeer still was a great musician who wrote memorable pages in this opera and knew how to compose so as to satisfy the public.

SZ: After the *Ugonotti* performances the world expected that you would undertake heroic roles. That had been the pattern for tenors: when a tenor had success in heroic parts, he continued in the same vein. You surprised everybody by undertaking French repertory calling for a relatively light voice.

FC: After *Ugonotti* they asked me to undertake *Guglielmo Tell*. *Ugonotti* is difficult, but you arrive at the high notes little by little via a beautiful legato, without forcing. *Guglielmo Tell* is heroic, more rhythmic. In *Tell* leaps between the middle voice and high voice were too difficult. It doesn't have the legato of *Ugonotti*, which would make the music easier for a throat such as mine. Also, for me to do *Guglielmo Tell* would require six or eight months of study because the opera is very difficult. For voices such as Giacomo Lauri-Volpi or perhaps Mario Filippeschi it was easy, but not for my voice. I needed time, which I didn't have, so in the end I didn't accept the part.

SZ: Why did you undertake Rodolfo, which in Italy at least ordinarily is the province of tenors considerably more lyric, as well as parts such as Faust, Roméo and Werther?

FC: Rodolfo was my first lyric role, and I really liked it. I must repeat a phrase said to me by Lauri-Volpi. When he was about 84 or

85 I asked him, "What is the role in which you take the greatest pleasure?" "Rodolfo," he said. I asked, "Why." He said, "I'm an old man, but inside I'm Rodolfo." I too like the opera, maybe because it reflects youth, it exudes youth, and has beautiful phrases, beautiful *slanci* [surges]. The beautiful surge of the part appealed to me.

SZ: Did the Italians ask why is this dramatic tenor doing a light part? Did they say this is not the voice for Rodolfo?

FC: In that epoch and before, we divided tenors into four categories: lirico-leggero, lyric, lirico-spinto and dramatic. Tenors in each of these categories have their particular roles. It was not customary for a tenor from one category to invade another. The maestros wouldn't permit it. Singers were expected to sing with their voices. It was known that Puccini wrote Johnson for lirico-spinto, Rodolfo for lirico, Calàf for spinto tenor. The classifications of voices were more rigid than now.

SZ: After 1962, after *Ugonotti*, why did you mostly stay in America?

FC: I had taken an apartment and put in soundproofing. Because of it I am able to sing without people outside going "Ooooo!!" In Milan some people went outside my house while I was singing and repeated my phrases. I became so nervous that I stopped singing. On the Met tour I had to sing in hotels, which was a real problem. To warm up my voice I needed an hour to an hour and a half. My voice wasn't always ready for singing in a theater.

Anyway, I was happy to stay here—perhaps because the Met gave me nice operas and nice fees.

SZ: But in Italy you took part in many important exhumations, whereas here you sang *Trovatore*, *Ernani*, repertory operas. You didn't revive operas unless one considers *Roméo* and *Werther*, which were little known here at that time. Were you tired of learning all those new scores?

Corelli in 1953

FC: The maestro who was in love with exhuming operas that had lain dormant for 100 years was Francesco Siciliani. Each season he sought out a forgotten opera for the Maggio Musicale fiorentino. Thus I came to sing *Agnese di Hohenstaufen* [Spontini] and *Guerra e pace* [Prokofiev]. I was glad to study these works as well as *Pirata* and *Ugonotti*—I was a quick learner, and doing so represented a very agreeable coronation with excellent artists and choreographies. *Pirata*, for example, had not been given at La Scala since Gigli [1935]. I loved doing it—it really was an interesting night.

SZ: Please tell us about singing *Turandot* with Nilsson.

FC: I sang *Turandot* with her for fourteen or fifteen years, and believe me it was tough, for she had an important strong voice. I did *Turandot* with many sopranos, but I don't think that since she undertook the role there has been anyone in her league.

Frank Darby, a member of the audience: Reviewers have called you the prince of tenors, but I disagree. You are the king of tenors. Maria Callas played an important role in your life; she helped you, did she not, in connection with your La Scala debut?

FC: Yes. My repertory was still extremely limited. I was very young to sing an opening night at La Scala, something that in that epic was very important. Three people insisted I sing Centurione di Cigno, the tenor in *Vestale*, at La Scala: Callas, Votto and Visconti.

Giuseppina Gosman: I was one of your biggest fans in the 60s; you're the reason I came to love opera. Two years ago in my town of Little Falls there was a very wonderful tenor who said he was studying with you. Are you teaching now? Can you give us a name or two of singers we may one day see at the Met?

FC: I don't enjoy teaching because I don't like sitting for hours at the piano. I must move. The first time I went to see a friend sing in a room in Pesaro, I opened the door and there was an old man with white hair in front of the piano. This image remains in my mind. I don't want to finish my life in this way.

Mel: Would you like to say something to young people who are going to pursue singing?

FC: Study well with a good teacher. Don't run around from teacher to teacher, but find one who's good for your voice. Make some sacrifices. After you finish your studies, assuming the outcome has been good, you'll need immense good luck to make a career.

SZ: I think your real position, as it has emerged in various conversations, is that it's very difficult to make generalizations. Instead, you prefer to tailor advice to individual singers.

Judd Jones: I never was into opera until I went to the old Met and heard you and Leontyne Price do *Il trovatore*. I was appearing on Broadway in the play *The Royal Hunt of the Sun*. A friend of mine connected with the Met got me tickets. I've never been so overjoyed as seeing you two try to outscream one another. You did it so magnificently that I got into opera and followed you and Leontyne Price through the years. I'd like to ask, why did you quit so soon?

FC: I had many beautiful nights with Price. I met her before we came to the Met, at the Arena di Verona when we did *Aïda* together. Afterwards I did many operas with her; she was and remains a wonderful soprano. Her voice still is all there. With regard to quitting, I was singing too much. My throat was a little tired but more, my nerves were broken. I tried to relax for three months, but that didn't help. When I began to rest for the three months I thought I would return afterwards. I was a bundle of nerves; I wasn't eating or sleeping. I was very nervous. After three months I had no desire to sing. Jerome Hines said to me, "Why don't you sing?" I said, "I really don't want to." Although the voice was there. I had the same problems as three months before. I preferred to relax and not think of singing.

SZ: Before going onstage tonight we both were suffering the tortures of the damned. For me it was very much like walking onto the stage here [Merkin Concert Hall] to sing a performance, with one important difference. Two days ago I was in wonderful voice; tonight I have allergies. If I had to sing it would go badly. That I'm speaking with difficulty is less important. But the physical problems of nerves were the same. Franco, once you came onstage, you relaxed totally and came to feel at home. You don't seem to be particularly nervous now. After this trial, do you think you could make a return?

FC: Singing is easier than this because I have the score. I'm always nervous when I go onstage. So is everyone else. I sang with important artists. Each one was nervous, indeed trembled. Some turned white; others perspired. I was very nervous because you have in front of you a theater such as the Met with 4,000 people, each asking from you your best. For example, they were accustomed to hear me hold the high note at the end of the first act of *Turandot*. If I didn't, they came to my dressing room and asked me why didn't you do it? Singing always is difficult. The public demands more and more of you, and if one night you don't deliver, they come to you and ask why.

SZ: For nine years on WKCR we've had singer popularity contests, and they've been publicized widely by *USA Today*, *New York Magazine*, *The New York Times*, *The Newark Star-Ledger*, a total of about twenty publications. For the first time a living singer won one of the historical contests. By historical contests I mean not a contest of current singers such as Domingo, Pavarotti, etc. but of singers throughout the century. And that singer is of course Franco Corelli. I thought I would take the opportunity on everybody's behalf to present him with an award. The plaque reads "Franco Corelli was voted Favorite Tenor of the Century by the listeners of 'Opera Fanatic' in 1989-90." The contest took nearly two years. He received 185 out of 600 votes,

Stefan presents Franco with a plaque in honor of his having won an "Opera Fanatic" radio contest for Favorite Tenor of the Century. The celebration took place at Merkin Concert Hall in New York City, June 5, 1991. Because Franco considered his looks "spoiled" nearly all the photos of us were shot from a distance.

or 30.8 percent of the vote. There were 47 singers who received votes, and the plaque says, "Presented June 5, 1991, at Merkin Concert Hall by Stefan Zucker." On behalf of us all, Franco, it's my privilege.

FC: Thank you very much. I'm very glad to receive this plaque. This means that my New York fans haven't forgotten me.

Ben Scott: In 1954, when you sang *Vestale* with Callas, would you have imagined that a mere eleven years later you'd be singing *Norma* with her, with her voice really broken? In retrospect, would you have had advice for her that possibly could have saved her voice, and did she ever give you advice that helped or possibly hurt your voice?

FC: I think Callas sang well until she met Onassis. Then she became one of the beautiful people and forsook a singer's life, staying up until 2 or 3 in the morning, laughing, maybe drinking. That is not good for the artist. I met Callas at the beginning of my career and admired her voice and acting. By simply staying near her you could learn many things from doing what she did. I tried to answer what she did onstage in the same way, in the same manner, in the same style.

Dielda Kunc: How did you like singing with my sister-in-law, Zinka Milanov?

FC: I sang with her early in my career in about '56. We did *Tosca* in London. She was a wonderful singer. I admired her beauty. I also admired her style and technique. She had a voice that was both free and beautiful. I loved to sing with her. Later we did *Gioconda* and *Chénier*.

SZ: You, of course, were notorious for being nervous. Because of your nerves, did you ever have problems when onstage?

FC: Yes. Every time I sang *Bohème*, in the fourth act I forgot the muff.

Ralph Marino: Did anyone ever try to use hypnosis to help you with your nervousness?

FC: No, I never tried hypnosis, maybe because I was content to stop my career. When I began my career it was not that I had at my disposal all the vocal means that an artist could have. I had studied for less than two years. At that time they needed a spinto tenor to sing parts sitting in the middle register, such as *Carmen*, *Tosca* and *Norma*.

Miguel Fleta as Cavaradossi. To perfect his diminuendo, Corelli not only listened to but also sang along with Fleta's recording of "E lucevan le stelle."

Auditioning is more difficult than simply studying singing, for today there are not as many theaters as sixty years ago. You have to be lucky to make a career.

Neil Eddinger, New York City Opera baritone, New York City: *Lei è una gloria d'Italia* [You are a glory of Italy—wild applause]. I was lucky enough to hear you in nine of your roles at the Met: Chénier, Don José, but one of the most memorable moments was in *Tosca*, in "E lucevan le stelle." You did an incredible diminuendo. Many who know your voice only from records might think this an engineer's trick, but you did it in every performance in which I heard you. How?

FC: At the beginning of my career, I always pushed my voice. I listened to recordings of Miguel Fleta and imitated him. I tried to open my throat and emit a sound like his.

Esther Braun: I have particularly fond memories of you in *Turandot*—your voice, your presence and your costume with the long red cape. You have so many fans, would you consider giving a concert at this time?

FC: It's not singing that worries me, but singing as I did before.

An audience member: Why don't you at least sing Neapolitan songs?

SZ: Let me share my observations since I've heard Franco Corelli sing several times this past year. It's not that he's worse than before, but he's different, subtler, with more *mezze voci* and diminuendos, more gradations of every kind. As I see it, his real fear is that he might not be in perfect voice for this comeback, because of the misfortunes of the day, the kinds of things that can defeat a singer during the course of a week or a day. And he can't stand the idea of being heard at less than his best.

FC: It's true.

Corelli as Ernani

Charlotte Gilbert: Franco Corelli, I've been in love with you for years. You are my favorite tenor. I was wondering who your favorite tenor was, other than yourself of course.

FC: The choice is between Domingo and Pavarotti.

SZ: Don't believe him. [Audience laughter]. Your favorite tenor of the century?

FC: I heard many beautiful tenors and sang in the 50s when there were a number of them, including Gigli. His *falsettone* was angelic. When I went to Florence for my first competition, I heard Gigli sing *L'elisir* entirely in *falsettone*. I've never heard a voice so beautiful.

Goeffrey Riggs: In the earlier part of your career you sang such bel canto roles as Sesto in *Giulio Cesare*, Gualtiero in *Pirata*, Poliuto, Pollione. Which one was the most demanding in terms of flexibility and agility?

FC: The most difficult passage I did was "O dolci baci, o languide carezze" from *Tosca*. It was also the most interesting because the public understood what I was doing. It was difficult to do softly and sweetly late in an evening of singing full voice. But I always did it that way, even when I wasn't at my best. It always was one of the more exciting passages I did, but every opera has challenging, beautiful, difficult moments. If you are in love with your profession, you are glad and happy to undertake them.

Daniel Salzberg: I've been in love with your singing for many years. Can you think of one American tenor of the first quality in the last forty years, and why isn't there such an example?

FC: I admired Richard Tucker, who had a beautiful voice. He respected the audience and dedicated his life to singing.

Fabio Osaben, Italian baritone: I always was very impressed with your diminuendo at the end of "Celeste Aïda." I'd like to pay honor to you and that note in particular with a little something that I made. That particular note was one of the most exciting moments on the opera stage. This is a little something for you in return for the many years of enjoyment.

SZ: I have before me a very lovely painting. There's a paper attached to it that says, "A Franco Corelli in onore del suo Radamès." [To Franco Corelli in honor of his Radamès] Sincerely, Fabio Osaben. On the left half of the painting there's an Egyptian motif, on the right a portrait of Franco Corelli. The painting is done in gold, white and green. It's an extraordinary work.

FO: I've heard you so many times, but I have a magnificent wife sitting here who never has heard you sing. It would be fabulous for her if she could hear you perform, even once.

Ann Plegianos: Of all the roles you've done which has touched your soul the most?

FC: If I had to choose one, it would be *Carmen*. It was my first opera, the one I did more than any other, and the one that remains most in my heart.

Chris Stavrou: Which opera houses have the best acoustics and which have the worst?

FC: Italian houses from the seventeenth and eighteenth century for me were the best. I also liked the old Met although I don't dislike the new one. If I had to single out one for sound, it would be La Scala.

John D. Vorenzo: Do you still go to the opera today? Do you have thoughts on miking singers in opera performances?

FC: I never heard a performance that was amplified.

Diana Fanizza: Not only are you the greatest tenor in all our hearts, but you are still, as we can see with you standing there, the handsomest man in the world. [applause]

Kenneth Lane, dramatic tenor: I heard you in 1961 in *Carmen*, where you made a wonderful diminuendo on the A-natural, and you reveled in it.

Anthony Coggi: You've done a number of French operas. When they were first announced, a number of people felt that an Italian tenor could not do justice to them. I always felt you brought an Italianate quality to, say, Werther or Roméo. To what extent does the French language color your interpretation? Did you interpret Don José differently when you sang it in French than when you sang it in Italian?

FC: I sang José better in Italian, because in Italian I can open my throat so that the sound emerges freely. Pronouncing in French tires my throat. I sang José many times in Italian before undertaking it in French, but I did Roméo, Werther and Faust only in French. I only recorded Faust but never sang it in the theater. When I sang in French I tried to keep my throat open as if I were singing in Italian. Italian is the perfect language for singing.

Anna Schumate: Let me say something I've wanted to say for years. Thank you for giving me supreme joy every time I listen to one of your recordings.

Filippo Compo: Did you have your breath support at the beginning of your career, or did you develop it as you went along?

FC: I found that right away. It is the basis for everything.

Bert Wechsler, editor of *Music Journal*: There was a period at the Met where many commentators thought you were singing repertoire

Corelli as Roméo in Roméo et Juliette

more natural for Nicolai Gedda, and he was forced to sing your repertoire. What are your thoughts about this switch of repertoire and about Gedda?

FC: I heard Gedda many times. He was really wonderful, particularly in *Puritani*, in Florence. He was wonderful for emission, technique, style, figure and musicality.

Donald Foul: Do you feel you were treated kindly by the New York music critics?

FC: I never concerned myself with them. Please keep in mind that Callas every night had more unfavorable than favorable reviews. I try to sing with my own qualities. No one is perfect. I tried to do my best; I knew I wasn't perfect. No one is.

SZ: Franco Corelli leads an extremely complicated interior life. Since his first appearance on my show, February 3, 1990, we've been written up quite a few times in this country and Canada. I usually cannot even bring him to read the write ups, even though they mostly express ecstasy about the possibility of a Corelli comeback.

John Ely, tenor: Mr. Corelli, I've been your fan since the late 50s, when I heard you sing *Turandot* with Nilsson and Stokowski, in Boston. I've always heard that you had an abnormal palate, that you were born with it very high up and that therefore it was easy for you to sing super-high notes without working at them as other singers do. Is that right?

FC: I think high notes come from the vocal cords, not the palate. [laugher]

Jerome Hines, basso, Scotch Plains, NJ: Italians don't make the error we do of calling them high notes, they call them acute notes. Recently I found myself in possession of one of those tapes we're

Corelli as Don Alvaro in La forza del destino

not supposed to have, of *La forza* with Corelli, Price, Merrill and Hines. I must say in all honestly that I thought Price, Merrill and Hines did pretty good. Franco Corelli sounded like somebody had come down from Valhalla to sing with us mortals. I know that the runner up in the contest for Favorite Tenor of the Century was Jussi Björling, with whom I sang many times. The first opera recording I ever bought was with Jussi. On that recording he sounded like six tenors wrapped into one. If you want to make a judgment, talk to somebody who sang onstage with these people. Jussi was a magnificent technician with a beautiful voice, but when you went out into the theater, it was very light. Franco's voice had everything—he is the tenor of the century. [applause]

I've been wanting to ask you this for the last fifteen or twenty years: There was a performance in Atlanta, GA, on the Metropolitan Opera tour. We got the word at 7:30 that something had happened and that you were very upset with Mr. Bing, that you had left your apartment at 2:30 and hadn't come back. Loretta called Mr. Bing and said, "I don't know if he's going to come to the performance or not." So we all were wondering who the tenor was going to be that evening. Mr. Bing, in a fit of repentance, had prepared a giant table of food in Franco's dressing room because he had not eaten dinner. We started the show at 20 after 8; I'm sitting at my table in the *Bohème*, Franco comes in, sits down, and I say, "Come va?" He says, "Male, la vocé è ingolata" [Bad, my voice is stuck in my throat.] I come offstage. He sings "Che gelida manina" like the father eternal. It was incredible. The audience went insane! I was standing there smirking next to Mr. Bing, as the audience was screaming their heads off. I said, "Well, Mr. Bing, was it worth waiting for?" He looked at me and said [imitates Bing], "Unfortunately, yes." Franco, I wonder if you would confide in us now: what did Bing do that afternoon that made you so angry with him?

FC: Mr. Bing was speaking with me about the contract, and something was wrong—money. [audience laughter] He insisted that I accept what he offered. I didn't accept and, in leaving his room, said, "OK. If you don't give me more money, I'll not sing tonight." I walked some distance from the hotel and thought no one would find me. But my wife and Zeritsky and Elman turned up in a car and said, "C'mon, Franco, it's ten of eight." I accepted in order to save the performance. I arrived at my dressing room and found that Mr. Bing had set a table with four platters of food. That was his way of calming me.

Franco Corelli as himself

FROM DEL MONACO TO CHRIS MERRITT

The following conversation is excepted from the May 12, 1990 "Opera Fanatic" broadcast. Audio for this program is available as a Digital Download and on VHS at belcantosociety.org.

FC: Del Monaco had a great deal of *squillo* [ring or ping]. Although he made his center extremely dark, his voice was made of bronze and steel and rang.

SZ: By the late 50s, according to me, he became constricted in the *passaggio* (the area of the voice where head resonance begins to predominate over chest resonance). Do you agree?

FC: Yes.

SZ: What caused that?

FC: Sometimes to open too much in the *passaggio* and to sing too loud there can be dangerous. And he found that if he took care with the *passaggio* without spreading his voice, without dispersing energy, it was a useful thing for his high notes.

SZ: In a radio program about twenty-five years ago Martinelli said that it is important to keep the *passaggio* concentrated. When people speak of the *passaggio*, unless they define it differently to deal with special cases, they usually mean notes in the area of D up until about G. Different singers have *passaggios* located in slightly

Del Monaco as Otello

Pier Miranda Ferraro as Otello

different places. Would you care to tell us where your *passaggio* is?

FC: F, F-sharp.

Del Monaco's brother studied in part with Melocchi and, as a teacher, followed Del Monaco's advice, Del Monaco being the path breaker for Melocchi's method. Del Monaco always said he had revised Melocchi's method to a degree. Only because of study did Del Monaco succeed. When he went to Melocchi he did not have a big voice. On the contrary, his voice was rather small. However, he studied with Melocchi for many years and emerged with an immense voice. If he went in with a twenty in terms of volume he emerged with a ninety. I looked upon him as a maestro because he had studied with Melocchi for a long time and went before me. But there are others besides Melocchi who taught the laryngeal method, even if it was Del Monaco who carried the banner throughout the world, because he applied Melocchi's method 100 percent. There were a number of similar tenors: Turrini had a laryngeal method. Francesco Merli was another singer who sang entirely from the larynx, although he didn't study with Melocchi. Even some singers before Melocchi were using essentially the same method. Lauri-Volpi sang that way as if by nature and had the perfect voice, if not in sweetness then in emission.

SZ: In what sense do you mean emission?

FC: The purity of the notes. [He demonstrates "ah" with a lowered larynx.] Lauri-Volpi's sound from a technical point of view was perfection. It emanated directly from his larynx in this way.

Pier Miranda Ferraro, a tenor who divided Otello with Del Monaco during my time, also sang from the larynx. Although he was not quite a celebrity, he was a very good singer. A certain Merola sang that way. I heard him; he had a tremendously beautiful voice. Gastone Limarilli sang from the larynx, as does Giuseppe Giacomini, who has high notes that are produced from the larynx and are truly exceptional.

SZ: Were you able to speak with Del Monaco? Were you friendly at all?

FC: We were not very friendly, but many times I went to the mountains near to Del Monaco, and I always called on him, and we always ended up speaking about vocal technique.

SZ: You were a rival to him, no?

FC: I don't think so because there are more theaters than good singers, so you don't run into one another that much. When one is in New York the other is in Milan.

SZ: No one disputes that with a lowered larynx one can sing powerfully, but can one sing sweetly or color one's voice? I'm of the opinion that many of those—you being the exception—who lower their larynxes have a brassy sound. With some of these voices it's as if a pitch has both 441 vibrations and 439 vibrations at the same time. The pitch itself becomes fattened or spread. [He shakes his head in disagreement.] In any event my question is, with the laryngeal technique can one color one's voice?

FC: Yes, if you master the laryngeal technique perfectly you can do all the nuances you want: sweet singing, *chiaro* and *scuro*, strong singing, hard tones. But the voice needs to be free with a good emission. The voice needs to have a percentage of laryngeal sound. The laryngeal sound makes the voice sound like a man. The larynx needs to be lowered a touch for the voice to sound masculine. Otherwise it sounds isolated.

SZ: Maybe the objection to lowered-larynx singing is that many of the practitioners, you being the exception, do it with such rigidity of the larynx that they are capable of only one vocal color.

FC: The laryngeal method needs to be used carefully. Otherwise it yields undesirable results.

SZ: Could one sing in the manner of Gigli, Tagliavini, McCormack or Olivero with a lowered larynx?

FC: Gigli had several manners of singing: He had his famous falsettone, which he had had as a boy and held onto for his entire life—a falsettone the likes of which perhaps no one else ever had. He had two ways of singing high notes. One was to keep them small, brilliant and highly focused, the other was a rather big, defiant way. He had a *passaggio* that he could focus and open until high A-natural, He could transition from bright colors to dark. He particularly developed dark colors in the last twenty years of his life. He was a singer with natural gifts. It's difficult to evaluate a singer

Beniamino Gigli as Andrea Chénier

and compare him with another. One singer makes a career because of his gifts, another because of his, which may be entirely different. There are many theaters, so there's room for all singers, especially today. Many things that go well in Milan don't at the Met. Many things that go well at La Scala don't pass muster at Covent Garden. The publics are different.

SZ: Do examples come to mind?

FC: Aureliano Pertile was a tenor who flourished in Italy in the twenties and thirties. For us he was great. He was very modern and interpreted with an exceptional line and a heart that was the equal of Caruso's. Yet, when he came here, in America, it seems he wasn't liked. That can happen for many reasons. Not every singer sounds equally well in every theater. Some theaters reveal brilliance of voice, others beauty or warmth. You really can't divorce the sound of a singer from what he sounds like in a particular theater. For example, a theater where I enjoyed singing and felt most at my ease was the Teatro dell'Opera di Roma. It gives more sheen and metal to a voice. Tenors lacking brilliance did well there. But particularly important is that at Rome a voice can expand, can enlarge itself.

My voice sounded better at La Scala than at the San Carlo of Naples or the Massimo of Palermo. You can't conceive of a voice without considering the theater in which you hear it. A voice cannot be considered in the abstract. What it sounds like in a room is not important. Each theater shapes the sound of a voice. This could explain why Pertile was highly successful at La Scala but not at the Met.

SZ: You certainly are describing my experiences as a singer. My voice sounds small at The Town Hall or at Merkin Concert Hall, in New York City, but not at the Sylvia and Danny Kaye Playhouse, let alone at Harvard's Sanders Theater, which is built of wood.

Listening to Del Monaco I wonder, with the lowered-larynx method is legato a problem—you of course being the exception?

Aureliano Pertile as Nerone in the world premiere of Boito's Nerone *(1924)*

Mario Del Monaco as il duca in Rigoletto. *The part is associated with a light voice. Early in his career Del Monaco sang it.*

FC: Listen, Stefano, you need to premise that the lowered larynx is needed by every singer, because "lowered larynx" means "open throated." It's important to see how a singer pushes his larynx down, if he presses on the larynx or not. Without a touch of laryngeal sound a voice has less strength, presence and character.

SZ: And legato?

FC: If a person presses down excessively legato disappears and the tone gets broken apart by the consonants.

SZ: It may be that what I'm objecting to is not the laryngeal method per se but the laryngeal method carried to excess.
   Did Del Monaco carry the method to the extreme?

FC: Yes, because Del Monaco based his singing on the dramatic rather than the romantic.   He conceived of his voice that way. Still, he often strove to have legato.

SZ: What is your opinion of Alfredo Kraus?

FC: Alfredo Kraus is a very good tenor and a very intelligent man. Because now he's at this moment in full voice.

SZ: Why does Aragall go flat?

Jaime Aragall as Roland in Esclarmonde

The Metropolitan Opera Archives, photographer James Heffernan

Miguel Fleta as Canio in Pagliacci

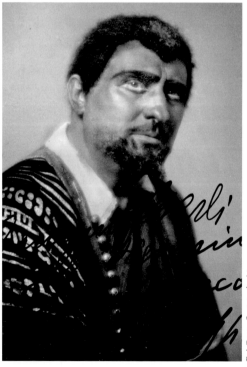

Francesco Merli as Otello

FC: I don't know why. He had a really beautiful voice. I heard him in *Tosca*, and he really was good. He did go flat at moments—I don't know why.

SZ: What made Fleta's voice waver as he made diminuendos, when he went from full voice to mezza voce?

FC: They say he abused mezza voce too much. If you sing too much in mezza voce, abandoning the diaphragm, the voice loses support. More, they say he was a handsome man. [Smiling] Do you know what he did—I don't.

SZ: They say that, like Aragall, Fleta lost it in bed. Why is that significant? In what way is sex incompatible with singing?

FC: Gobbi said singing is like sport, and for a sport you must be strong. Do you think a boxer could win a fight having had sex the night before? Francesco Merli told me, "If I only could be able to go a month without having sex my voice would become like steel."

SZ: And what do you do? *[We both laugh.]*

[Helen Kamioner, a singer's publicist, alleged to me, "I was backstage at the Munich opera. Out of the blue Aragall, whom I had never met, came up to me and put his hands all over me. We had sex in his car, in a Munich side street."]

SZ: Pavarotti: what do you like and what don't you like?

FC: I heard Pavarotti most recently on the radio in the last act of *Rigoletto* and liked him. He sang it with great spontaneity and abandon. I did notice that he sang his first octave unduly rounded, a prelude maybe to his singing some other opera. I don't think the approach suited to *Rigoletto*.

Pavarotti as il duca in Rigoletto

Gigli as himself

SZ: To what opera is his rounded first octave suited?

FC: You can hear from what he's doing that he's preparing himself to sing dramatic roles.

SZ: Yes, he's announced to sing Otello among other places at Carnegie Hall next season [1990–91].

FC: He may be trying to copy the first octave of some tenor with a round voice. But otherwise he sings well and easily, with bel canto.

SZ: According to me Gigli did not have a great deal of *squillo*, and to be exciting a voice must have *squillo*. As I see it, Gigli created excitement with impetuosity, with phrasing and with interpretation but not the notes themselves. Do you agree?

FC: Yes, Gigli singing was suave and caressing. He carried away the public with the sweetness of his tone color, which made people dream. His *falsettone* was unique to him. In the theater it was like a lighted lamp. It had a boyish quality, but in the theater it carried like a strong voice.

SZ: And Caruso?

FC: Caruso had a beautiful, marvelous voice, both in forte and in piano. But his heart was still greater than his voice. When you put together a beautiful voice and a great heart, that's the most beautiful thing that can be.

SZ: You have a long breath span, yet you apparently don't concern yourself with breath control because you think more than anything about the larynx.

FC: When you become master of a technique you don't have to think much about it. You focus on basic things. If you think about

Caruso as Cavaradossi

The Metropolitan Opera Archives, photographer Herman Mishkin

how you are singing note by note, you'll end up sounding like a machine. You need to concentrate on being Roméo or Chénier and what the phrase is saying. You don't have to control your voice a lot. By now your throat is open, and you need to go with your voice without thinking day and night about technique.

The most important thing in our work is breath. You sing on the breath or with the breath. You gather together different thoughts and weld them into one, consisting of technique, breathing and the manner of singing. Singing on the breath perhaps is the most difficult thing of all. Only through the breath can one achieve the elasticity one seeks, including strong singing, mezza voce and long phrases. Thus breathing is one of the most important aspects of the laryngeal method. Only through breath control can one make of oneself an able singer. Perhaps I shouldn't continue in this vein or we'll speak until tomorrow morning about nothing but vocal technique.

From the March 3, 1990 broadcast:

SZ: I've maintained that, under circumstances including lack of preparation, pallid interpretation and directorial willfulness, booing is justified. What is your position?

FC: Yes, I agree. Either an artist is good or he isn't. If he's good he should be applauded. If he isn't he must be booed. There's no middle ground. It's useless to excuse him.

Sometimes people don't boo because they've been taught not to or because they don't want to ruin the evening. But that's bad for the theater. Standards need to be upheld. At the Scala opening this year [1990] there were many boos for *I vespri siciliani* with Studer and Merritt. The performance as a totality was not at a high level, and the Scala public is accustomed to the best.

SZ: Have you yourself ever booed?

FC: No.

SZ: Why?

FC: It's against my temperament, but still there are times when it is necessary.

From the May 12, 1990 broadcast:

SZ: Maybe this is the occasion to explore the booing of Chris Merritt at La Scala on December 7. Maestro Corelli said on our last broadcast together (March 3, 1990) that booing is justified under certain circumstances, citing in particular the booing of Merritt. Since last summer we've had here a series of confessions of booing, where about forty people [ultimately 120 people] have come forward to confess their booing and in some cases to justify it. The discussions sometimes have been heated. What I'd like to do is play an example of Chris Merritt from his commercial record on the Bongiovanni label, singing an aria from Rossini's *Tancredi*, and then play you the actual example from La Scala where he was booed. Also booed then was the soprano Cheryl Studer. They were doing a duet from *Vespri Siciliani*, with Riccardo Muti conducting, this from the seasonal opening night. Cheryl Studer will be my guest here on September 29, and no doubt we'll have occasion to discuss this episode. In any event we'll hear Chris Merritt first in a record he approved, so that you'll hear him in something he presumably deems worthy of himself, and then we'll hear him together with Cheryl Studer in a tape of this episode from La Scala, made from the audience, just a brief segment. I'd like to thank Joost van Berge of Maastrichtland, the Netherlands, for providing me with the tape.

I played the tape.

Neither Franco Corelli nor I will stake our high Cs on this, but from the sound of the *Tancredi* aria we suspect that some of the recording may have been taken not from the live performance.

Franco Corelli, what did you think of it all?

FC: Unfortunately he didn't sing this opera with Verdi style but Mozart style.

SZ: I who sing a certain amount of Rossini am tremendously impressed by Merritt's agility and velocity. Hearing him in *Tancredi* at Carnegie Hall my reaction was that never had I dreamt that a singer with such a large voice, in the middle, in particular, could have such agility in that music, which moves extraordinarily quickly. Usually when you have to sing that quickly you have to reduce volume some, but he didn't, and I was amazed. What did you think of his Rossini?

FC: I liked it very much, but it's clear that he's not suitable for Verdi—perhaps his voice is suitable but his manner of singing isn't:

Chris Merritt as Idreno in Semiramide

he sang it too sweetly, suavely and lightly. Verdi calls for a certain volume, consistency and weight.

SZ: Do you think that he simply doesn't feel the requirements of the music?

FC: It's likely that he was coached to sing it this way. Maybe that's the way Muti wanted him to sing it. He after all was the one who asked him to sing it in the first place. Merritt has an ample middle voice and a voluminous bottom.

SZ: Do you think the Scala public was justified in booing?

FC: La Scala is a foremost theater, with a severe, correct public that takes offense when things aren't just so. I believe that Merritt, if he had wanted to, could have sung the music more strongly. He has a heavy, strong middle voice. I don't understand why he wanted to sing Verdi in that manner. I also fail to understand why the management trained him to sing Verdi that way.

SZ: Cheryl Studer, what do you think?

FC: She has a beautiful voice and a beautiful agility. Stefano, we are hearing her voice through a recording. It's not possible to gauge the body, size and strength of a voice that way. She's a prepared singer who sings well and sings all the notes. But to assess the size of her voice she needs to be heard in a theater. Also one aria is insufficient to define a voice.

SZ: Merritt is slated to sing Manrico at the Met in a few seasons.

FC: He's got the voice.

SZ: The question is, does he have the personality, the temperament.

FC: Yes. Also we must see how he does in the theater—how he works the stage.

SZ: One thing you haven't commented on that bothers me is that, to my ears, his Italian sounds terribly American.

FC: When he sings sweetly he sings well. I don't know this opera, for I never saw it. I can't determine if he sang it too sweetly, without personality, without the phrasing that one typically finds in Verdi. But it's clear that the public dissented from what he was doing. The public knows how Verdi ought to be sung. Yet Verdi style includes sweet singing and mezza voce. But given the reaction of the public one can conclude that he was doing something inappropriate.

[SZ: I feel the music calls for singing along the lines of Merritt's.]

SZ: If you had the chance to do it all over again, what would you do differently?

FC: Undoubtedly I would strive to make more colors and not always sing with strength. Instead I would make my singing heartfelt, passionate, and I would emphasize melodies and contrast forte and piano to avoid monotony. I see that the public today is very prepared. Above all they like bel canto—bel canto in the true sense of the word. They love notes sung strongly—those always are loved—but they are captivated more by singing in the Gigli mold, singing emphasizing sentiment more than high notes. That is what I myself today like most of all.

SZ: During the course of an evening a singer in a lead role performs hundreds of phrases and hundreds of notes. Inevitably at one time or another he has sung nearly all of them better than on this or that occasion. It seems to me that this situation, that no singer can be at his best on this or that occasion, is so frustrating for you that it is intolerable, and that's why you don't perform.

When you sing for me on the phone you have more variety of dynamics and color, more warmth and nuance than in the 70s. Your singing has become more mellow and has more bloom. Although you haven't sung high for me and haven't sung for more than thirty seconds at a time, I believe the only thing standing between you and performing is unwillingness to accept human frailty and unwillingness to risk failure—to risk being heard at less than your best.

FC: My voice is there, but consider the case of Lawrence Tibbett: After some years of silence he made a comeback. He wanted to sing Rigoletto, which had been a great part for him, but his return did not go well. Making a comeback always is something that weighs on you a great deal. It's not an easy thing when you have had a certain career. You must avoid missteps. If not you'll be haunted by the

Corelli as Andrea Chénier

consequences. You know well that I am of a mind to determine what I'm capable of doing today. But a serious circumstance has held me back these last months, a circumstance of which I'd prefer not to speak but which you know, Stefano.

SZ: Well, yes, it's got absolutely nothing to do with singing. [He had problems with the Internal Revenue Service over back taxes.]

FC: Still, I'm mulling the possibility of a comeback and before returning to Italy will record one, two or three arias. Afterwards we'll see what happens.

SZ: Do you sing for acquaintances?

FC: At this time I sing for myself.

SZ: I think that singing for acquaintances makes singing for strangers easy.

FC: I think that's true because the public is unknown. You don't know who's out there. There can be people or no people. You aren't preoccupied with these people. The theater can be empty or full. In the darkness you don't see anyone. You're not preoccupied about the people in general but with those you know.

SZ: Have you thought of forcing yourself to sing for people you know?

FC: For the moment, no.

Listener calls

Ken Swenson, New York City: Who is the greatest Otello of the post-War era?

FC: Without a doubt, Del Monaco.

SZ: Why?

FC: He was suited to Otello, particularly because of his voice, phrasing and ability to erupt. He was lacking somewhat in legato, but he had three positive qualities against one negative one. First of all, he had the right voice for the part, secondly his sculpted recitatives, his ferocity. His rotund, bronzed color.

Dave Weinberg, Brooklyn, NY: What are your recollections and comments about Gianni Raimondi and Mario Filippeschi?

FC: Two beautiful tenors. Raimondi's color was more warm and round. The high notes of Filippeschi were more interesting, easier, more electric, suitable for *Guglielmo Tell* and *Puritani*. I admired the

Del Monaco as Otello

beauty of their tone colors and the facility of their high notes—two great tenors.

SZ: What were their shortcomings?

FC: I can't say. The favorable aspects of their singing far outweighed any unfavorable ones.

Dr. Dave Marcus: You're doing a wonderful job, Stefan. It's simple to listen to you—your translations of the Italian.
   Franco, what is your evaluation of Björling?

FC: I never heard Björling. I heard some records. His color really was beautiful, and he sang very easily. He had a beautiful technique, a beautiful throat and a beautiful legato. Everyone knows he was a great tenor.

SZ: What didn't you like about him?

FC: At times he was too classic and sang with insufficient heart.

Barbara Travis: What a surly audience at La Scala that night! Merritt's high note in the *Tancredi* aria made me sit up, but then he slumped back into being an ordinary tenor.

Gianni Raimondi as Rodolfo in La bohème

The Metropolitan Opera Archives, photographer Louis Mélançon

Mario Filippeschi

John Short, New York City: As the greatest Italian tenor of the postwar years, what is your view of Vickers, Tucker and McCracken?

FC: They were three wonderful tenors with strong voices who did the lirico-spinto and the dramatic repertories. They each had wonderful although different qualities.

SZ: What were their qualities, good and bad?

FC: Tucker sang a higher repertory than the others, more lirico-spinto. For example. I don't think Tucker sang Samson [which is low lying; actually he did]. He sang a big repertory, *Forza*, which is almost dramatic, *Bohème*, *Ballo*, *Rigoletto*, which for a heavy voice like Tucker's is difficult but for him was very easy. I heard him do it in Atlanta, and he was great.

Björling in Manon Lescaut

Richard Tucker as il duca in Rigoletto. *Although he was a heavy tenor, he sang il duca throughout his career.*

McCracken as Otello

The Metropolitan Opera Archives, photographer Louis Mélançon

I heard Vickers in *Otello* at the Met, and he was very good, also in Wagner, where he was great. He had a large voice with a beautiful, easy mezza voce. He can manage with the strong voice easily. His technique is admirable.

McCracken was the biggest and darkest of these tenors because his low voice was very strong. I heard him many times as Otello, and he was very good.

SZ: Singers come in two varieties: those who can sing mezza voce and everything in between mezza voce and full voice and those who essentially have two voices, mezza voce and full voice. What sort of mezza voce did Vickers have? Was it related to his full voice?

FC: I think that singers who have a mezza voce and a full voice without much in between use too much falsetto. If you force the mezza voce you can end up having a large voice. A complete singer is able to go gradually from mezza voce to full voice. But singers who have a falsetto and a full voice find it difficult to go gradually from one to the other. Yet any number of people are able to do exactly that. It's a matter of technique.

SZ: Examples?

FC: There are many.
 I don't want to say something out of place, but I was able to go from mezza voce to full voice gradually. I also could go from full voice to pianissimo gradually. It also has to do with birthright; I was born with this disposition. But ordinarily he who has a good technique can do these things.

SZ: Tagliavini according to me was of the two voice types.

FC: Yes. He had a falsetto and a full voice, yet on some notes he was able to arrive at full voice from falsetto, but more often he was not.

SZ: And Vickers, did he also have two voices?

FC: Yes, absolutely.

SZ: What were the faults of McCracken, Vickers and Tucker?

FC: Tucker was a complete tenor. He had great facility in singing. His high notes always were at the ready. His weakness was that he didn't sing in mezza voce often although he was able to.

SZ: And Vickers?

FC: Vickers had a very easy mezza voce—a mezza voce that permitted him to save himself in any situation. If he was tired at a given moment he could switch to mezza voce and arrive at an aria's end.

I don't recall hearing McCracken use mezza voce in *Otello*. In *Le prophète* he sang a B-natural in falsetto—it was very good. He was very professional.

SZ: Vickers swept me away as Siegmund and Florestan. I found him less satisfying in Italian repertory although I did respond to his passion.

FC: Perhaps his voice was born in this way. Every artist has composers in which he is at his best.

SZ: On this show many listeners have taken exception to McCracken's Italian. Even some who don't speak Italian find his objectionable. Do you agree with them?

FC: I heard McCracken perform Otello a few years ago on Long Island. He was good. Maybe these people are thinking of what he was like twenty years ago.

Marco Lampas: Thank you both for a wonderful program. Corelli and Gigli are the best Chéniers.

Enrico D'Amicis, New York City: Do you use falsetto in practicing? If so, do you use the vowel "u," and how high do you take it?

FC: I do use the "u" vowel, but I've never tried to see how high I could take it.

SZ: Do you sing in falsetto?

FC: Sometimes, yes, but not a falsetto for a theater but a chamber falsetto—a sweet, small falsetto.

Vickers as Otello

The Metropolitan Opera Archives, photographer Louis Mélançon

SZ: For what do you use this falsetto?

FC: I use it only when I'm learning music, to avoid tiring my throat.

Carmine Rizzo, Brooklyn, NY: You, Corelli, are in agreement with Douglas Stanley that technique is based on the pharyngeal sound, and you agree with the Lo Monaco brothers that it's not a question of placement.

SZ: I know from discussions with Maestro Corelli on the phone that he is not familiar with the Stanley method. Stanley after all was an American phenomenon. I think there may be agreement on rejecting placement, but, based on my understanding, it would be erroneous to conclude that the agreement extends further. Stanleyites, I think you are mistaken in thinking Corelli agrees with you. The matter is difficult to discuss because Stanley wrote many books, they are not easy or agreeable reading, they are not in print, and Maestro Corelli for understandable reasons has not read any of them.

Carmine Rizzo: Are dramatic tenors the only ones to have the pharyngeal sound?

SZ: Did Schipa have it?

FC: No, he did not.

SZ: What is your evaluation of Schipa?

FC: [chuckles] He was a big master of sweet and legato singing but certainly not of singing that approached the heroic.

SZ: What of lyric tenors in general?

FC: Of course lyric tenors are able to produce laryngeal sounds.

Artie Conliff, Brooklyn: Franco Corelli, you are my favorite tenor. But when I started to get interested in opera you just had retired. Do you agree there are no more great tenors even though there were a number in the 50s? Is it simply the case that they're not coming here from Italy? What lies ahead in the future?

FC: Only a handful exist today: Pavarotti, Domingo, Carreras, Giacomini. I'm detached from the scene, so there may be ones with whom I'm not familiar. At any rate the theaters are open.

Nick Pangas: Yes of course, Franco Corelli, you are one of the greatest tenors. But Del Monaco was the greatest Chénier, hands down.

Kenneth Lane, Lake Hiawatha, NJ: When you hear your voice on disc does it sound higher to you than it does in your inner ear?

SZ: I think he is asking you to compare your voice as you hear it when you sing to your voice when you hear it on records.

FC: I can't know from records what my voice really sounds like in the theater.

SZ: The first time you heard your voice on tape or on a record were you surprised?

FC: A bad surprise.

SZ: How did the sound compare to what you heard as you sang?

FC: I recall that I didn't like the sound on the record. As a result I began to study to make my sound more pure, clean and interesting.

Ken Lane: Your voice shot into the auditorium and had more projection than Caruso's, to judge from his records. You have more dynamism in the voice and a greater sweep although I miss Caruso's warmth. A technical question: How do you breathe —do you push in or out?

FC: I push my diaphragm out.

SZ: So many others push in. How come?

FC: Pushing out is the normal breathing for everyone. I took this from babies. If you watch a baby in a crib, you'll see him do like so [demonstrates].

Robert Steed: Which conductor do you favor and why?

FC: Karajan, because of his finesse and command.

Joseph Krenus, Assistant Chief Usher, The Met: Franco Corelli, your intelligence and clarity in this interview are sensational. You are the Einstein of tenors. You are the most intelligent singer I've ever heard and give the lie to those who say singers can't think.

SZ: Remember, this is the man who was depicted by John Culshaw in a book, *Ring Resounding*, as a moron, and his view was accepted until these programs.

Scotto's interpretation of Lady Macbeth was full of interesting inflections and unusual emphases. Adelaide Negri, who sang a couple of the performances, provided the temperament, vocal color and power one associates with the role. I applauded them both.—SZ

BOOING: TRUE CONFESSIONS
(EXCERPTED FROM THOSE ON THE
"OPERA FANATIC" RADIO PROGRAM)

"If you keep your mouth shut you are complicit."
—*Gino Mariani, booer*

PUTTING FRANCO'S POSITION IN PERSPECTIVE:
SOME OPERA FANATICS BOOED HIM

SZ: Booing has a history older than opera. At the turn of the century the Neapolitans booed Caruso, whom they found less imaginative and nuanced than Angelo Masini. (De Lucia came from the same tradition as Angelo Masini, who, however, never recorded.)

Booing is to applause what yes is to no: the significance of the one is linked to that of the other. Without booing how can one protest the *La sonnambula* production directed by Mary Zimmerman? She defiled the opera by burlesquing it. She treated the work not as an opera *semiseria* but as an opera buffa. To cite only one example, the first finale is full of rage and grief. She loaded it up with shtick, as if it were the first finale to *L'Italiana in Algeri*.

Among the confessions is that of Claude François Etienne. He and his cohorts ruined Renata Scotto's career with their booing. When she was booed at the Met *The New York Times* predicted management would stand by her until the furor subsided and then drop her. That more or less is what happened.

What a person will or won't boo tells you something about his attitudes and values. For me, the interpreter's intent is paramount. I am prepared to boo cynicism of purpose and, at times, failure of sensibility but not failure of voice.

I wouldn't boo creative non-traditional direction that illuminates a work of art (although in general I would prefer to see the original staging and replicas of the original sets and costumes). Nor would I have been among the booers of Patrice Chéreau's interpretation of the *Ring*, even though it misrepresented the work by fixing it in one time and place (the nineteenth-century industrial age), denying its universal and mythic qualities. At least the undertaking in no way was cavalier.

I should have booed Peter Sellars after the first act of the Purchase *Così fan tutte*. He had Despina revive the Albanians by wiring their genitals to a "Die-Hard Machine," awakening first the genitals,

Peter Sellars

then the men. The audience broke up in hilarity, rendering most of the remainder of the finale inaudible. I too laughed—for a moment. Like a demagogue, Sellars co-opted us into destroying the work of art. No one booed him. That I had press seats inhibited me.

I hadn't booed in fifteen years—not since Giuseppe Campora hadn't bothered to learn Loris for the Newark *Fedora* with Olivero. But I did boo Shicoff's Werther. (My girlfriend then, Fighetta, who liked Shicoff's voice, tried to cover my mouth.) He did vocalize the role pleasantly (though some of the few notes above the staff sounded a little effortful). He communicated the music's pulse and didn't fall behind the beat—unlike at his *Bohème* and *Macbeth* performances reviewed in *Opera Fanatic* magazine, issues 1 and 2. But *Werther* is fragile and particularly vulnerable to misrepresentation; I might not have booed him in anything else.

Shicoff's were sins of omission: failure to convey the character's sensibility—his loneliness, remorse, suffering, torment, anguish and despair. His passion. Shicoff's voice didn't change color in response to words or music. In his mouth the opera merely was pretty. He trivialized it. *Werther* should intensify our sensibilities. Shicoff numbed them. (The same goes for Leona Mitchell's Butterfly.) *Werther* and *Butterfly* shouldn't be performed if the title roles aren't going to be sung with expression.

What do you think? Is booing sometimes justified? Have you ever booed and why? Have you seen unjustified booing? Some of you boo frequently. Come and confess!

Joe Rolof, New York, NY: Stefan, since you don't like Shicoff, why did you go to his *Werther*?

SZ: I was slated to interview Kathleen Kuhlmann a couple of days later on this program. She wanted me to see her Charlotte first.

Frank Dunand, New York, NY: I boo at the Met to let management know that the people they are putting onstage aren't worthy. If you have Scotto making a mess of *Norma*, you have to let management know that knowledgeable people won't stand for it. That's why I booed her. Jessye Norman is all right, but not at the level of Milanov or Tebaldi; in comparison, she's Curtis-Verna. The audience needs to be taught about quality. When Shicoff screams his lungs out in roles he shouldn't be singing, such as Hoffmann, you should boo. Gedda captured the subtleties in the part; he knew the style. He was part of a line consisting of Rogatchewsky, Thill and D'Arkor. Shicoff stood on the sofa in *Werther*—ridiculous! Management forces these things on you and wants you to accept them as high style. Levine may want to do the works but shouldn't if he can't present them properly.

Claude François Etienne: Callas was opera. One should not blaspheme against her. I have adored her since age nine, when my father played her "Tu che invoco" from *La vestale*. I must hear Callas's voice every day and will not listen to another singer until I have done so. I cannot be friends with anyone who doesn't like her and have broken up friendships over her.

Scotto said that when she and Callas did *Medea*, Callas had her music cut. Callas was right. Who cares about the part of Glauce! In an interview in *The New York Times* Scotto said she had a better voice than Callas and could do her repertory. How could she pretend that? Scotto never dared speak against Callas when she was alive.

I broke every Scotto record I owned, except for the '68 *Lombardi*, because of Aragall and Pavarotti, and the *Prophète*, because of Horne and McCracken. When I played those records I skipped the parts where Scotto sang. I walked the streets all night long, writing on the Scotto and Levine posters at bus stops, "Scotto, you are shit. Levine: corrupter of minors."

I had already booed Scotto's *Luisa Miller*, shouting, "Callas, brava Maria Callas, soprano assoluto del mondo. Scotto, tu sei una stronza! [You are a shithead!]" Levine stopped conducting for a moment. It was a broadcast and the mikes picked up everything; you can hear it on the tape. Someone from security asked me to leave. Subsequently, whenever I came to the Met, they watched me.

Speaking about Pavarotti during a TV interview from San Francisco, Scotto referred to her audience as "gente di merda [shit people]." Well, when she came to the Met to do *Norma*, I shouted, "Callas, brava Maria Callas. Scotto, tu sei la merda, tu sei una stronza! [You are the shit. You are a shithead.] Brava Callas." Others then booed Scotto. I knew them well. They too adored Maria. There were ten of us. We agreed that I would scream at Scotto right before "Sediziose voci" [Norma's entrance]. Then they would boo. It went like clockwork, although Stefano Milano did get into a fight with security guards. (He died of AIDS in '87—10 years after Maria's death. He loved her high E-flats.) Maria created the disaster for Scotto, to punish her for talking against her. The little bitch dared to speak against Maria in Maria's home town. New York belongs to Maria. It required a great deal of love to do what I did to vindicate Maria, in response to the words of that viper.

Because some ushers were looking for me, I had gone to the performance disguised as a beggar. I didn't want to be recognized, but as a matter of honor, I had to defend Maria. To avoid arrest or a beating, I had left open the doors leading to Damrosch Park, at the side of the Met. The ushers upstairs knew what I was going to do—word had leaked—and they were delighted because of love for Maria and hatred for Scotto. An usher stopped me from opening the doors but then said, "I didn't see you." After I yelled at Scotto, I ran out. Security guards came after me. But I am a jogger, and Maria protected me from heaven.

I normally wouldn't boo for a bad night or for a vocal defect, because you don't know the circumstances. I once heard Shicoff crack on a high C in *Hoffmann*, but I didn't boo him, because he had sung it well three days before, holding it forever. I wanted to boo the *Trovatore* production; I would really have been booing the management and the producer.

I hate Levine because of his casting, his favoritisms, such as putting his lover on the stage—the lover doesn't even belong at the La Puma Opera—his hypocrisy in telling singers like Negri he wants to perform with them and then dropping them, and above all his

I agree with Etienne: the Met should have reengaged Negri (top), Galvany (right) and Deutekom (bottom).

treatment of Marisa Galvany. He told her he couldn't continue to allow her to perform at the Met because he is responsible for having only the best. Yet Galvany is the closest to Callas, with a similar lower register and top, even if her technique is not as good. Levine also threw out Irene Dalis—a theatrical revelation—and Deutekom. I had to go to Hartford to hear Deutekom and Negri. Every time you fall in love with a singer, the Met lets them go. Levine miscasts

Kathleen Battle. She's all very well in Mozart, but Zerbinetta should be sung by a coloratura. She sang it out of her cunt. Give me Sills, Streich, Moser or Gruberova. Levine tried to make Scotto queen of the Met, the way Maria was queen of La Scala, but Scotto didn't have the goods. The Met's "secret service" should allow you to boo—as in Europe. I don't boo Levine, but I also don't applaud him.

I'm sorry for Scotto's fans: by booing their idol I hurt their feelings—but I had to do what I did for my Maria. Scotto crushed my idol. I act against anyone who dares to open his mouth against Maria—especially those queenly followers of Scotto. I took karate and am very strong. When I am crossed, I turn myself into something animalistic. I am Maria's defender. When I was playing a tape of Maria on the standing-room line, somebody once told me to turn her off. I screamed, "You never turn Maria off"—and almost killed him. Maria will not be silenced after death. Life is beautiful—as long as there is opera.

SZ: There was bad blood between Etienne and myself. Our first encounter was at one of my concerts, during applause after a group of songs: he emerged from the audience to hand me a rose. I pricked myself, drawing blood—the rose hadn't been de-thorned. Taking his action not as tribute but as bedevilment, I made an amusing caustic remark [which I wish I could recall]—to the audience's delight and his mortification.

In the greenroom afterwards, Etienne bragged of having made a bootleg tape of the performance. My accompanist Mayne Miller chased him down the street. A practicing attorney, Mayne wanted Etienne's name and address, so he could sue.

After Etienne booed Scotto later that season, some of her fans told me they planned to ambush him and beat him up. Part of me rejoiced, but in the end when I saw him on the street I warned him, so he could stay away. One of Etienne's lovers, the opera-pirate Ralph Ferrandina, told me I needn't have bothered, since Etienne is a street fighter who can take care of himself. Etienne alleges that Bob Lombardo, Scotto's manager, put the fans up to attacking him.

Callas as Tosca, March 19, 1965—her Met comeback

Gino Mariani, Bellrose, NY: On the standing-room line Etienne's nickname is Carmen Miranda. Etienne is a tremendous admirer of Gwyneth Jones. Etienne has been arrested on account of violence. She [*sic*] tried to scratch someone's eyes out. She is a Puerto Rican hairdresser affecting a French accent who got thrown off the [Met standing-room] Line by the other queens. At 7:30 in the morning, she used to get weepy whenever somebody played a Callas cassette. Sure she's French—French and Greek! She's a disgrace to the Callas queens—just a fucking demented pain in the ass.

If I am allowed to yell "bravo," I should also be allowed to boo. There is very good and very bad. Interpreters don't have the right to change what the composer and librettist wanted. Sellars should be booed—often. If you keep your mouth shut, you are complicit. Opera is semi-sacred and must not be treated in a cavalier manner. Singers and directors have the mission to reawaken the basic impulse that made the composer write the way he did. *Così* is Mozart's, not Sellars's. It is up to directors and performers to interpret, not change.

Recently, I booed at the Met's *Aïda*—before walking out. Tocyska didn't understand what she was doing, likewise, Petrov, who was not trying to communicate and acting like a fishmonger. I used to boo Kurt Baum for acting like a pig. I booed Milnes for his insensitivity in *Don Carlo*. However, I won't boo a singer whose voice has deteriorated. When the singer had it, he gave it to us. But when somebody tries to lie to an audience, he should be booed.

I booed Carlo Bini the night Domingo canceled *Gioconda*. Management shouldn't have put him on. I booed Morley Meredith: he was no Scarpia, especially next to Tebaldi's Tosca. (She wasn't spontaneous, but she didn't lie about it—she didn't pervert it.) The opera house is my church—which some performers and directors try to muddy. Sellars drags opera down to his level.

I've seen more unjustified ovations than unjustified booings. The Met has a coterie of fools who scream and bravo everything. Years ago, I saw only two standing ovations: for De Luca and Jeritza. Now they are commonplace. What are you going to do when you see something truly great—drop your pants?

Italian booing is intelligent: they do it when a singer misses a high note. They booed Lauri-Volpi because he was a fool—gifted with more voice than brain, strutting about like a prize fighter. They booed Marcella De Osma, who thought she was wonderful but overdid everything with fake crying. I remember when in *Fedora* she fell down for effect. Italians used to boo foreigners who had bad pronunciation as well as people who didn't follow tradition. But they never booed good-looking blonde German sopranos!

The first time I booed was at the American San Carlo—the Bonze was so bad. I didn't boo at the Brooklyn Academy of Music when Bechi had no voice: he apologized after the first act but continued because they had no cover. Everyone else booed him mercilessly.

When Anni Konetzni was over-age, she was booed in Vienna because she didn't have high notes. The foreigners booed her—unfortunate. The Viennese don't usually boo old singers.

I remember when Tebaldi backers booed Callas in Milan, around '53. After '56, Callas treated people in a high-handed manner and became a snob. The poor people began booing and laughing at her. She had started to believe her own hype.

Leonard Tillman, Brooklyn, NY: Etienne would be doing himself and everyone else a favor if he went to the opera and enjoyed or didn't enjoy it but saved the street fighting and terrorist tactics for more important causes. If he doesn't, he may press his luck and end up joining Maria, wherever she is.

Someone like him could spoil the enjoyment of a number of people.

Cantor Don Goldberg, Host of "Opera Celebration," WRHU-FM, Hempstead, NY: Anyone who carries on a love affair with the dead is sick. Anyone objective has to admit that after the 50s Callas gave some pretty miserable performances, despite her great acting. After '60 she had practically no voice left. Did Etienne boo with a Callas wobble? I hope he doesn't karate chop me.

Andrew Gurian, New York, NY: What's Goldberg kvetching about? He's carrying on a love affair with Björling.

Greg Gregory, New York, NY: I don't like booing; it sometimes spoils performances for me. Moreover, a bad performance can sometimes be exciting. When a singer sings badly, the silence in the

Dalis (top), Fernandi (right) and Sereni (bottom)

audience should be deafening. When you boo a singer, it takes great effort, and you acknowledge him.

Etienne isn't playing with a full deck. He is sick and should be treated kindly.

Russ Tyser, New York: Etienne is said to have thrown a chicken at Scotto. Did he?

Robert Carpenter, New York, NY: I agree with Etienne totally and am glad Maria has such a champion. Once, when I started to boo Scotto in *Macbeth*, I laughed instead, because she sang out of the corner of her mouth.

Tom Lanier, former Assistant, Editor, *Opera News*: I was famous for having named Irene Dalis "The Toilet." I booed her fairly consistently because the Met gave her opening nights and new productions—all the more intolerable since it was the period of Simionato, Barbieri, Dominguez and Rankin. I also booed Eugenio Fernandi and Mario Sereni on their worst nights, of which there were many. These three stood out as undeserving members of an otherwise marvelous company. I would go to hear Milanov, Rysanek, Price, Sutherland, Albanese, Nilsson and Tebaldi—it was a glorious time for sopranos—but the patina of the evenings was tarnished by these three. In later years, having become involved in the field, I felt it unprofessional to boo, so I often had to bite my tongue.

In any case, I booed to educate the audience and try to keep opera alive. Today the level is so low that booing is futile. Behrens—a great artist, to be sure—has a small voice, unsuitable for Brünnhilde, but is nevertheless accepted in the part. Maria Ewing is allowed to sing anything anywhere. The silly schoolboy shenanigans of Peter Sellars pass as great staging and are considered important by a few serious, intelligent critics who really should know better, such as Peter G. Davis in *New York*.

I am very much opposed to the kind of booing that took place at Scotto's first Norma—booing an artist on her entrance—because it is doubly stupid: it shows the booer to be angry, prejudiced and hostile, and it totally defeats his purpose by shifting the sympathies of the rest of the audience. Etienne's booing of Scotto on the *Luisa Miller* telecast backfired: she had a tremendous success. I was glad to hear he was brought out of the theater bloody.

SZ: I must say I agree with Etienne that the Met should have renewed the contracts of Deutekom, Galvany and Negri.

Claude François Etienne: No one dared lay a hand on me. However, security summoned me to an office where they asked me why I had disturbed the performance. After I explained, they asked me to leave. I said, "That's fine, because I came here not to listen to the performance but to disrupt it."

SZ: On September 28, 2017 I wrote to Scotto's son, Filippo Anselmi, to obtain her side of the story. Here is my note and his reply:

Dear Mr. Anselmi,

I am publishing a series of opera books. *Franco Corelli and a Revolution in Singing: Fifty-Four Tenors Spanning 200 Years*, vol. 1 is in print. Vol. 2 is at the printer. And I am at work on vol. 3, which contains a chapter on booing.

I have a statement from Claude François Etienne who, together with cohorts, booed Madame Scotto at performances of *Norma*, *Luisa Miller* and *Macbeth*. The man is a malicious lunatic who claimed he carried out instructions he received from Callas after she died.

I'd welcome publishing Madame Scotto's account of her reactions and of the impact of the booing on her career.

I'd be grateful if you would put me in touch with her.

Warmest wishes,
Stefan

September 29, 2017

Dear Stefan,

My mother in no way would EVER discuss this with ANYONE.

Please respect her privacy and mine!
Do not contact me again.
Thank you.

Filippo

Corelli as Andrea Chénier

Kurt Groat, New York, NY: One season Corelli got me so angry that I finally booed him. In an *Adriana* he was completely uninvolved. Tebaldi had to drop down on top of him to make it seem like something was happening. They had a fight backstage, and neither one came out for curtain calls. The audience was frustrated, wanting to boo him. At a *Tosca* a month later once again he was uninvolved, and he cracked at the end of "E lucevan le stelle." The audience clapped anyway. I couldn't stand it and yelled, "Fuck you, Corelli!"

Tobias Kronengold, New York, NY: When I was in high school in '69 or '70 Corelli came to Minneapolis to sing Cavaradossi. After

"E lucevan le stelle" I booed him because he held the first A-natural practically longer than the rest of the aria. When I was that age I had little appreciation for pure sound. Phrasing and expression were everything—which is why I loved Callas at first hearing. If I heard Corelli do the same thing today I probably would appreciate the sheer voice and control—although I still think it a piggish way to sing.

I booed in the Rome Opera—and they kicked me out. I once booed Corelli in *Forza*. He was scooping. I wouldn't boo a lady. I would boo Tagliabue in tonight's recording, for his hollow voice. [I was playing a 1953 *Trovatore*, with Callas, Stignani and Penno as well as Tagliabue.]

Cantor Don Goldberg: Several years ago, I heard a story that may be apocryphal concerning tenor Giuseppe Lugo, who had a beautiful voice and made a nice career in France, Italy and in films. Supposedly Lugo was performing *Tosca* in Parma and singing well, until his voice broke on an A natural in "E lucevan le stelle." The audience booed him unmercifully, and he left the stage. The following week he sang *Tosca* again and, filled with fear, broke on the same note. The audience howled him off the stage, and he never sang another peep.

Should one boo a singer who takes his audience for granted and gives less than his best? I did so at a 1966 Met performance of *Gioconda* with one of my favorites, Corelli. I first heard him around '59, in a film of *Tosca*. So taken was I by his handsome appearance and thrilling voice that I bought his three Cetra recital albums. What a joy to hear Werther's aria from a voice able to pour forth glorious tone yet diminish any note to mezza voce. During Franco's first two years at the Met, I revelled in his Manrico, Radamès (with a diminuendo on the final B-flat of "Celeste Aïda") and Calàf (the best ever). As the years passed, however, Franco began scooping into notes, paying less attention to rhythms and preening instead of acting. So, when in *Gioconda* he slobbered through "Cielo e mar," I refused to applaud. That was until Franco's claque began braying bravos, with Franco basking in them. Only then, in anger over his

Giuseppe Lugo
in Bohème

apparent callousness, did I let fly with three long, loud boos. The claque almost made chopped liver of me.

Claude François Etienne: New York, NY: I don't see how Cantor Goldberg could boo a singer he loves, such as Corelli—no matter how he sang.

SZ: I have recordings of Corelli singing "O paradiso" throughout much of his career, with piano as well as orchestra. In each recording at one point or another he loses track of the beat. If I heard him do that live I might boo, just as I did Campora in *Fedora*. Why didn't they respect music and listeners enough to learn the piece or simply not sing it? Why were they content to approximate the rhythms instead of getting them right?

This doesn't mean that I'm not Corelli's friend or that I don't find him a highly exciting singer.

John W. Freeman, Associate Editor, *Opera News*: Booing spoils the performance for both the performers and the audience. When I buy a ticket, included in my expectations is that there won't be booing. If people don't like the performance, let them leave, and if they like, demand their money back. Booing performers demoralizes them and doesn't help them overcome their problems. One has to think of how one would feel in that situation. I'm not sure what the booer is saying, other than "Get off the stage." If anything, the booer is saying, "Get upset, get worse." Booing at the end of a performance, however, doesn't do harm. It may be justified, but it also is bad manners. In this country, booing is relatively tame. In Italy, they boo if some poor tenor cracks on a high note and wait around to heckle him at the stage door.

When I was young, I booed *Rigoletto* at the New York City Opera, with Reggiani and Mascherini. They were quite good but weren't singing the music the way it was written; I thought they knew better. My booing most likely failed to make its point. How were they to know why I booed? When somebody just can't hack it, booing is offensive and unjustified. However, when something unsportsmanlike or intentionally bad occurs, then perhaps it's not unwarranted. At the end of the trio in *Trovatore*, there was a competition between Price and Corelli over who could hang onto the D-flat the longest, as if they were in a sporting event to see who could make the longest throw: very unmusical. It annoyed the hell out of me. I resent unmusical things that turn opera into carnival to such an extent that I might consider booing. I'm no fun: levelheadedness is not one of the ingredients of opera fanaticism. I was glad we had both Callas and Tebaldi.

Booing is antisocial behavior, disruptive and unpleasant. And what if you don't agree with the person booing? Then it's perplexing and irritating. Unless I know why the person is booing, my

Tebaldi in Tosca's *title role*

Gianna D'Angelo as Gilda in Rigoletto. *I heard her sing a lovely Lucia in Hartford in '61.*

reaction is "Shut up, already!" Not applauding, not responding, can be perfectly justified and isn't offensive. Mediocrity is not enough reason to boo—one should simply withhold approval. Why go back to a restaurant if you don't like the food?

Robert Cohen, New York, NY: The worst thing I ever heard was Gianna D'Angelo's Gilda. At her first word, "Padre," I couldn't help laughing. Not one note came out right. After the cadenza in the aria the auditorium sounded like a wrestling ring, with little ladies' yelling, "Prostituta!" D'Angelo walked offstage holding the candle, smiling, as if on drugs. After a long intermission Osie Hawkins came out and yelled at us, saying D'Angelo was indisposed. For months afterward the programs contained notices saying, "Please refrain from any sign of disapproval." It was wild to watch practically the whole house booing. She never again sang at the Met.

Kenn Harris, author of *The Opera Quiz Book* **and a Tebaldi biography, New York, NY:** Booing is an excellent way of teaching discipline to wayward singers. However, like all strong weapons, it must be used with restraint. I would not boo an excellent singer who cracked a high note, but I would boo someone who was chronically sloppy and demonstrated general musical incompetence. It was fun to reminisce with Etienne about the notorious Scotto opening-night *Norma* fiasco, although I never booed her. But I feel it is wrong to boo an artist before he has sung a note, even if one doesn't like him. It would be better to confront the singer at the stage entrance and attack him with cream pies and water pistols.

I wish there were more booing at the Met and City Opera, because there are many in both houses who meet my criteria. Milnes is at the top of my list of singers who ought to be booed.

Bea Solomon, Brooklyn, NY: I am glad others boo. People usually boo for good reason. I shouldn't be cursed just because I booed Tebaldi. It was her fault. She should have quit before she did. I saw her when it was too late and had to boo her. When I said that on the show, Kenn Harris told me to drop dead. Scotto should have quit singing a long time ago—although I never booed her, because she's a grand lady. I only heard her at Brooklyn College, when she could no longer sing.

John Centenaro, Livingston, NJ: Under certain circumstances booing is justified. For example, the New York City Opera *Nabucco* and *Lombardi* are a joke: bad casting, ridiculous sets and staging. People laughed at the *Lombardi*, and there was lots of booing. I agree, however, that it's not a good thing to boo entrances.

Richard Paduch, Passaic, NJ: I'm incensed anyone would even consider booing at a performance. Opera isn't the Roman circus. If you don't like what you're hearing, simply withhold your applause. In forty years, I've sat through the worst: Baum, Poggi and others who have been plain bad or have had bad nights. However, when you're in somebody else's house, you don't boo.

Sherrill Milnes as Iago

Carlo Bini as Don Carlo

Giuliano Ciannella

Gino Mariani: If you're quiet instead of booing, the singer will merely think you don't want to interrupt the beauty. Quiet doesn't bother a singer. Booing is the only intelligent way of telling a singer, "You'd better do more work."

I caused the Bini booing. He was so wretched! My laughter got him upset. He came to the front of the stage and shouted, "Why you no like me? Leave the opera house. Don't laugh on me!" Every time Morley Meredith fucked up a line in *Tosca*, I booed him, and at the end of Act II I yelled to Tebaldi, "Use a real knife!" I also booed him in *Boccanegra*.

John Basileo, Bronx, NY: I booed Ciannella during a *Bohème*, as a way of letting management know that kind of singer is unacceptable even though he presumably was doing his best.

*Morley Meredith
as Dappertutto in*
Les Contes d'Hoffmann

Wolfgang Wagner

Jeff Selby, New York, NY: I went to hear Kleiber conduct *Traviata*. Instead of him we got Woitach—the worst conducting of anything I've ever heard. Shicoff wasn't up to the demands of Alfredo. Brendel was absolutely dreadful as Germont. Gruberova was OK, sometimes. It was primarily the conductor I booed, but I was pretty unhappy with the others. I've never heard or seen anything worse. It cost us $100, and we're not rich—a terrible evening! Perhaps some day somebody will contest the Met's no-refund policy, to see if it's legal. [I never saw Woitach conduct but thought him a wonderfully sensitive piano accompanist to opera singers. He gave you the feeling you were listening to an orchestra.—SZ]

Miss Manners, Syndicated Columnist, *The Greenwich Times,* **July 13, 1989:** GENTLE READER—Whether your sport is opera or baseball, expressing dissatisfaction by refraining from clapping is for the timid. Miss Manners admits to this timidity on her own behalf, but defends the right of the more robust to demonstrate displeasure with the traditional boo.

One should keep in mind that the booing tradition predates and is unrelated to the psychological strategy of building confidence. It merely identifies lapses—of skill as well as of honorable intent—without asking why they happened.

Professionals in fields where this is a custom understand that when the audience has a way of expressing its negative judgments—to its favorites as well as outsiders—ovations and other forms of adulation are correspondingly more valuable.

W. Randolph van Liew, Upper Montclair, NJ: I think booing completely inconsiderate. I've seen about twenty operas and do not remember any booing. One performance was spoiled for me, however, because two people nearby were giggling and smirking in a condescending way.

I don't go to operas now, because of cost and travel, so booing is not my problem. Still, I think the question that needs to be asked is, "Do booing and other bad manners hurt opera as a business?"

Richard Woitach

Opera and other classical concerts may soon be in trouble, for a young audience isn't taking the place of the older generation. Do we really want to add booing to this problem? Inconsiderate people in movie theaters are driving movie fans to their VCRs. This could happen to opera, for as history shows, inconsiderate operagoers in London helped to ruin things for Handel, as more refined people opted to stay home and listen to private concerts.

Bad manners had some effect on the careers of two of the greatest opera singers in the world: Farinelli was willing to retire from the stage in his prime and join King Philip's court in Spain; Pacchierotti admitted that he preferred concerts in the home over the stage. He was glad to take leave of the stage and retire, doing occasional concerts in church.

Eric Neher, Brooklyn, NY: At Bayreuth this summer many of us booed Wolfgang Wagner for his new *Parsifal*. After forty years he should know better and try harder.

Gino Quilico as Belcore in L'elisir d'amore

Joanne Grillo as Maddalena in Rigoletto

Very often singers can't help it when they have problems. Booing isn't fair unless you feel the artist hasn't tried.

Rod Cushley, Brooklyn, NY: I'm glad you're speaking of booing. As an usher at the Met in the 60s I booed on two occasions: I booed the judges at the auditions for not awarding a contract to Jessye Norman. I also booed McCracken—his sounds were unmusical and ugly. For the life of me I can't understand how McCracken and Poggi had international careers and recording contracts. Why would anyone want to preserve their singing for posterity? Can anyone explain their positive qualities?

I agree, I would never boo a singer for having a bad night. A cracked note is nothing to boo. So long as the singer has some clarity of intention, I'm with him.

Peter Dvorsky as Gustavo in Un ballo in maschera

The Metropolitan Opera Archives, photographer Winnie Klotz

Ermanno Mauro as Cavaradossi

The Metropolitan Opera Archives, photographer Winnie Klotz

Livia Budai

Bel Canto Society Archive

Harry Theyard

Jean-Pierre Ponnelle

Carol Neblett as Amelia in Ballo

The Metropolitan Opera Archives, photographer Winnie Klotz

Leonard Tillman, Brooklyn, NY: Most who boo give no explanation. It must be very confusing as well as painful for those onstage. The singers don't intend to perform badly. That's why if I don't like a singer I don't applaud—at best I tap two fingers together. Booing is too blunt. If I do enjoy a performance, I applaud until my hands ache. I enjoyed Shicoff hugely in *Hoffmann*. I would only boo Karajan because of what he was—a man who joined the Nazi party twice.

Paul McGinley, Waldwick, NJ: I've only booed once: Peter Dvorsky. He had no refinement or phrasing, giving us flat-out yelling and defiling Puccini as well as Marton's tremendous *Tosca*.

Bill McMullen, New York, NY: I booed *L'assedio di Corinto* when Rita Shane substituted for Sills and Joanne Grillo took over for Verrett. Grillo was atrocious and should have had the sense not to

Schuyler G. Chapin

The Metropolitan Opera Archives, photographer Louis Mélançon

sing the role. Lacking the technique for the part, she just screamed it. I didn't want to boo but couldn't control myself. After I booed, she just screamed more.

Kenn Harris: Braving the wrath of three female Danish tourists who were threatening me and my friends with bodily harm, I booed Gino Quilico during the curtain calls after *Lucia*, Act I, because I thought his singing offensive and sub-professional—off pitch, badly phrased, insensitive. I felt his performance was scandalous! Departing from my usual practice of waiting until curtain calls before booing, I booed Mauro as loudly as I could, after he had butchered the "Fontainebleau" scene" in *Don Carlo*, because his every appearance at the Met has been marred by disgusting singing and lack of artistic standards. I often boo stage directors and designers because we have to endure their abominations until a production is changed, unlike singers who may merely be having bad moments. I booed

McCracken as Gherman in The Queen of Spades

Budai because she plainly had no aptitude for Verdi in a major house—a glaring example of bad casting. At the opening night of *L'assedio di Corinto*, I booed Theyard because he couldn't handle the music. An old lady said I was a jealous fool. I told her I would hardly be jealous of Theyard.

I booed Ponnelle's *Dutchman* vociferously, at curtain calls. He had perverted and destroyed the drama in Wagner's libretto and foisted a self-indulgent, ridiculous and incompetent production on the paying public. I only began to boo the alleged soprano Neblett when as I was booing Ponnelle she shook her fist at those who were booing. I was threatened by several in the audience, so I showed them I walk with the aid of a stick and said, "Come on, beat up a cripple, impress your girlfriends." Had Wagner wanted the

Herbert von Karajan

Dutchman to be the steersman's dream, he would have indicated it. Furthermore, for the curtain to rise on the second scene with the ladies working at their spinning wheels on the ship's deck was ludicrous.

I booed Sir Peter Hall and his choreographer at the *Macbeth* premiere in '82. I boo Corsaro because most of his productions do a disservice to the drama and the music and consist of vulgar liberties calling attention to him, without contributing to the opera. I've booed him innumerable times at the New York City Opera, especially after the premiere of the "Spanish Civil War" *Carmen*. He had a volley of rifle fire at the end of Act I, destroying the light-heartedness of Carmen's escape. (I only wish the City Opera chorus would use real bullets!)

If I feel in advance that a production has no chance of succeeding with me, I usually stay home. After a City Opera *Rigoletto* with the most idiotic staging I've ever seen, I absented myself from the company's performances, excepting one *Street Scene*.

I was frustrated by the precipitous downturn in singing under Chapin's regime and gleefully admit to having been *la voce di vendetta* who shouted obscenities about him, before the baton came down at the start of each act, yelling, "Bring back Bing!" I obtained Chapin's home number and used to phone him at 4 AM to tell him to drop dead and go fuck himself—he mentions this in one of his books.

I don't hold with booing somebody just because you don't like him in general. If a singer I haven't liked on five nights sings well on the sixth I will yell bravo. A singer should be judged on the basis of his performance that night, not on his career.

In New York, booing isn't condoned. The practice might be likened to spanking: it is necessary at times but ought not to be overdone.

Jeannie Williams, USA Today: I'm rising in defense of Gino Quilico. In the Met's *Barbiere*, he was fabulous as Figaro.

Charlie Handelman, Live Opera, Queens, NY: I have never booed in public. No guts? Afraid they would throw me out? Probably both. I do a lot of booing at the radio, especially when I am alone and the Met is on. So I'm still chicken-hearted.

Booing should be a conscious protest on the part of knowledgeable fans, to educate the public that what they are hearing is not worthy of the stage. I'm not talking about the occasional cracked or off-pitch note nor even the singer with a third-rate voice (let him make a living).

Booing tells people what is really wrong. Of course, this is arrogant: it presumes that I am the one who can tell others when booing is appropriate. When it comes to my favorite subject, opera, I get vehement enough to wish I could break into some of the

Met broadcasts and BOOO my guts out, so truly ignorant individuals could hear a dissenting voice and wonder if maybe they couldn't start to educate themselves before they blindly endorse everything just because it's on a great stage and the rest of the audience is applauding.

I like to compare the Mets ball team to the Met Opera: The batter is slumping, the third baseman lets the ball roll through his legs constantly. Everyone understands, everyone recognizes. So the manager benches the player and works with him on fundamentals or maybe sends him down to the minor leagues. The fans do not tolerate the inadequacies of the player; they know the game. Not so with the Met Opera: who really knows what is wrong?

Stefan Zucker knows, Don Goldberg knows, even Charlie Handelman thinks he knows. But we are a tiny minority and we are frustrated. Frauds should not be perpetrated on the public. When a singer is clearly (whatever that means) miscast by his or her own choice or a so-called "famous" singer cannot sing his role adequately, then we should give forth with loud booooos to signal that this is not worthy of the money nor of the reputation of the company.

To my distress, on live tapes of Italian performances, audiences sometimes even boo a bad note sung by a fine singer but bravo some of the greatest mediocrities of the age, so "knowledgeable" Italian audiences are not necessarily true judges of great art.

Maybe I have an unrealistic or exaggerated idea that any singer who knows his onions would not dare to get on a stage or make a recording that is substandard and would even feel like booing himself if he heard what came out. But they obviously do not hear what we great critics hear. An example in question would be Leontyne Price's singing of "Melancholy Baby" on the RCA "Right as Rain" album. I used to think it a parody, until I found she really thought it good pop singing. Now that is a booable selection. Apparently she cannot hear that it is not worthy of any fine artist. We might also use the Theresa Stich-Randall *Italian Opera Arias* album, in which she does a "Sempre libera" that sounds like a cat being murdered. Can't the woman hear?

That kind of stuff should be booed, but tame audiences would not dare. Many of us suffer because this substandard singing is tolerated.

Having booed Baum during a performance, we standees were waiting for him at the stage-door entrance. Mrs. Baum came out and screamed at us, "You're all a bunch of faggots!" It was true!

The next time you hear one of those Milnes Bert Lahr imitations, the next time Kiri puts you to sleep, the next time Plácido announces he is indisposed, so he might not sound so good on top—GIVE A GOOD BOO.

Speight Jenkins, General Director, Seattle Opera, WA: The booing of the Seattle Opera *Ring* caused people in the city to view opera as a dynamic and controversial form—in short, as theater. The problem with opera—the reason we get called a museum—is that people know what they're going to see (even if they don't know what they're going to hear). To achieve a *Gesamptkunstwerk*, opera must be as surprising visually and dramatically as it is vocally. When our *Ring* was new, booing and fistfights made us something to talk about. If what we did was not based in the music and not honestly done, with no attempt to provoke, then it would die of its own worthlessness. But if it's honestly done and gets protests because of its sincerity, then you're on the way to getting art.

SZ: Never having heard Cheryl Studer before this, I'm bedazzled by her musical sensitivity, with each note weighted so as to correspond to its place in the harmonic structure. To me, it's churlish to hold minor vocal blemishes affecting this or that note against her. Rather than booing her, La Scala should have gone down on its knees. Merritt strikes me as a sensitive singer who went flat, owing to vocal problems. Unfortunately, his Italian pronunciation betrays that he is American. His mezza-voce singing of the word "addio," at the end, struck me as a thoughtful effect. Sensitive singing compromised by physical limitations at least should be respected: the people who booed Merritt and Studer are *caffoni*.

Kurt Baum as Radamès, Mexico, 1950

Since the early 90s there's been little booing at the Met—apart from new productions of *Rosenkavalier*, *Macbeth*, *Tosca*, *Ballo* and *Sonnambula*. In a couple of cases conductors have been booed: Domingo, when he conducted Netrebko and Villazón in *Bohème*—he was deemed unduly metronomic—and Daniele Gatti, when he conducted *Aïda*. The booing tradition, however, continues in Europe. (See the Filipova and Alagna chapters, below.)

The Death of Klinghoffer was booed not for artistic reasons but because the Met disregarded the Klinghoffer's daughters' request that his murder not be used as the subject of an opera and because the work widely was perceived as anti-Semitic and as glorifying terrorists.

SZ: What do you think about these confessions?

FC: They don't change my view about the necessity of booing.

Corelli in Turandot

Carlo Bergonzi as Rodolfo in Bohème. *"Each one of these great tenors at the apex of tenors, Bergonzi, Pavarotti and Domingo—I don't think you can find defects. He who doesn't have one thing has another. They all are worthy of the names they have."—Carlo Bergonzi*

CONVERSATIONS WITH CARLO BERGONZI (1924–2014)

For me Bergonzi's best qualities are his warmth, his legato, his clarity of diction, his observation of composers' markings, his diminuendos on high notes. Such virtues are self evident and require little comment other than to say that it's easy to have good legato if you sacrifice consonants. It's easy to have clear consonants if you sacrifice legato. He managed to reconcile the conflicting demands of both.

I interviewed Bergonzi, in Italian, on April 27, 2002 at the Mayflower Hotel, in New York City, and in phone conversations on September 14, 2007, May 22, 2011 and January 10 and 13, 2014. (The 2002 interview was available as a Webcast at BelCantoSociety.org for four years.)

SZ: Were you received more favorably in New York than in Italy, Parma, in particular?

CB: Parma treated me coldly after I sang the B-flat at the end of "Celeste Aïda" softly, but New York loved the effect. As a result I came to sing the B-flat softly only in New York. But since I'm no longer singing Parma treats me with respect!

SZ: I have the impression that you did fewer portamentos than others in the 50s.

CB: Yes, I tried to abstain from them and give the notes their full value. [Time taken for a portamento shortens a written note.] After all, the composers didn't write all those portamentos others used. The only time I used portamento was when the composer indicated it.

SZ: My theory is that because you gave the notes their due the American public thinks you are more musical than other tenors.

CB: I think you're right!!

Bergonzi always has avoided criticizing recent colleagues but is more forthcoming about singers of the past:

CB: De Lucia, Pertile, Merli, Schipa, Gigli and Galliano Masini had their personal styles but weren't faithful to the composer, because they introduced ritards, rests and effects. Toscanini and Bruno Walter were the only conductors who heeded what the composers wrote. Del Monaco was the first singer to respect the composer.

SZ: Did you hear Merli and Masini in person?

CB: I heard Merli in *Otello*. He sang very easily, his voice carried very well, and he was very communicative. But he performed the music his way, not Verdi's.

SZ: Do you recall examples?

CB: He took too many liberties. More recent singers get closer to what's in the scores.

SZ: And Masini?

CB: When I sang as a baritone [see below] I performed with him. He had a gorgeous voice but didn't know music and learned everything by ear. He didn't interpret words and wasn't very expressive. But you accepted that on account of his voice.

SZ: Merli recorded *Trovatore* and Masini *Forza*. Did you listen to those recordings when you prepared those operas?

CB: Yes. I also listened to Merli's *Manon Lescaut*, in which he sings fabulously. [I feel he is too muscular in it but find him compelling in *Pagliacci*, to which his approach is better suited.]

SZ: Did you make use of anything they did in your own performances?

CB: No, their approaches were too free.

SZ: Masini placed in the mask, but Merli had a laryngeal technique.

CB: Yes, that's correct. Merli had a technique that was his own.

SZ: You also sang with Gigli. Was his style also too free?

CB: Yes, he sang too many portamentos—he made one whenever he had to go up an octave.

SZ: And what of Del Monaco?

CB: He was the first to sing the music as the composer wrote it. I admired his diction and declamation, and he admired my musicianship. We were friends and felt free to give one another advice.

SZ: Do you recall some advice he gave you or that you gave him?

CB: Well, I urged him to sing mezza voce, but he couldn't because he forced too much.

SZ: Sometimes he did sing mezza voce.

CB: Yes, but it was ugly.

Corelli also didn't use mezza voce often enough.

SZ: What did you like about Schipa?

CB: As a baritone I also sang with him. He had a small voice but a wonderful technique, for you could hear him even when he sang in ensembles with a chorus.

SZ: I studied with him. He had nothing to say about technique other than that the vowel "ah" should be pronounced with the mouth in a very wide position and with the sound very open.

CB: That technique is mistaken completely. It's a grave error to sing like that.

SZ: Please describe your technique.

CB: I expand the diaphragm during inhalation, contract it during exhalation and place the voice in the mask at no one spot, and I cover. [The breathing method he describes may sound obvious to non-singers but in fact is anything but, and there is little agreement among singers about the myriad approaches to breathing.—SZ]

SZ: Do you use the same amount of covering from role to role?

CB: The difference between my singing of *Bohème* and *Trovatore* is the degree to which I cover. Rodolfo is a lighter role, so I cover less, but Manrico is more dramatic, so I cover more.

[To illustrate the point he demonstrated the openings of "Che gelida manina" and "Ah! sì, ben mio" with a marked difference in the degree of covering.—SZ]

SZ: On the 1959 *Aïda* with Karajan and Tebaldi you cover less than you did, say, twenty years later. Why is that?

Bergonzi as Turiddu, 1971. "I tried to abstain from portamentos and give the notes their full value."—Carlo Bergonzi

CB: You don't need to add covering above F; the voice does that by itself [a decidedly controversial statement].

SZ: I'm thinking about your use of covering in the middle voice.

CB: By 1959 I had been singing only for a relatively short time. By 1979 my technique was more profound.

SZ: Consider Tamagno's records. At La Scala he created the revision of *Simon Boccanegra*, the four-act version of *Don Carlo* and of course *Otello*. He coached extensively with Verdi. According to reviews from the time he sang open, and on his records he doesn't cover a single note. You instead are against not covering, in Verdi in particular. How come?

CB: The true Verdi style is covered. It is a mistake to sing uncovered in Verdi.

SZ: Giuseppe Oxilia, who performed Otello at La Scala in 1889, two years after Tamagno, also didn't cover, as you can hear on his records. Giovanni Battista De Negri, Verdi's favorite Otello apart from Tamagno, recorded "Ora e per sempre addio" without covering although he does cover in "Niun mi tema." [See the Tamagno chapter, in vol. 1.]

CB: Not covering in Verdi is a grave error.

SZ: Who are the pupils who best exemplify your teaching?

CB: Michele Pertusi, who is particularly intelligent, and Roberto Aronica.

SZ: What of Giuliano Ciannella?

CB: He had a beautiful voice but didn't know how to sing and wasn't expressive.

SZ: Vincenzo La Scola?

CB: He was excellent in lighter repertory but shouldn't have undertaken Manrico and other heavy parts.

SZ: Giorgio Casciari?

CB: He was a fine singer but with a small voice.

SZ: I've heard many times that you and Salvatore Licitra had a falling-out. What happened?

CB: No, that's not correct. I haven't seen him in a long time. That's all. [Licitra died September 5, 2011 at age 43. According to the Associated Press, "Licitra crashed his scooter into a wall near the Sicilian town of Ragusa the night of Aug. 27 after suffering an interruption of blood in the brain…. (He) died without ever regaining consciousness…."]

The following interview took place on "Opera Fanatic," on WKCR-FM, October 12, 1985. Carlo Bergonzi spoke in Italian (I translated). Also present in the studio were the late Dr. Umberto Boeri, pediatrician, a close friend of Bergonzi; the late Bob Connolly; Kenneth Rapp, accompanist; Annamarie Verde, Bergonzi's New York concert producer and Michele J. Cestone. Throughout the evening we interspersed records of Bergonzi in songs and arias.

SZ: With whom did you study?

CB: I first began to study as a baritone, beginning at the Parma Conservatory with Maestro Ettore Campogalliani.

SZ: Campogalliani is still active. Americans sometimes go over to study with him. Even at an advanced age he chases sopranos around the piano. [Born September 30, 1903 he died June 3, 1992.]

Did he think of you as a baritone?

CB: That was not the maestro's mistake but perhaps mine. At 15 I was too young. I had a strong will to sing, to study, to go on stage: that always had been my aspiration. My voice hadn't changed yet. Since boyhood I always had a rather dark voice, so the maestros were misled. I continued to study as a baritone and made my debut in 1948, in *Barbiere,* as Figaro. I continued to sing as a baritone until October 12, 1950. I performed Figaro, Germont, Don Pasquale, Belcore, Enrico in *Lucia* and one performance of *Rigoletto*—a turning point. We were on tour in Puglia (Bari, Molfetta, Barletta). Tito Gobbi was to have sung the performance. But as suddenly happens to singers, owing to a banal draft my late, dear friend's voice deserted him. This was at eight in the evening, with the performance scheduled to start at nine. The maestro asked me if I knew Rigoletto and wanted to sing it. I had studied it to the point that I was musically secure and, carried away by enthusiasm, said yes. During that performance I began to understand I was no baritone, for I didn't succeed in finding the power, also the velvet voice for the pathetic moments, that the part demands, particularly in Act III. Still, I saw the performance through. I was very happy to have worn the costume, but the experience gave me the first suggestion that I should change repertory.

Kenneth Rapp: Who were the Duke and the Gilda?

CB: Gilda was Signora Baruffi, a singer with a beautiful voice of whom I heard nothing further. The Duke was Gino Sinimberghi, who made a good career, including several films.

I went on to further performances as a baritone and, since the maestros said I was very musical, they signed me for parts for *baritono brillante*. Indeed, as a baritone I sang with some great maestros: Serafin, De Sabata, Votto, Gavazzeni. No one ever said I was a tenor instead of a baritone.

I am much indebted to my wife, Adele, for my career. One evening she was present at a *Butterfly* performance. The tenor was Galliano Masini, the soprano was one of the first Japanese to come to Italy, Tosiko Segava. In the dressing room that evening I sang C natural—the famous C from the chest; I don't know what "C from the chest" means—at the end of Act I. Masini had sung it badly, so I did it in the dressing room. Perhaps it was a stroke of fortune or because I didn't know what it really meant to sing high C: to me came perhaps the most beautiful C of my career. From that point, I really began to think of changing register. Three months later—January 12, 1951—when my eldest son, Maurizio, was born, I made my tenor debut as Andrea Chénier at the Petruzzelli, in Bari. From then on I sang as a tenor. Nineteen fifty-one fortunately was the 50th anniversary of Verdi's death, and RAI signed me to sing the tenor leads in *I due Foscari*, *Giovanna d'Arco*, *Oberto, conte di San Bonifaccio*, *Aroldo*, *Forza* and *Boccanegra*.

SZ: Are there any tapes of you as a baritone?

CB: Unfortunately not. If they existed, they'd be something to laugh about, but at least we'd spend some happy moments.

SZ: Did you experience problems in switching to tenor?

CB: Since my voice really wasn't a baritone, in the three years I sang as one I had to force my voice in order to fatten it. For my first fifteen days as a tenor I had some difficulty in lightening the sound, especially on low notes. But I quickly found the right way, vocalizing on the breath, lightening the voice and concentrating on legato.

SZ: As a baritone, what was your range?

CB: Not very high. I went up to F-sharp or G, but on G I was forcing, because I wanted to fatten it, to make myself a baritone by strength.

Bergonzi as Riccardo in Ballo. *"The difference between my singing of* Bohème *and* Trovatore *is the degree to which I cover. Rodolfo is a lighter role, so I cover less, but Manrico is more dramatic, so I cover more."—Bergonzi*

SZ: When you began to retrain as a tenor did your range change quickly?

CB: Over three months. When I was studying I listened to records—not to imitate them—of four great tenors of the past: Caruso, Gigli, Schipa and Pertile. Caruso, for the inimitable purity of the sound. Gigli, for a vocal technique that sang on the piano and carried the note, linking it to the forte. Schipa, for his inimitable technique, achieved by no one else, that allowed him, without having a beautiful vocal quality, to become a great tenor. Pertile, for vocal technique and technique of interpretation. I tried to steal a little of this technique. Imitation is never good and in the end is impossible. But I tried to understand the vocal position and the way in which they emitted sound. I sang Belcore in *Elisir* and Marcello in *Bohème* with Gigli and a tour of *Elisir* with Schipa, and I learned a great deal.

SZ: As a baritone, what was your lowest note?

CB: My voice really wasn't made for low notes. The lowest you truly could call a note—not a half noise—was B-flat.

SZ: After you switched to tenor what was your lowest note?

CB: For a tenor, as you well know—for I know that you are one and they tell me you sing quite well—the lowest note is a C. They say you are an artist, and therefore you must know that a tenor must never force the low notes but sing them lightly. They are called for, but there's no need to exaggerate them. Today is October 12. At this hour thirty-five years ago my elder son was born, and it was a pleasure to receive the telegram announcing that, right after Act I and the "Improvviso." That night a career also was born that—with some sacrifices on my part and the part of my wife, who has participated in my career—we have carried on for thirty-five long years of successes.

SZ: What sacrifices?

CB: We sacrificed everything. My wife and I have traveled around the world perhaps three times. The satisfactions have been few. We have gotten to know New York a little in recent years, but in the other cities we have known only two things: hotel and theater. And my wife has prepared the luggage many, many times.

SZ: What happened after your emergence as a tenor and those first Verdi performances?

CB: Radio was then the most effective system of propaganda and today still is very effective. Impresarios and agents took an interest in me, and I was able to begin my career.

SZ: When did you make your Scala debut?

CB: In 1954, with a modern opera by Jacopo Napoli, *Masaniello*. I have seventy-one operas in my repertory, including works by unknowns: Bianchi, Napoli, Rocca, Pizzetti, Rota and Franchetti. That was before I began my great career with repertory operas.

SZ: Did you study music as a boy?

CB: No, I went to elementary school, and then I worked with my father, making parmesan cheese. At 14 I entered the conservatory, studying piano for five years. In making the switch from baritone to tenor I was self taught. I also learned the seventy-one operas entirely by myself.

SZ: Do you not have a coach or repetiteur?

CB: No. But I'm not suggesting to young singers not to have a maestro, for they are needed. Since no maestro told me I was a tenor I studied on my own and went ahead on my own.

Listener calls

Bill DiPeter: Was it a help or a hindrance to begin your career as a baritone?

CB: Without doubt it was an advantage. Singing as a baritone gave me the fundamentals and helped me focus the sounds and have a base from which to build that which I built as a tenor.

Rosina Wolf: What's the Due Foscari—I'm not speaking of the opera?

CB: You're speaking of my restaurant and hotel in Busseto, at the Piazza Verdi. Traveling around the world I found restaurants named after every other Verdi opera, from Oberto to Falstaff, but no I due Foscari, so I chose the name.

Bill Masterson: You and Di Stefano caress phrases. But Dano Raffanti, Pavarotti, Gianni Raimondi and Ciannella don't phrase well. Is that because of their voices or their techniques?

CB: The question's a little mischievous. Mr. Masterson's is a personal opinion of the sort made by all opera fans. Pavarotti has his personal singing that reaches the summit, and he is the most famous tenor in the world today; thus I don't believe he doesn't even know how to phrase. In the time of Caruso, Schipa and Gigli some liked the way one phrased but not the others, and today nothing is changed. Someone may like Bergonzi, someone else may prefer Pavarotti, someone else, Domingo. Each one of these great tenors at the apex of tenors—I don't think you can find defects. He who doesn't have one thing has another. They all are worthy of the names they have.

Michele Simone: The name of Bergonzi has joined those of the century's greatest tenors: Pertile, Gigli, etc. Will you sing at the Met ever again?

CB: It's up to the Met's administration to sign Bergonzi. I can't intervene in these things, first of all because I've never asked anything of any theater. In thirty-five years of career I've never forced a maestro or a theater to hire me. I've always been signed for my natural gifts, and that's my great satisfaction. For a season or two a theater can do without a particular tenor, because they haven't appropriate repertory and thus have no need of him.

Irwin Petri: Why is your upcoming concert a tribute to Gigli?

CB: That was my thought, which I transmitted to my dear friend Eclesia Cestone [who put up the money]. Having sung with Gigli and being a great fan I wanted to have the satisfaction of transmitting to the Carnegie Hall public the songs and arias he sang in his films. Gigli is the tenor who gave me the greatest satisfaction.

Michael Tortora: What about Wagner, Lohengrin, in particular?

CB: I've only sung Lohengrin's arias.

Howard Hart: Are there roles you'd like to sing?

CB: By now I'm on the threshold of a long road. I still have the pleasure of singing and of diverting myself, and I am happy that the public that comes to hear me diverts itself. But there's no point in speaking of new parts.

Peter Wilson: Who are the great sopranos and mezzos with whom you've sung, and what made them great?

CB: I have the misfortune that the years have passed and now we are heading into old age, but I have the good fortune to have taken part in the period of great sopranos. I'll tell you some names but may not remember them all: Callas, Tebaldi, Milanov, Albanese, Kirsten, Scotto, Freni, Sutherland—with whom I sang *Lucia* at

Covent Garden in April, where I had the great satisfaction, still, at my age, of having an optimal success.

Bob Rideout: You are the great tenor stylist of recent years. What did you think of Callas as performer and singer?

CB: I think about Callas as you perhaps do, as everyone does: she was unique in singing and onstage.

Greg Gregory: You are the tenor of the world. I want to hear you sing all my life. When I die I want you singing in the background.

CB: I thank you. It would be a great honor. But I hope the occasion will be far, far away.

Eclesia Cestone: For a young singer what's the most important thing in pursuing a career?

CB: First and foremost you need great discipline never to tire of vocalizing, to do exercises for diaphragmatic breathing, to work on vocalizes by Concone and on sung solfeggios.

Barbara Travis: Why do singers burn out early? Could it be because of the pace of life today or because of their impatience to make careers?

CB: Youngsters want to do, to arrive quickly, to get to the finish line before the right time, and they burn the candle at both ends. As a result they tire themselves out, ruining their vocal qualities. A recommendation: When you are young time seems to go more slowly. Never tire of waiting. Wait until the right moment to decide repertory. It's of no importance if you make a career as a tenore leggero, for there is a vast repertory for tenore leggero, as for lirico, lirico spinto and drammatico. Later, if nature takes you from being a lirico to being a drammatico you'll gradually get to do the entire repertory. But never tire of studying.

Anthony Frezola: What is required to be a Verdian singer?

CB: First of all you must listen to the repertory a lot to understand the composer. For you to transmit what he wants the music has got to enter into your blood.

AF: Why is there a paucity of Verdian voices today?

CB: I have a contest at Busseto for Verdian voices and can assure you they still exist. But they don't get ahead because young singers are in a hurry and accept roles unsuited to their voices. Hence they are constrained to force, and the voices lose enamel and velvet instead of acquiring Verdian color.

SZ: Wasn't it ever thus?

CB: I have two authentic Verdi letters, given to me by Busseto's Carrara Verdi, one dated 1872, the other from '86. Verdi laments the lack of voices for his operas. Verdi is very difficult to interpret. It's also difficult to get to the point where you can emit the sounds he wanted, particularly for tenor parts, because the music tends to sit in the *passaggio*, and to sing on F-sharp, G and A-flat for an entire aria is very difficult. That's why there always have been few Verdi tenors.

SZ: When was Verdian singing at its peak?

CB: If an appropriate tenor, soprano and baritone came forward it would be at its peak today. But the material is lacking. Sometimes you can't play around and must tell the truth: if theaters would begin to hire young singers for the right repertory I assure you that Verdian, Puccinian and Wagnerian voices still would come forward. Today when a tenor with an easy high C comes on the scene they don't consider the color—whether it's of a lirico leggero, a lirico spinto or a drammatico. He has the C so they quickly hire him for *Trovatore*, for only the "Pira" is important. In Verdi high notes are important,

Bergonzi and Antonietta Stella in rehearsal for joint Met debuts in Aïda, *1956*

for he wrote them, even though in the "Pira" he didn't put in a C but a G. However, the C is a beautiful tradition and thus one should do it. Phrasing, portamento, tonal velvet and the bronze of the color—these things are Verdian singing. Not just the high C. Thirty-five years ago, when I began my career, there were the following kinds of tenors: leggero, lirico leggero, lirico, lirico spinto and drammatico. Today there's no difference: they have a *Barbiere* tenor sing *Rigoletto* and a *Rigoletto* tenor sing *Otello*. Thus the categories are lost.

Russ Tyser: Is there a tenor now singing *Otello* who should be singing *Rigoletto*?

CB: I don't know one.

SZ: Are there interesting singers in Italy we don't know of here?

CB: I don't know which young singers are appearing here.

SZ: Did any careers start as a result of the Busseto competition?

CB: Yes, Giacomo Aragall, Rita Orlandi Malaspina, Ángeles Gulín, Piero Cappuccilli and others. Today there's a truly good lirico-leggero tenor, Vincenzo La Scola.

SZ: Has he been engaged to sing in the States?

CB: No, but he sang *I Lombardi* with the contest and has been engaged by the Paris Opéra for *Fille* and *Sonnambula* and by Lisbon's São Carlos for *Rigoletto*.

Stewart Manville: I adore the caressing quality of your singing. Is that quality what is meant by "*slancio*"?

CB: No, *slancio* is something felt in the person.

SZ: "*Slancio*" applies to interpretation, not vocal quality. Would you care to define it?

CB: When you interpret a phrase, putting in that vocal expression, that signifies *slancio*—giving expression to the words.

SM: I'd like to listen to you forever.

Dr. Umberto Boeri: "*Slancio*" may best be defined as "oomph," "propulsiveness" or "a springing forward."

Miguel Nicoletta: I heard you sing with Leontyne Price some years ago at the Teatro Colón. Please reminisce about those performances.

CB: I remember them with great enthusiasm. I also recall the enthusiasm of the public, the management and the press. Thank you for calling the experiences to mind.

Now, Stefan, I have to ask you a question: tell me something about your career. I've heard a great deal about you but have never head you sing. What repertory do you do?

SZ: I specialize in Bellini's high tenor parts. For example, I sang the actual world premiere of Bellini's last setting of *Adelson e Salvini*. My repertory includes Fernando in *Bianca e Fernando*, *Puritani*, *Sonnambula* in the original keys, which are as much as a third higher than those in scores published in this century. I also sing stratospheric parts by Rossini and Donizetti, as well as music written by the nineteenth-century tenor Giovanni Battista Rubini.

CB: Well, in *bocca al lupo* (into the mouth of the wolf), with my very best wishes, because having gotten to know you I'll tell you the truth: I've gotten to know someone of notable intelligence regarding drawing distinctions and speaking of vocal technique. [For particulars

Bergonzi as Canio, 1959.

about Bergonzi's voice placement, see *Opera Fanatic* magazine, Issue 1, p. 34 and Issue 2, p. 11, both still available from Bel Canto Society.]

SZ: *Crepi il lupo* (may the wolf croak). On behalf of the listeners and myself, let me wish you *in cullo alla balena* (up the asshole of the whale).

CB: Yes, that's very important. Very good. *Che non scorreggi* (may he not fart). (Bergonzi's entourage applauds.)

Bob Connolly: It's almost as much a pleasure to hear Grande Uffiziale Bergonzi speak as to hear him sing; the speaking is so beautifully produced it makes me realize that most of us Americans speak and sing in the throat.

SZ: For me it's a diction lesson. We're all high as a kite here.

CB: I thank you all for listening and phoning. For me it was a real treat. The time flew. Arrivederci.

Bergonzi and I enjoyed talking and kept in touch. In person and on the phone he exuded a beautiful warmth. He was endearing. Sometimes this comes through in his singing, for example, in his Nemorino.

We weathered a dispute over his adherence to Lyndon LaRouche who, on specious grounds, was advocating a tuning pitch of A = 432. (For the details see the 1989 issue [issue 3] of *Opera Fanatic* magazine, available at belcantosociety.org), and he took in stride an unfavorable review I published about his singing, which includes the following paragraph (it's possible no one translated it for him):

> Bergonzi's defects as a musician are considerable. He sings all music in a manner appropriate, at best, to Neapolitan songs written around 1920. In the concert under review he slithered and slurred his way through two songs by Caccini and Bellini, freighting each phrase with a heavy overdose of portamento. He places accentuations and sometimes crescendi as well on

Bergonzi as Chénier with George Cehanovsky as Fléville, 1959

The Metropolitan Opera Archives, photographer Louis Mélançon

rhythmically weak notes and weak syllables, thereby dislocating the climactic points of the phrases, inappropriately transferring the climaxes from points of structural tension to points of structural repose. And he sometimes obscures musical structures by blurring phrases into one another. His intonation is often vague, and he lacks both rhythmic solidity and a sense of rhythmic proportion: he doesn't borrow time, he just steals it.

With regard to the last sentence my premise was that if you take time away from a note or group of notes you should pay it back elsewhere.

Bergonzi was a lyric tenor whose covering made his tone opaque but not dramatic. He had enough volume for dramatic roles but not

Bergonzi as Rodolfo in Luisa Miller, 1988. "Not covering in Verdi is a grave error"
—*Bergonzi*

the bronze timbre. He never excited or moved me. On a YouTube video of a 1989 *Elisir* rehearsal he does little covering. Pity he didn't sing Nemorino more often instead of heavy repertory.

For many people his worst qualities may be less obvious and require some exposition. If I dwell on them it's not because I wish to emphasize unfavorable things but because I think them of some importance. They include his insensitivity to harmonic structure—he emphasizes and prolongs resolutions of dissonances, weak syllables on weak beats—instead of the dissonances. The dissonances are moments of harmonic tension, whereas their resolutions are moments of harmonic repose. His emphases go against the music's harmonic structure and minimize both its tension and its repose. He thereby dislocates phrase climaxes and phrase shapes.

Bergonzi as Riccardo in Ballo

Also, he lacks chiaroscuro both of dynamics and of timbre. And his top notes seldom are thrilling.

In the mid 80s Bergonzi videotaped and performed a program called *Bergonzi Celebrates Gigli*, declaring Gigli his favorite tenor and the one who influenced him the most.

But compared to Gigli, Bergonzi did little soft singing and almost never contrasted covered with closed and open tones. In general he sang with no—or minimal—chiaroscuro. Compare him to Gigli in the material they both recorded, *Aïda*, say.

Bergonzi had performed the baritone part of Belcore, in *Elisir*, to Gigli's Nemorino. When Bergonzi came to perform Nemorino himself he imitated Gigli's alternation of covered, open and closed tones and even his timbre. (See his Florence *Elisir*.)

In general, however, Bergonzi's singing didn't have a lot of chiaroscuro.

Alfredo Kraus as Roméo, 1986

KRAUS (1927–99)

After he made his debut in 1956 Alfredo Kraus quickly became a foremost tenor. He was secure technically, and his method became a reference point among singers. Because it has nothing in common with Melocchi's precepts, I am including Kraus's description to put matters in perspective. The interview took place on "Opera Fanatic," October 22, 1988.

SZ: Please describe your vocal technique.

AK: You have to send the air and the sound to the mask and to produce all vowels in the position of the "ee." According to my technique "ee" is the easiest vowel and the best for projecting the voice. It has the most overtones and the most *squillo*.

SZ: Quite a few singers believe that "ah" is the easiest vowel. Yet the first vowel over which I myself had control was the "ee." Perhaps there are two kinds of tenors, those for whom "ah" is the easiest vowel and those for whom the "ee" is. [Gigli was an "ah" tenor.]

AK: No, I don't believe that. The basic sound is the "ee," not "ah," because "ah" is in the back of the throat. We don't have resonance there but here, in the mask.

SZ: Alfredo Kraus is pointing to the area beside his nose, just above the nostrils.

SZ: Do you have a most-preferred vowel for high notes?

AK: No, no longer. At the beginning it was the "ee" and the "eh," but now for me there's no difference. What I do is place the "ah" and the "eh" and the "oo" in the same place as the "ee." That way each vowel has the same sonority.

SZ: Is one vowel better for making diminuendos?

AK: No, they are all the same.

SZ: Sometimes I am a tiny bit preoccupied about the "oh" vowel, as in "sole."

AK: The "oh" shouldn't exist in singing, especially up high. Change it to "ah"—"Un trono vicino al sal" [instead of "Un trono vicino al sol," from *Aïda*].

SZ: Very interesting. What is your opinion about covering?

AK: There is no need for it.

SZ: At last a singer who agrees with me!

AK: I am so happy to. You have to manage your voice just with the pressure of the air, using more pressure on high notes, that's all.

SZ: Let me take a guess. Since you don't cover, for you the *passaggio* is not a problem.

AK: For me the *passaggio* doesn't exist.

SZ: According to me covering leads to the very thing it is supposed to solve, *passaggio* problems.

Kraus as Tonio in La Fille du régiment. *That his mouth is lopsided presumably is unintentional.*

I've had this discussion with many singers who were sitting in the same chair in front of the same microphone as you. They told me, "You must cover." When I mentioned to Virginia Zeani and Nicola Rossi Lemeni that I do not cover, they said, "If you do not cover, you will lose your voice. You still are young. We never have heard you sing, but in a few years you will lose your voice simply because you do not cover."

AK: They told you that?

SZ: Yes. They tell everybody that. If a student comes to them and does not cover they make him cover. That is the first requirement.

AK: I sang so many times with Zeani, but I never realized she covered.

SZ: They demonstrated here and so for that matter did Bergonzi and many others.

In the nineteenth century covering by no means was ubiquitous. I maintain that it limits the possibility of inflecting the tone. It gives only one color of voice.

AK: Yes. If you cover you change the color of your voice, and the voice has to be the same from the top to the low notes. Properly produced, the voice changes registers by itself, without the need for covering.

SZ: Do you believe in mechanistic techniques involving manipulation of the larynx, the soft palate, the tongue, the lips or the cheeks?

AK: No—except that I do pull up the muscles around the nose to help the high notes.

[In speaking of that Alfredo Kraus smiled with the corners of his lips raised, lifting the cheeks slightly, causing a furrow in the cheeks about midway up the face.—SZ]

Kraus as il duca. Notice the position of his mouth and cheeks and his bared upper teeth.

AK: To avoid having the voice go back you have to help with the muscles around the cheeks. As you sing higher, little by little you bare the upper teeth. You have to place the voice in the area from the bottom of the upper lip to the top of the forehead, at the hairline.

Imagine that you have here a piston with which you push the air and then obtain the high notes.

To sing higher I spread my mouth wider and wider, sideways, with the upper lip pulled up and the corners of the lips raised slightly. If you try what I have described you'll discover that it is the correct way to sing. But you know what happens in general—the teacher says, "Oh, no, no, no. Your voice is too light. Sing heavier, more dramatically, with more darkness in the voice." It is wrong because the voice has to go where the real voice is, and the real voice is the "ee" in everybody. Of course a dramatic tenor will have a darker "ee" than I do, but if the voice already is dark why put more darkness in it? For the student to have a more dramatic quality the teacher says, "No, no. Don't be so light on top." This is the mistake.

SZ: How do you breathe?

AK: This is a good question. Normally, people don't know how to do it. They push the stomach out, and that's all. The technique I use is the intercostal diaphragmatic. You move the ribs all around, not only here but in the back too.

SZ: Mr. Kraus is moving his hands from the side of the ribs to the back of the ribs.

AK: Yes. The diaphragm is completely open and elastic and very tense. This is the support for the air.

SZ: So you push your ribs out?

AK: Out. And I take in air at the same time.

Kraus as Werther. *"Del Monaco never had a high C. Probably with my technique he could have had it."*

SZ: You are breathing through your nose.

AK: Yes.

SZ: Is it possible to do that and take a breath very quickly?

AK: It depends. But the ideal is to breathe through the nose.

SZ: Why is that?

AK: Well, it's normal. When you take in air you do it by nose. You also feel the freshness of the air coming inside, and you feel the place where you have to put the voice at the same time.

SZ: With whom did you study?

AK: My first serious studies started in Barcelona with a Russian lady named Gali Markoff. I studied with her three months one year and another three months a year later. Then I stopped to continue my studies [of electrical engineering] in my city [Las Palmas, on Grand Canary]. In Valencia I found another teacher, Maestro Francisco Andrés, who was about 90, and I studied with him for six months. Then I interrupted my studies for two years, but I decided to go to Milan in 1955, where I found Maestra Mercedes Llopart [who also taught Renata Scotto], and I studied with her before I made my debut.

SZ: Did you always use the same vocal technique?

AK: Maestro Andrés and Mercedes Llopart taught the same technique. Gali Markoff explained her technique differently—more technically, more scientifically—but the results were about the same.

SZ: How long did you study?

AK: I continue to study now. But before my debut, three and three months, twelve months and then from March to December another one year and nine months.

SZ: So it is not necessary to study for five or ten years.

AK: No. It's bad when you study for more than four years.

SZ: Why is that?

AK: Because you must understand singing from the very beginning. If you don't understand then you never will. Maybe you never will find somebody who will teach it to you. But after five or ten years of studying, if you didn't find it, it's too late to start a career.

SZ: According to me the conceptual content of vocal methods is very small. One can explain everything a singer needs to know about vocal technique in a few minutes.

AK: Yes. It's very, very simple: breathing to tense the diaphragm and going up little by little, trying to place the other vowels in the same place where you feel the "ee." That's all.

SZ: You mentioned a moment ago that if one studies for many years it is too late. Is there an age after which it is futile to try to make a career?

AK: No. It's too late because in so many years you develop so many bad habits that your voice gets worse and worse. This is irreversible.

SZ: Among the listeners tonight there certainly are many singers who are thirty-five, forty, forty-five, perhaps older, who would like to start careers.

AK: The challenge is to find somebody who will engage them at those ages. The managers and people who hire singers for opera companies think that someone who does not have an established career at forty is too old. [Francisco Araiza, Corelli and Hines also said 40 was the cutoff age.]

Listener calls

Cathy Wall: When you extend your chest or your rib cage, what do you do with the rest of your body? Do you push out, push down or pull up? What you described is insufficient as a basis for breathing.

AK: I push out.

SZ: What do you push out?

AK: All around. All the body. The stomach gets very hard, like stone.

SZ: Is there a danger of becoming musclebound?

AK: No. Some teachers say you must help the sound go out by pulling the stomach in. But if you do this, after a few seconds you have no more air, and you make the diaphragm cave in. The diaphragm always has to be elastic, and to be elastic you have to push out the whole time during which you are projecting your voice.

Patrick Moscato: Your views on humming?

AK: I think it is good to prepare the sound—the open sound. If you use it in the right way and you use the mask to make the sound, it's ok. [He demonstrates a note.] I like this preparation of the real sound.

PM: What about singing falsetto? Is it a bad thing or a good thing?

Kraus as Edgardo in Lucia di Lammermoor, *1982–83. "Techniques other than the one I've described are erroneous."*

AK: I don't say it's a bad thing. It's another way to sing. If you use this way, and it's good for you and you make a good career, I have no objection. But it's a different technique and sound. It's not a real one. Many famous singers sang very high notes, above high C, this way. It's ok. It's not bad.

SZ: Is there a difference between head voice and falsetto, and do you ever sing in falsetto?

AK: Of course it is different, but I don't know exactly where is the difference. I never sang in falsetto and I don't know how to make it. I know theoretically—they say it's more of a head voice. But it couldn't be a normal voice, since head voice is what I do.

SZ: Do you ever sing in *falsettone*?

AK: No, I never tried—I never felt the need—and I don't know how to do it. The two techniques are completely different. If you do one you can't do the other.

SZ: Can you develop head voice from falsetto? Here in New York City many voice teachers, Cornelius Reid and Conrad Osborne come to mind, teach falsetto, hoping that pupils will develop head voice.

AK: Everything could be possible, but what I believe is that if you start to have a falsetto on high notes you of course develop the falsetto but never a real voice.

SZ: What about *voix mixte*? What is it, *falsettone*?

AK: It's a kind of *falsettone*, a reinforcement of the falsetto. What Gigli does I think is *falsettone*.

SZ: What is a reinforced falsetto?

AK: It's a development of the falsetto, something closer to the real voice.

SZ: Gigli, at the end of the 1931 recording of the *I pescatori di Perle* aria and Lauri-Volpi, when he sings mezza voce—is that really falsetto?[a]

AK: Yes, it is falsetto.

SZ: How can you tell the difference between falsetto and head voice?

AK: You feel that it is not a real voice—it is not a metallic voice but a note of a different intensity, without timbre.

Peter Turner: The difference between falsetto and head voice is that with falsetto you cannot crescendo to a fortissimo, whereas with head voice the pianissimo can be expanded. If you try to go from falsetto to full voice there is bound to be a break, whereas if you go from head voice to full voice it can be done without a break.

AK: I agree.

SZ: Today there are some falsettists so skillful that they manage to do that.

AK: It could be possible, yes.

SZ: How do you sing in mezza voce?

AK: The support has to be greater. You have to continue to press the voice out, and the diaphragm has to be even more tense to be able to remove weight, strength and volume from the voice. You might think that pressing the voice out results in more volume, but that isn't necessarily so. You need a column of breath that pushes

---

[a] On YouTube, as of this writing, you can hear Alain Vanzo in "Je crois entendre encore" from *Les Pêcheurs de perles* with top notes in *falsettone*. I believe the final high note in Gigli's 1931 version, likewise available on YouTube, also to be in *falsettone*. Pavarotti in "Credeasi, misera" from *Puritani*, once again on YouTube, sings the high F in falsetto. For a fuller discussion of this last see p. 303. (Sound on YouTube is so compressed as to be highly misleading; yet it is adequate for judging the difference between mezza voce, *falsettone* and falsetto.)

the sound continuously, without interruption. It's as if you wanted to project your voice to the horizon.

Charlie Handelman: Do you agree that yours is a vanishing breed, that you are among the last great singers?

AK: Maybe this is true. I continue a tradition that is now going to disappear. But it depends also on the taste of the public, if they like it or not. I think there is more contrast in my voice. I try to give more colors. But the people who sing verismo think only about volume. Maybe it's too early to say the tradition will disappear.

SZ: From what I have seen in the world of provincial opera companies, whereas in the 60s there still were a handful of older singers who smiled, there are none today.

In this country instrumental singing is very popular. Some people believe that each note should have the same color, the same inflection, in the manner of today's instruments, not those of, say, the eighteenth or early nineteenth centuries. Other singers, Adelaide Negri comes to mind, favor having different colors of voice for different phrases. What is your view?

AK: The color always has to be the same. But if you are expressing love, hate or talking about war the inflection and the emphasis in your voice must change. Then when you have to reduce the voice it has to be the same color. Only the intensity has to change. I dislike many singers who have different voices—it seems like different voices if you change colors.

SZ: What about Callas?

AK: Callas changed colors but not because of inflection. She changed colors because of technique. Wrong technique.

SZ: Is that why she lost her voice?

AK: Probably.

SZ: What was she doing incorrectly?

AK: She sang heavy repertory—operas not good for her voice—*Turandot* and heavy Verdi. She also had personal problems, sentimental problems. Many things can have an influence.

SZ: At the Lisbon *Traviata* what was she like as an artist and as a person?

AK: She was very nice to me. I was a little worried about her because I had heard terrible things. When I started to sing my aria during the rehearsal she was a perfect, completely good professional. When, after my aria, the whole theater gave me tremendous applause—when I was the discovery of the evening—I feared her reaction. But she came to me and said, "Bravo, Alfredo, you're fantastic." Even at the end of the opera she never went out to take the applause alone. She took my hands and said, "You come with me, you come with me." She was the protagonist, and in all the theaters of the world she was accustomed to take the applause alone. She has been faulted on account of her quarrels with Del Monaco and others but, who knows, perhaps her anger was justified.

SZ: What is your feeling about the *coup de glotte* [glottal stroke]?

AK: I am against it.

SZ: Caballé advocates attacking with the glottis.

AK: Yes, I know.

SZ: I happen not to like it, both for vocal reasons and musical ones. Sometimes when there is an upbeat beginning on "ah" she imparts an ictus, a kind of emphasis, with a glottal attack, whereas an upbeat is meant to build toward a climax, perhaps on a dissonance on the final downbeat of a phrase. With Caballé you get an accent because of her glottal attack. What is your feeling about her way of attacking?

AK: I think it's wrong. But in any case she said on television in Spain that Alfredo Kraus's technique is not good for everybody. But I would like to say to her, "Have you ever tried my technique?" How could you say that it's no good without trying it? In any case I feel that everybody would be better off never touching the glottis. I've been singing for thirty-two years, yet my voice still is fresh, I still have my high notes, and I never canceled one performance. Something must be good in my technique.

SZ: Do you think it is unhealthy to make a glottal attack?

AK: First, it is unhealthy. Second, the full voice is not in the head—it's not head voice. Then, the quality could be much better if she used head voice, head placement for the voice. She uses it when she does falsetto or mezza voce, but she doesn't use it when she sings in full voice.

SZ: When she sings in full voice her sound a little bit lacks a center, a core. When she sings with less than full volume, at its best the tone has remarkable sheen, *smalto*. But the full voice, no.

AK: Because it's not in focus.

SZ: Yes. Sometimes it's a tiny bit spread in pitch.

AK: I am happy when somebody agrees with me. In general, I disagree with all singers and teachers.

SZ: For me it's a thrill finally to find a great singer who agrees with me!

AK: We are talking about a very high level. Because we are analyzing with a magnifying glass I said what I said. She doesn't need your advice or mine. She's a great singer, a fantastic singer.

SZ: Agreed.

Peter Turner: Have you had training as an actor?

AK: No. Training is by experience. One theater, another theater. One year, another year. Working with other great artists like Tito Gobbi, Sesto Bruscantini.

PT: You sound as covered as any other singer.

AK: No, I don't cover. One doesn't need it. Your voice is covered by your head.

Robert Rusk: It sounds as if you have changed your vocal method to make a darker sound. Is this to accommodate the passing years?

AK: No. The technique is the same. Maybe I discovered that using this same technique you can give more cavity in your voice—more space—but that's all.

SZ: What do you mean by "more space in the voice"?

AK: If you think your head is your harmonic box and that your head is bigger than in reality you can turn your natural sound into a bigger one. Just by thinking, you augment your cavity in the head; to have more sound you think that you are growing your head. It's unbelievable that in this profession it works—the intensity in the way you manage your mind.

You have to imagine that the sound comes from outside the top of your head, goes inside and then is projected out through your mouth. You don't think about your glottis or your throat.

Alfredo as Alfredo in Traviata. *"Callas changed colors not because of inflection but because of technique. Wrong technique."*

SZ: Just now it was as if you used my particular placement, with the sound coming in from the top of the head, from a point between the ears but higher up, in the area of the sphenoidal sinus, where a baby's skull comes together. Yet you advocate placing in the cheeks, by the nose. How do you reconcile the sound coming in from the top of the head with the placement beside the nose?

AK: This is a mental explanation. Because you can't touch or see your instrument you have to make examples inside your body. You have to work with sensations and imagination.

SZ: Is your voice different today than at the start of your career?

AK: Of course it is different, but not much.

SZ: What are the differences between now and thirty-two years ago?

AK: My voice today is less fresh than at the beginning of my career, but I sing with more colors and nuances. Then it was too incisive. Now it's a little rounder, and I have more volume in all registers.

SZ: Given that your voice was more incisive, did you have more *squillo* at that time?

AK: Not more *squillo*—it was a little thinner and higher than now.

SZ: Are there roles that you sing today that you would not have sung thirty-two years ago?

AK: The parts I sing now are the result of thirty-two years of singing. Just little by little, you have to build something and you have to start at the very beginning, from light operas and more lyric operas. Don't abuse too much and don't sing too much. Rest and let things mature inside you. The roundness I have now is not artificial; it is the result of a natural development.

SZ: At the beginning of your career, or near the beginning, you sang Nadir, in *Pêcheurs*. Would you have sung Hoffmann, for example, or Werther?

AK: No.

SZ: How about as an interpreter—are there specific differences between now and the beginning of your career?

AK: At the beginning I concentrated more on perfecting my technique than on deepening my interpretations. I think that musical and dramatic sensitivity and acting onstage are something you have inside you that have to be developed. I am much more of an actor than before, in part because it's not the same to sing *tenore di grazia* parts like Almaviva or Ernesto as it is to do more demanding romantic-dramatic roles like Roméo, Fernando in *La favorita*, or Hoffmann or Werther.

John Mangini: Do you have a ritual on the day of performance?

AK: Ritual?

SZ: How do you prepare yourself to perform?

AK: No. I try to have a nice sleep; I try to get up not very early, about 10 o'clock in the morning or 11 sometimes. I make a normal life. I have a big lunch around 2 or 2:30, and that's all. I walk a little. I watch television or I read or I do something like that—something light. And then I go to the theater an hour and a half before the show.

SZ: Do you not eat certain foods? Do you practice exercises of one sort or another, and do you do vocal exercises?

AK: No. I don't do vocal exercises every day. It depends. It's not a mathematical system. It depends on the opera I'm going to sing. It

Kraus as Tonio in La Fille du régiment

depends on how I feel. Sometimes I feel I need more exercises than other times. Normally one hour before the performance I do ten minutes, and that's all.

SZ: You're not a vegetarian, say?

AK: No. I prefer vegetarian—I don't eat a lot of meat. I try to eat more fish, but I prefer vegetables and salads. The most important part of my diet is vegetarian.

SZ: How can a singer keep his voice for many years?

AK: Before everything you have to have good health. Then you need to rest your voice, never force, limit your repertory and have correct technique. Techniques other than the one I've described are erroneous. Natural gifts are of far less importance than having a brain with which to understand technique, taste, style, personality, musicality and how to make a career.

When Kraus sings high B or C he introduces an extreme smile with a very wide mouth. I've always found the sound unpleasant—shrill and too open—and have wished he kept his mouth in a vertical shape.

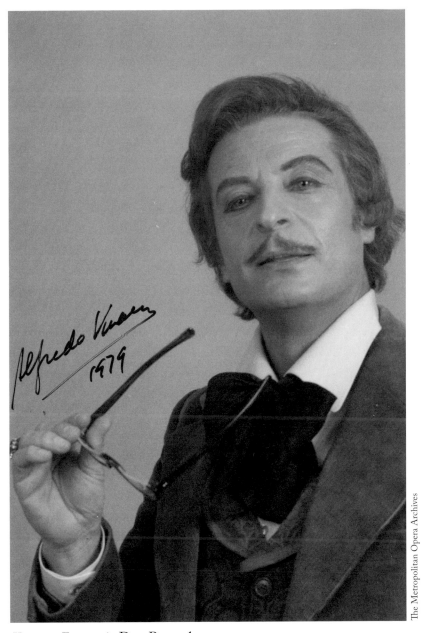

Kraus as Ernesto in Don Pasquale
"*Natural gifts are of far less importance than having a brain with which to understand technique, taste, style, personality, musicality and how to make a career.*"—*Alfredo Kraus*

Mario Del Monaco as Lohengrin, La Scala, 1957. By his account he was unsuccessful in the part because it was "too lyric." He performed Siegmund in Die Walküre, *in Stuttgart in 1966, and contemplated singing Tristan but found that Wagner calls for "falsetto and mezza voce." In the end he forsook German repertory, apart from Siegmund's "Ein Schwert verhieß mir der Vater," which he often sang in concert.*

THE ORIGINS OF LOWERED-LARYNX TECHNIQUES

As discussed in vols. 1 and 2, in the 1820s Donzelli introduced the *voix sombrée*, a darkened tone quality—sometimes referred to by voice teachers as "covered"—soon widely adopted in Italy. In 1837 Duprez created a stir at the Paris Opéra by singing a pair of high Cs in *Tell* with the *voix sombrée* with a lot of chest voice. (This was called the *ut de poitrine*.)

Several voice teachers began to experiment with the *voix sombrée*. In 1841 voice teacher Manuel García II maintained in a letter read to the Académie des Sciences that since 1832 he had been experimenting with the lowered and fixed position of the larynx, as a way of producing the *voix sombrée*. Although García seems to have regarded singing with the larynx thus positioned as little more than a curiosity, his pupil Camillo Everardi taught the technique in Russia. So far as I have determined, Melocchi, who learned it from a Russian, was the first to teach it in Italy. Where Merli learned it I have been unable to ascertain.

On a few occasions Franco remarked that the lowered-larynx technique originated with García. García, however, appears to have set it aside. Sir Charles Santley maintains in the *Art of Singing and Vocal Declamation* (1908):

> Manuel García is held up as the pioneer of scientific teachers of singing. He was—but he taught singing, not surgery. I was a pupil of his in 1858 and a friend of his while he lived, and in all the conversations I had with him, I never heard him say a

word about larynx or pharynx, glottis or any other organ used in the production and emission of the voice. He was perfectly acquainted with their functions, but he used his knowledge for his own direction, not to make a parade of it before his pupils, as he knew it would only serve to mystify them, and could serve no good purpose in acquiring a knowledge of the art of singing. My experience tells me that the less pupils know about the construction of the vocal organs the better; in fact, as I heard a master once remark, "better they should not be aware they had throats except for the purpose of swallowing their food."[1]

Indeed, thinking about physiology can be a distraction from monitoring sensations, which is at the heart of many older vocal techniques.

JEAN DE RESZKE'S LARYNX-LOWERING

According to repertory coach Amherst Webber and de Reszke biographer Clara Leiser, during performances the tenor used more than one method of voice production.[1]

After his retirement in 1904 de Reszke turned to teaching. Walter Johnstone-Douglas, a long-time de Reszke assistant, published a detailed and informative account of de Reszke's methods, according to which he "insisted upon the lowest possible position of the larynx for all heavy repertory."[2] He also maintained that, "[W]hen the voice is in the right place the tone seems to be resonating right on the hard palate, by the front teeth…."[3] Also "the great idea was to keep the line from the diaphragm, through the vocal cords into the mask."[4] De Reszke advised lifting the cheeks and smiling[5] and advocated subtle manipulations of the soft palate as well as the uvula.[6] Melocchi by contrast abjured mask placement and taught very different manipulations of the soft palate (see the chapter "A Corelli Student" below).

Jean de Reszke experimented with vocal technique. As Johnstone-Douglas puts it, "His ideas changed in focus and perspective very often…. Old pupils coming back would find new things that had been thought of, new 'places' found, new analogies, new metaphors."[7] And it is not clear if de Reszke lowered his larynx or placed on the hard palate during his career.

At the very beginning of the twentieth century Colonel Henry Mapleson recorded Met performances on cylinders. Unfortunately, those of Jean de Reszke are in horrible quality; not only was the recording done from the flies, as with all Mapleson cylinders, but noises usually obscure his voice. Still, when I listen to them the sensations in my face tell me that he is placing at the bridge of the nose or a little higher on the forehead. I don't hear evidence of his lowering the larynx. As he noted in his letter to Lilli Lehmann (see the de Reszke chapter in vol. 1) he studied first with Francesco Ciaffei, then Cotogni. To change from baritone to tenor he went to Giovanni Sbriglia. To judge from Lauri-Volpi's singing and Corelli's statements, Cotogni taught placement in the middle of the forehead but not lowering the larynx.

No studio recordings survive of Jean de Reszke but do of Sbriglia students Édouard de Reszke and Pol Plançon (who first had studied with Duprez). It is plain from those recordings that they placed on the forehead and did not lower their larynxes. To judge from her records another Sbriglia student, Lillian Nordica, placed on the forehead and may have lowered her larynx—I can't be sure. Vladimir Rosing, who studied with four Russian teachers as well as Jean de Reszke and Sbriglia, did lower his larynx, to judge from his singing, but from whom did he learn that? (In 1984 I interviewed Bidú Sayão, a Jean de Reszke student, on "Opera Fanatic." She said he made little mention of technique, did not speak of lowering the larynx and mainly concentrated on coaching, perhaps because she already was a finished singer who was performing.) It isn't known if Jean de Reszke was taught to lower the larynx or came on it later, during his experimentations.

Corelli never mentioned de Reszke and presumably was unaware that he used a laryngeal technique, nor is he mentioned in the books by or on Del Monaco. (I didn't ask Corelli about de Reszke because, although I had read Johnstone-Douglas in my teens, I had forgotten that de Reszke had written he lowered his larynx, until Gian Paolo Nardoianni [see vol. 1] reminded me of it.)

Jean de Reszke

Caruso in 1903 as il duca, in a costume from his Met debut. Many tenors preferred to debut in the role. In 1903 he hadn't yet come to sing at full volume most of the time.

DID CARUSO USE A LARYNGEAL METHOD?

In our interviews Corelli claims that Caruso used a laryngeal method. But Rosa Ponselle claims that Caruso told her he "kept a little stretch in the back of the throat to keep it open, open in the back and relaxed. It feels like a square, but only on the high notes.... The palate is high and the back of the tongue flat. This [makes] the square."[1]

Keeping the tongue flat in back would have had the effect of lowering the larynx a bit, as Jerome Hines notes in *Great Singers on Great Singing*, from which this quote is taken. But the larynx would have lowered as a *result* of the position of the tongue, which from a singer's point of view is very different from lowering the larynx by controlling it directly. Moreover, the amount of the lowering would have been far less than with the Melocchi method.

Gastone Limarilli as Dick Johnson in Fanciulla. *His teachers included Melocchi and Marcello and Mario Del Monaco.*

SOME LESSONS WITH MELOCCHI (1879–1960)

An undated seventy-eight-minute private recording survives of Melocchi giving lessons to Gastone Limarilli. Melocchi has him sing exercises mostly not on "ah" but "uh" and not on "ee" but "ih." He concentrates on emission, not sound. The sounds are thickened, rotund, have depth and mostly are covered. In my view the exercises are enough to erode any sheen a voice might have (but then I feel that way about most teachers' exercises). Limarilli clears his throat frequently. Melocchi urges him to raise his soft palate and criticizes Del Monaco for having sung Lohengrin with his palate down. (Del Monaco's only Lohengrins were six performances at La Scala in December 1957–January 1958, in Italian. By his account he was not successful because the part was "too lyric.") Melocchi intimates that Del Monaco has strayed from what he calls the "Melocchi school." He criticizes Del Monaco for sometimes not covering notes in the *passaggio* and says that Del Monaco and Corelli are too full of themselves to come to him for checkup lessons.

On the recording Limarilli's attacks of vowels sometimes have hard initiations or onsets (but not glottal strokes). Sometimes he goes off pitch, usually sharp, and sometimes he sounds labored. Scooping is the order of the day. Melocchi never comments on such things. He advises him to sing with a yawn.

Melocchi demonstrates frequently. When he finishes an utterance the last note sometimes has a hard offset (a glottal stop or kind of grunt). And he doesn't criticize Limarilli for ending notes the same way. Melocchi never mentions the larynx or breathing, perhaps because Limarilli already is making a career and presumably has mastered such things. Melocchi's question, "How long have you been performing," suggests that Limarilli may not have been studying with him very long. (Limarilli answers, "For two years.")

The big surprise is that, although Limarilli has trouble when Melocchi asks him to make diminuendos and can't sing mezza voce when the maestro requests it, Melocchi himself has no difficulty demonstrating both. He declares, "To make diminuendos and mezza voce you have to keep your throat open [that is, sing with a fully lowered larynx] and reduce the volume of sound."[1] He doesn't sound thick, spread, leathery or old. Lowered-larynx techniques in general limit musical expression. But Melocchi's brief demonstrations suggest that this result is not inevitable.

In passages from *Turandot* Limarilli sometimes sings the note before a high note open. After Limarilli sings "ti voglio ar*den*te d'amor" Melocchi exclaims, "Are you crazy? You don't take a breath before a high C?" He advocates taking every opportunity to top off the breath.

Limarilli says that Corelli has a good center but a tight top.

In one of his many asides Melocchi adds, "Del Monaco's wife [Rina] is a cretin. I saw a photo of him standing behind her on a ship. If Del Monaco really understood what she was he'd have grabbed her by the ankles and thrown her overboard, so he'd be free of her." [Rina had studied with Melocchi in the thirties. Bulgarian soprano Elena Filipova—see her chapter below—had studied with her in the eighties and said she was gracious and caring.] Melocchi also declares, "Corelli lives with a concubine, a comprimaria—a woman of mediocre intelligence. [I can't imagine thinking this of Loretta.] She's not beautiful, but he is, physically."

FC: Melocchi was superior to all other teachers because he was exacting. More, he had an exhaustive reply to any question and was able to explain the reasons why it was opportune to sing a note in a certain way. He also told you the consequences and risks if you used a different method. Mario liked to study very much. Melocchi's method limited a little his *mezze voci*, but Mario, studying with the will and tenacity that were his, succeeded in obtaining them and even very beautiful ones.

The lowered-larynx mafia

At that time La Scala's head coach was conductor/composer Antonio Tonini. Melocchi says on the recording that Tonini was his pupil. In the interest of full disclosure I should mention that in 1963 Elisabeth Schwarzkopf wrote me a letter of introduction to Tonini, with whom I then coached repertory. He referred me to voice teacher Arturo Merlini, a Melocchi adherent, Melocchi himself having died in 1960. I sat in on some of Merlini's lessons, only to conclude that I did not want to take my voice in the direction of his method. All the pupils were loud, ear splitting, even. None of them could sing softly, vary tone color or attack "ah" without slapping it. And along with Del Monaco, Merlini pupil tenor Luigi Ottolini was the model. He is heard on a number of recordings, including a commercial *Aïda* highlights with Nilsson; if you listen to it you'll get the idea.

Schwarzkopf, a doctrinaire advocate of mask placement, subsequently told me that Tonini coached her without mentioning lowering the larynx. Maybe he sensed that she'd have flayed him alive. (Actually, contrary to her well-known usual behavior, she was very nice to me. But I did see her tell a wonderful soprano to quit singing because she had a fast vibrato—although it was less extreme than Conchita Supervia's.) Tonini expected unknown singers to convert to Melocchiism.

In the late sixties Merlini became La Scala's head coach. The influence of Tonini and Merlini undoubtedly contributed to the ascendance of the lowered-larynx approach.

Franco Corelli and Simona Dall'Argine in Tosca, *offstage*

CORELLI'S REAL VIEW OF THE STANLEY METHOD

As you can hear in some of the calls from listeners during the Corelli interviews, adherents of the vocal technique taught by Dr. Douglas Stanley and his pupils claimed that Corelli vindicated them by advocating the lowered larynx. In the wake of these broadcasts a number of Stanleyites—students of Cornelius Reid, Conrad L. Osborne, Jerome LoMonaco and Thomas LoMonaco—auditioned for Corelli and for our master classes. He came to feel that his comments were being used to justify what he termed a "laryngomania" that was causing many voices to sound old and tired—that the men were singing with their larynxes slamming into their balls.

Nicola Martinucci as Radamès, Met. He could be stolid onstage. To wake him up in Manon Lescaut, *Act II, at the Rome Opera in 1994, Elena Filipova took his hands and put them atop her breasts (so she told me).*

SOME MARIO DEL MONACO SUCCESSORS

Marcello Del Monaco taught a number of singers—tenors, in particular—who came to dominate the Italian operatic scene from the 60s onward: Besides Limarilli (who studied with both Marcello and Mario Del Monaco in addition to Melocchi) they include Giorgio Merighi, Bruno Sebàstian, Corneliu Murgu, Gianfranco Cecchele (who, after his debut, modified the method), Amadeo Zambòn, Vincenzo Bello, Robert Kerns, Silvano Carroli, Josella Ligi, Angelo Mori, Giorgio Casellato Lamberti, Rita Lantieri, Maria Luisa Nave, Peter Lindroos, Nicola Martinucci and Giuseppe Giacomini,

Elena Filipova in the Manon Lescaut *in question*

among others. Although more men than women have used the technique successfully, another Marcello Del Monaco pupil, Alain Billiard, taught mezzo-soprano Sonia Ganassi.

Of the post–Del Monaco, post-Corelli Italian dramatic tenors none was more prominent than Giacomini. His tones were bronzed, and his breath span enabled him to encompass in one breath phrases others sing in two or three. True to the breed his sounds were not sweet, romantic or poetic but ringing and brilliant. Unlike some of the "laryngists" he seldom was throaty. He sang some blazing B-flats, and he even made a diminuendo on the A-flat of "paradi*so*," in the first-act *Otello* duet.[1]

Martinucci's tone had core, ring, bite, excitement, brilliance on high notes. He generally sounded like he was singing "Sì! pel ciel!"(*Otello*). He didn't—couldn't—sing softly and was without sweetness, caress, romance. Still, unlike many who lower their larynxes, his tone had a nice spin and wasn't muscular or constricted.

In an *Aïda* from Parma, he begins Act III with tones gleaming like Radamès's spear. Spectacularly, abruptly, he runs into trouble and drops down an octave at a high B-flat, apparently having strained his throat. Will he make it to the end of the act? Will the audience boo? He continues in the correct octave but is a little cautious. They applaud him.[2]

Unlike the others Lindroos doesn't have to cover A, B-flat, B-natural and C above the staff. As a consequence his singing doesn't seem manufactured and predictable. He even sings high notes with some head voice. As a result his tone on occasion is sweet, beautiful, even. Unlike Giacomini and Martinucci he doesn't sound ungainly in lyrical material. He also has greater ease above the staff. Like them his voice rings.

Did Marcello Del Monaco not invariably insist on covering, or did Lindroos revise the technique on his own? (Marcello Del Monaco was his final teacher; his studies with him pre-date his recordings. Before that he studied with Jolanda di Maria Petris, Licinio Francardi and Luigi Ricci.)

Giuseppe Giacomini. Corelli admired his emission, but he makes me squirm when he is sharp.

Lindroos's shortcomings? They are typical of Marcello Del Monaco pupils. He sings as if there never was a Gigli: no tenderness or caress, no pianissimo or mezza voce, no chiaroscuro, little response to words. Often he sings not phrases but mere notes, which don't head in a direction. He is a vocalist first and foremost who makes one piece sound much like another. On an unpublished CD-R[3] the second rendition of "De miei bollenti spiriti" and the second of the "Flower Song" afford glimpses of what he might have been: they are impassioned and have moments of dynamic variety.

Limarilli, Giacomini and Martinucci were Mario Del Monaco spinoffs who, like their model, frequently sang sharp in the middle voice. Del Monaco–style laryngeal tenors flourished outside Italy as well. From the 1950s onward there has been a plethora of such singers; the above list is but a small sample.

Del Monaco as Canio. His upper teeth are covered, his lower teeth are bared, and his jaw is dropped.

Peter Lindroos

Del Monaco as Don José in Carmen, *Met, 1952*
"Del Monaco was a highly passionate Don José, complementing my own portrayal. And yet he never hurt me—never a bruise, a scratch or anything even though he was a very physical Don José. He threw me to the ground, knelt down, bent over me. We were very effective together—an intense, passionate couple—and audiences were excited. Yet, despite his apparent violence toward me and his apparently brutal treatment of me, he never caused me any pain." —*Giulietta Simionato, in outtakes from the film* Opera Fanatic

MY LESSONS WITH MARCELLO
AND MARIO DEL MONACO

by Emilio Moscoso as told to Stefan Zucker

I studied with Marcello and Mario Del Monaco from January 1977 through March '79. I would travel from Wuppertal, where I lived and where my wife was engaged, to Treviso, where they lived, and stay for ten or twelve days and take four or five lessons a week, sometimes with a day of rest in between. Marcello taught technique through the use of arias and phrases of arias rather than exercises. You were expected to come in with your voice warmed up. My first lesson started with the first phrases from the *L'Africana* aria, with him telling me, "Yawn to lower the larynx"—which became the theme of the first lessons. He constantly would repeat "Yawn!" while you were singing. We spent the whole first lesson working on that process. (Luckily I already had some experience with yawning while singing. My teacher at the Boston Conservatory had taught it as a means to "open the throat" but had not said that the larynx was to stay down.)

At the end of the lesson Marcello had me vocalize on "u," starting on G above the staff, going up by whole steps for just three notes, holding the top note briefly and coming back down to G. We repeated the exercise a half step higher so that the high note was the C. Then he had me rest for five minutes while he explained that the "u" vowel helps lower the larynx but that it works like a file on the vocal cords and should be used only when one is warmed up completely. We repeated the exercise, and then we did the same thing using "io"—"iiio"—holding the "i" on the top note and then sliding into the "o" very slowly. This forces the tip of the tongue to stay forward, behind the lower teeth, and the forward feeling of the "i" gets integrated into the "o," keeping the tone forward-sounding but with the space that the lowered larynx gives.

At the end of my third or fourth lesson I had to return to Germany. Marcello gave me a regimen of practice to do on my own, and for the first time in the years of taking lessons someone told me how to utilize my practice time. Do a few vocalises to get warmed up, then work on an aria or two but not for more than forty-five or fifty minutes. Then do the "u" and "io" exercises for five or seven minutes. No more! Next day, rest! And again he emphasized the effect of a file on your vocal cords and that you should use the "u" with great care.

Some of his favorite exercises were from *Turandot*, "Gli enigmi sono tre, una è la vita"; from *Tosca*, "la vita mi costasse, ti salverò"; from *L'Africana*, "tu m'appartieni." He wanted the vowel on the top note to have the feeling of the "u," so that it felt like "suno tre," or "costusse." We did these exercises, starting in a lower key and then going up by half steps to the correct key and beyond. That solidified the feeling of security on the top notes and gave tremendous *squillo*.

Mario's visits to Marcello's studio seemed spontaneous. One time he showed up in riding boots and jodhpurs, and Marcello asked, "Are you on horseback?" while Mario's Rolls was parked in the courtyard instead of his horse. His participation was more as a coach. He wanted to hear how you sang certain arias, interjected his comments and would sing to show the way he wanted a phrase sung. He thought I should sing the *passaggio* notes more open; he would interject "Open, more open!" especially in "Ma se m'è forza perderti" from *Ballo*. He wanted me to open the notes before the B-flat on "Come se fosse" and carry that open "o" up but then darken the vowel on the high note, making it almost "fousse".

In "O tu che in seno agli angeli" from *Forza*, in the passage "Leonora mia," he had me carry the "i" up to the B-flat and then slowly turn it into the "a," obtaining such ring on that note that it bounced off the walls of the studio. He also demonstrated how to achieve legato by placing consonants at the last instant possible

Emilio Moscoso as Andrea Chénier

before the next word, giving the full value of the note to the vowel without anticipating the consonant. He sang the whole "Amor ti vieta" for me, and the sound was connected and at the same time fluid, with the text not compromised, so that you were able to understand every word. It was such a huge sound!

On the days I didn't sing they encouraged me to come to the studio to hear other students. I saw them work with Cecchele, Murgu and Kerns. The approach basically was the same. Of course by then these singers were coming for tune-ups, since they already had successful careers. Kerns had just finished the *Butterfly* film and album with Freni, and Murgu got his contract with the Vienna State Opera shortly thereafter.

Marcello forbade me to audition until he gave his permission, which he did after eight months. As a result of my first audition I received a contract to do ten performances of *Chénier*, in Landshut, Germany. When I told him and went back to coach with him he insisted that I should approach the role in the manner of a lyric tenor. He also told me that when Mario coached it with Giordano for La Scala he told Mario that the final duet should be a half-tone lower—otherwise it becomes a screamfest.

Shortly after, my wife and I returned to the States and did not go back to Treviso. I went into the restaurant business where I remained for twenty-five years until I had to retire because of illness. I did sing Canio in a couple of productions here in Boston and was involved in several other productions with a local opera group. I still sing in church.

I feel it is important for young singers to understand what was going on in the fifties, sixties and seventies with regard to the development of the tenor voice.

DEL MONACO'S DIAPHRAGM

by Chris Stavrou

Chris is a top donor to Bel Canto Society. Here he recounts one of his experiences as a supernumerary at the Met, as a teen, from 1956–58. He understudied a speaking part in *Andrea Chénier* and understudied the corpse (Titurel) in *Parsifal*. He explains:

> "We supers made $2 a night. But for a speaking part of over a certain number of words, perhaps four or five, you got paid $10 or $20. But the supers who did those parts always showed up."

For seven years, until recently, Chris studied voice with John Macurdy. Years ago he studied with Broadway star William Diehl. Below he reflects on Mario Del Monaco's speaking voice and breathing technique.

> As a super, I chatted with Del Monaco. I was surprised then (and am now) at how high in pitch his speaking voice could be—he almost sounded like a high soprano—although he also could speak with a baritone voice. You can hear that high voice on his radio commentary when singing *Forza* at Hartford's Bushnell (I think before he went to the Met) and on a few interviews on YouTube.
>
> But when he walked onstage and adjusted his palate and dropped that larynx (or however he did it) he pumped out that glorious, brilliant, dramatic, unique sound.
>
> Del Monaco designed his own costumes, and they were made of the lightest material to have as little as possible touching his chest, apparently, so I actually could see his diaphragm working during *Chénier*, during the trial scene. I would say it vibrated somewhere between one and two inches as he sang.

Mario Del Monaco as Lohengrin, La Scala, 1957

Enrique Pina. One of the handful of students to study with Corelli for a number of years, he is able to describe his teaching.

A CORELLI STUDENT

Many more singers have adopted the "fixed" lowered-larynx technique rather than Corelli's floating-larynx modification, in part because a number of teachers advocate the former, but also because Corelli made it difficult to study with him on account of his comings and goings, unreliability about appointments and generally being impossible. He rescued a student from exaggerated lowered-larynx teaching only to find a couple of years later that the man had reverted to his former ways and brutalized his voice, much to Franco's despair. (I heard the man in a *Nabucco*. To me he sounded like late Cecchele, only more off pitch. Returning home I played some McCormack to wash my ears.)

Over the years a number of Corelli students asked to sing for me, but Loretta in each case advised them they weren't ready. The students told me the Corellis always discouraged them from auditioning. Corelli's most famous pupil is Andrea Bocelli, but Loretta several times said I shouldn't judge Franco's teaching from Bocelli's work because he hadn't studied with him long enough. "He sings badly," she said of Bocelli.

I asked Franco if I could sit in on the lessons of one or more pupils, but he said he didn't want to invite me because I might think his teaching too aggressive and regard him as crazy.

A friend said a Corelli disciple wanted me to hear him. His name is Enrique Pina. On a video on YouTube he sings Annibale's "O' paese d'o sole" sweetly, with head resonance. On another video on YouTube, of *Carmen* excerpts, he makes a diminuendo on the B-flat of the "Flower Song."

Corelli dropping his jaw in front and in back while covering his upper teeth and lowering his larynx in a 1963 Met Tosca. *Yet in a photo of a 1964 Met* Bohème, *not shown, he is singing while smiling, with the corners of his lips raised, probably in imitation of Lauri-Volpi, with whom he was studying Rodolfo.*

SZ: How do you make that diminuendo?

EP: It's a result of the floating larynx. I position my larynx midway down and then lower it slightly to make the diminuendo.

SZ: For how long did you study with Corelli?

EP: For six years. I traveled from Rome to Milan every week to take two lessons with him, until he became ill in 2003. The most difficult thing was in the first year and a half, getting the larynx to stay down. It's like touching your toes: at the beginning your back doesn't like it. For six months my neck hurt and my voice was unhappy. Corelli said, "You don't perform with the larynx lowered as far as it can go, but you have to lower it that much at the beginning." He had me stand in front of a mirror and lower my larynx and the back of my tongue but without singing. For the first eighteen months I didn't sing songs or arias but only exercises to make the throat muscles stretch and become more flexible, to help lower the larynx and the base of the tongue. In the end he had me lower my larynx all the way for loud high notes but not for notes in the middle voice. By contrast Del Monaco–type singers always keep their larynxes lowered to the maximum. Watching *Corelli at His Zenith*[1] helped me because it gave me a good view of his larynx in action. "Remain conscious of the distance between your tongue and your soft palate," he used to say.

SZ: In a radio interview with me [February 3, 1990] Corelli said he believed in smiling while singing. Did he have you smile?

EP: Corelli never had me smile or raise the corners of my lips. He wanted me to sing with my lips covering my upper teeth. "The upper teeth never must be seen," he said. But he wanted me to bare my lower teeth. On the tape of his 1981 comeback in Newark you can see what he had in mind. He was proud of that performance.[2]

SZ: Many mechanistic teachers train the registers separately and have students sing in falsetto. Did Corelli do this?

EP: No, he did not train the registers separately or have me sing in falsetto.

SZ: Did he teach you a breathing method?

EP: When I came to Corelli I already had one that involved pushing out with the diaphragm. (I don't support from the pelvis, for example.) I had learned it from my first teacher, in Santo Domingo. Corelli concluded that my breath support was working well and decided by and large to leave it alone. He wanted my voice to be "seated on the breath." But on extreme high notes he had me push

Here is an enlarged version of the photo on p. 194 with Corelli dropping his jaw in front and in back while covering his upper teeth and lowering his larynx in a 1963 Met Tosca.

The Metropolitan Opera Archives

with my thighs. He was against breathing through the nose, saying that it reduces *squillo*.

SZ: Olivero told me she always breathes through the nose—and she is not alone.

EP: Corelli maintained that if you breathe through the mouth the throat opens automatically, but if you breathe through the nose the throat remains closed and it is more difficult to open it. [Mouth breathing may be what caused Corelli to become so dry that he sucked water from sponges while performing.—SZ]

SZ: When Corelli taught at Opera Music Theatre International some students protested that they didn't want to study with him because his teaching was too extreme [listen to the Dodi Protero interview on the March 3, 1990 tape, available as a Digital Download and as a bonus on the DVD D100, *Corelli in Concert*, www.belcantosociety.org/store/audio/musicdownloads/conversations-with-corelli-3-3-1990/]. What was the most aggressive thing he did as a teacher?

EP: He pushed down on my Adam's apple while I was singing. Many who studied with Corelli didn't stay long enough to learn his method in depth. He himself said, "It's not something you can learn in a day. It takes years and requires a great deal of patience." [From the point of view of the singer, having a teacher press on the Adam's apple is terrifying. Nilsson in her autobiography, *La Nilsson*, recounts that an unnamed voice teacher "began the lesson by gripping my larynx and pressing it down. For two weeks my larynx was so sore I could hardly speak."3]

Corelli made no mistakes with my voice. He never pushed it and never made my throat feel tired. He cared about my voice. [This may be the first time anybody ever accused Franco of altruism.—SZ]

SZ: What was Corelli's objective?

FP: For every note to have *squillo*.

To hear Pina live I rented a practice room. The voice was quite different from what I had heard on YouTube, which had compressed the sound to the point that the *squillo* was omitted. Live, Pina's sound was focused and never was thick or coarse. Unlike other mechanistic tenors he didn't sound like a pushed-up baritone, and his voice wasn't weighty like a dramatic tenor.

In an exercise he went all the way down to the B-flat underneath the range of most basses.

I asked him if he could trill—and he did.

On the "Chi son" of "Che gelida manina" he made a diminuendo on the "son" and gradually returned to full voice in an extended crescendo in the next phrase.

In "Celeste Aïda" he gave me a spinal chill before the final B-flat, on which he made a Corelli-style diminuendo. And he made another Corelli-style diminuendo in "E lucevan le stelle."

He was forceful and provided another spinal chill in Edgardo's entrance from *Lucia*.

On high B-natural his voice took on a more heady quality. Sometimes his mouth was lopsided, as were Corelli's and McCormack's on occasion (not to mention George London's). Sometimes he ended the last note of a phrase with a hard offset—a kind of extra-musical grunt. Corelli and Caruso, among others, did the same thing on occasion.

Pina illustrates that the benefits of the floating larynx are repeatable and weren't limited to Corelli's own singing. I don't mean to suggest that he is another Corelli. The voice and singing personality are very different.

On December 18, 2009 Pina had sung a concert with the Orquesta Sinfonica Nacional in the Dominican Republic which was broadcast on Television Dominicana and others. The program included "E lucevan le stelle," which Pina sang with a Corelli-style diminuendo. I asked him how he sang the piece from a technical point of view.

EP: I sing from "E lucevan le stelle" through "Mi cadea fra le braccia" with my larynx lowered almost to the maximum. Then I sing "O dolci baci, o languide carezze" with a floating larynx, without tension. After that I do "Mentr'io fremente le belle" with my larynx lowered to the maximum. I begin "disciogliea dai veli" with my larynx gently lowered and then relax it to make the pianissimo and diminuendo. The remainder of the piece I sing with my larynx lowered to the point of maximum *squillo*.

I practiced this passage with the diminuendo for a number of months, until at last I was able to sing it without the sound breaking or wavering. Even so, phlegm from a cold could break the thread of voice. Also, the effect easily could be shipwrecked by a communication failure with the conductor since the first violin is playing the melody with the singer, and the two have to stay together.

On October 6, 2010 I attended a concert at Zankel (a new hall inside the Carnegie Hall building), where Pina appeared as soloist with the orchestra of Best Buddies International, Demetrius

Spaneas, conductor. Pina sang "Donna non vidi mai" (*Manon Lescaut*), "Tombe degli avi miei.... Fra poco a me ricovero" (*Lucia*) and "E lucevan le stelle" (*Tosca*). At the end of the *Manon Lescaut* he gave a spinal chill. In the *Lucia* he made much use of mezza voce and in-between-levels of dynamics, reserving his fortissimo for the big climaxes, in the manner of many pre–Del Monaco tenors, and singing with lovely pathos and a sweetness evocative of them. In the *Tosca* he was similar to his YouTube version but with more passion toward the end.

SZ: I just viewed two of your latest clips on YouTube, the "Sanctus" from the Berlioz *Requiem* and "Tombe degli Avi miei.... Fra poco a me ricovero" from *Lucia*, and noticed that you have modified your technique.

EP: Yes, I believe in lowering the larynx but not as far. I push it down sweetly [*dolcemente*], to the point where my voice rings the most. That point varies from person to person because of differences in anatomy. Corelli believed in singing strongly. When I began to use his method I experienced problems of endurance and finished every performance with a tired voice. I feared I would have a short career and end up losing my voice on account of the effort with which I sang, but now I can sing for hours on end. The "Sanctus" requires pianissimi sung with a sweetness that is difficult to achieve with a more extreme laryngeal method.

Pina has modified his technique repeatedly. YouTube has many clips of him singing. To hear him using a technique closest to Corelli's teachings listen to the above-mentioned "E lucevan le stelle" on YouTube as well as "Por amor" and "O sole mio," also from the December 2009 concert.

As we saw from Corelli's letters in vol. 2, during his Met years, influenced by Lauri-Volpi, he was unfaithful to his own technique. What the letters don't tell us is that afterwards he returned to it.

William Matteuzzi

FRANCISCO ARAIZA (1950–): A ROSSINI TENOR WHO LOWERS HIS LARYNX

After declining for 150 years, vocal virtuosity is on the upswing. Around 1960 few tenors sang roulades or high Cs. The number who do steadily is burgeoning, though the singing sometimes lacks personality, passion and charm.

The differences between Nicola Monti on a Melodram recording of a Naples performance of *La cenerentola* in 1958[1] and Mexican Francisco Araiza on a CBS studio recording of the opera from 1980[2] are representative of the typical differences among tenors—I'm tempted to say singers—from the 50s and those from the late 70s onward. Monti is sunny and ingratiating, his mezza voce caressing. But he omits the trills, blurs the coloratura at conductor Mario Rossi's fast clip and sounds uncomfortable upstairs. The technical demands are beyond him and his range simply is too short: had the more difficult and high-flying passages not been cut, he probably would have been unable to sing the part.

Araiza sings it uncut, hitting all the notes—except the trills, which he too avoids. He has marvelous agility and velocity, and the high Cs hold no terrors. But, however proficient, he is charmless and mechanical. I have found no evidence that anyone in Rossini's day produced his tone like Araiza, with the locus of resonation far forward in the face.

The generation of Italian Rossini performers from the 1950s, 60s and early 70s had fallen behind not only Araiza but also Americans, in particular, in their ability to sing florid or high-flying passages. (The Americans Rockwell Blake, Chris Merritt and Bruce Ford

Francisco Araiza

flourished in Italy at the Rossini Opera Festival at Pesaro.) Italian tradition had come to sanction cutting the most difficult passages. Italian singers—tenors, in particular—omitted trills and high notes and simplified or smudged coloratura.

Part of the problem is that, since Del Monaco (since Caruso, really), Italian tenors haven't stopped striving for a macho image. In 1983 soprano Adelaide Negri told me tenor Dano Raffanti told her, "Horne promised me that if I sang the Rossini repertory she would help me. But if I don't sing Verdi and verismo people will say I'm a *froscio* [faggot]."

Still, *frosci* or not, as we shall see some Italians by now have caught up and then some.

Francisco Araiza

In a 1984 Met performance of *Die Entführung aus dem Serail* Araiza hit most of the notes dead on with big, bright tones so well focused as to make intonation lapses more noticeable. In the highly florid "Ich baue ganz" he was accurate in the stepwise passages, less so in the arpeggiated ones. He interpolated both a small cadenza before the repeat of the main theme and some ornamentation in the repeat itself—as well as a few extra breaths. He pronounced German well and acted energetically. But his singing was more impressive than beautiful. And he wasn't very interesting: His dynamics were sometimes random, sometimes inert. He failed to emphasize melodic climaxes and to distinguish melody from ornamentation through volume or accentuations. He sang with little tenderness and was boring in tender passages. He hardly ever shaded his tone and managed to be vigorous yet dull.

Singers sustain interest in many ways, interpretation and temperament among them. Pavarotti does so through charisma; Schipa, through charisma, charm and musical sensitivity; Di Stefano, through passion and feeling for words; Caruso, through warmth and emotion. Araiza isn't endowed with an extraordinary supply of these qualities. On a recording of lirico-spinto warhorses made in 1986[3] he relies instead on musical effects, such as contrasting soft singing with loud—chiaroscuro of dynamics. His interpretations of the album's two Puccini pieces, "Che gelida manina" and "E lucevan le stelle," are satisfying, for in addition to alternating dynamics, he does sing with some tenderness and fervor. But in the aria from *Eugene Onegin*, one misses Dmitri Smirnoff's plaintive quality, his wistful yearning. In the *L'Arlesiana* aria Araiza lacks both bitter melancholy in the opening and desperation and *slancio* (surge, oomph) for the end. He also lacks vocal punch and core on the high As, where the voice is unassertive and veiled, particularly on dark vowels ("ah," "oh," "oo").

Perhaps the recording's most underinterpreted selection is "Ah! fuyez, douce image" (*Manon*), where he sings as if he hadn't considered the importance of the notes in relation to each other or thought about which leads ahead to which. In the middle voice he produces a strong round tone, but he doesn't imbue the high B-flats with longing, pleading or desperation; nor is he able, in the alternative, to trumpet them forth. On higher notes, however, such as the *Bohème* aria's C or the interpolated high D at the end of "Possente amor" (*Rigoletto*) the voice takes on brilliance. Stylistically he is an anomaly: a Latin singer with a German sound who achieves legato in the German manner since the 30s—almost without portamento. The music on the record, mostly from the late nineteenth century, was first performed by singers who, to judge by early records, used portamento generously.

Araiza is never tasteless. At his worst he is earthbound, offering conscientious observance of interpretation markings in the score without going beyond them. At his best he is an excellent singer who just misses striking sparks.

On January 5, 1991, on "Opera Fanatic," Araiza gave me a brilliant, wonderful interview. (At BelCantoSociety.org the four-hour interview is available as music download #M43.) Here is an excerpt:

SZ: Where do you place your voice when you aren't covering?

FA: I place in the front of my hard palate, just above the front teeth.

SZ: Where do you place when you are covering?

FA: I go through the wide section of the soft palate into the nasal cavity, up above the hard palate.

SZ: Do you change the position of your larynx?

FA: When I started to study my larynx tended to go up. I did muscular exercises to make it go down or at least not go up. My sound was inside my body, throat and head. My teacher brought the sound back to the frontal position but with the larynx down.

Araiza as Belmonte in Entführung

SZ: I'm not aware that in the early nineteenth century anyone consciously lowered his larynx or placed so far forward in the face. Do you think I'm wrong?

FA: No, you may be right.

Aspiration

To obtain precise articulation of florid passages in *Cenerentola* and *Entführung* Araiza aspirated—which raises the question, when if ever is aspiration justified? In 1991 I asked Araiza this question on "Opera Fanatic." He rejoined that he preferred the clarity of articulation that can be achieved with aspiration.[4]

The subject is important enough to warrant a digression, especially since it is relevant to discussion of Ramón Vargas later in the book: With aspiration it is possible to discern each note without

205

ambiguity. Yet aspiration offends many ears. As a practical matter the question all too often boils down to this: Conductors frequently choose tempos that are too fast to allow a singer to articulate 16th notes clearly and cleanly without aspiration. Rockwell Blake brags that he can sing 16th notes at a metronome marking of 144 to the quarter note without aspiration, but I have difficulty pinpointing the pitch of individual notes when he sings them at that tempo. (His vibrato further clouds the issue.) As a practical matter when most singers go beyond tempos of 120 without aspiration accuracy of intonation and clarity of articulation suffer. So which is worse, loss of accuracy and clarity or light—as opposed to heavy—aspiration?

In special cases moderately heavy aspiration can be a virtue rather than a lesser evil. In the quartet from *La scala di seta* Rossini did something highly unusual for the period: he wrote triplets for the tenor against the other singers' duplets. To make certain the listener feels the triplets as such it is helpful that they be aspirated (at least that is what I did).

Pier Francesco Tosi wrote about aspiration in the 1743 book *Observations on the Florid Song*: "There are some [singers] still more ridiculous, who mark [divisions] above Measure, and with Force of Voice, thinking (for Example) to make a Division upon A, it appears as if they said Ha, Ha, Ha, or Gha, Gha, Gha; and the same upon the other Vowels." Tosi is telling us not only that he disapproves of aspiration but also that it was not uncommon in Bologna in 1723, when and where his book first was published, in Italian.[5]

In 1757 Johann Friedrich Agricola published a German edition of Tosi's book, with an introduction and annotations so extensive that in effect it constitutes a separate work. On aspiration he wrote: "This is a typical error of those poorly instructed basses, many of whom seek fame by bellowing instead of singing, especially on their highest notes. When they wish to sing divisions, they put an h in front of every note, which they then aspirate with such force that, besides producing an unpleasant sound, it causes them unnecessarily to expend so much air that they are forced to breathe almost every half measure."[6] In short, aspiration was not uncommon in Berlin either.

Any number of famous singers have aspirated. Are we to abstain from listening to Gigli because he was one of them?

Olivero worships Gigli but complained to me in 1996 that he aspirated turns in the fourth act of *Adriana*.[7] I asked her how she could reconcile his aspiration with her contention that he had a stupendous technique. She called it a minor fault. Ironically she herself aspirates at the end of "Sempre libera."[8]

Other things being equal, I prefer it when singers don't aspirate. (Sometimes I would learn a piece using heavy aspiration, then switch to light aspiration and then to none, striving all the while to preserve accuracy of intonation and clarity of articulation.) But if a singer needs aspiration to obtain accuracy and clarity I'm happy to pay the price.

In any case, granted that aspiration does help a singer achieve accuracy and clarity, I still don't understand why Araiza aspirated as heavily as he did in *Entführung*, where the tempos of the fiorituras only are moderate.

William Matteuzzi and Giuseppe Morino: Unaffected by Del Monaco and Corelli

Of recent Rossini tenors, Italian and otherwise, William Matteuzzi is the most accurate, agile-voiced and musicianly. In a 1998 *L'Italiana in Algeri* from Parma[9] he uses a crescendo to build a phrase to its moment of greatest harmonic tension (an appoggiatura or other dissonance), then tapers the following consonance, a moment of harmonic relaxation.

Because of the influence of such conductors as Gianandrea Gavazzeni and Riccardo Muti Italians since the war have done little or no ornamenting of vocal lines. Not so Matteuzzi, who decorates the repeat of his first-act cabaletta. But he sometimes sacrifices tone quality on the altar of brilliance of tempo and ornamentation, to the point that his tone turns white. (Giovanni David, a principal Rossini "creator," was accused of the same thing—by Giacomo David, his star-tenor father, no less.[10]) Matteuzzi's ornamentation itself consists not of divisions, as generally was the case in Rossini's day, but of interpolations. (With divisions, for example, each written eighth note is replaced by two sixteenth notes, so that the music becomes twice as florid.)

His mezza voce matches the timbre of his full voice even on a high B-flat in "Languir per una bella," but he has a bleaty forte C. It's hard to hear him in ensembles (the same was said of Rubini[11]). His tone isn't full bodied, his breath span is short and he has no trill. But he doesn't have to distort vowels by covering—yet he has no *passaggio* problems.

He ends the cabaletta on a high E-flat—a solecism. In music of this period it is not enough to end on the tonic; for the melody to be resolved one also must end on the tonic in the octave in which the melody is centered. This is true all the more in cases where the melody has not gone higher than that tonic in the phrases preceding the end of the piece. To justify ending on the high E-flat Matteuzzi would have had to relocate the tessitura upward so that it lay in that octave.

Giuseppe Morino: A Voice That Stays in the Ear

Mid-nineteenth-century British critic Henry F. Chorley remarked of Rubini:

> Before, however, Rubini came to England [in 1831] his voice had contracted that sort of trilling or trembling habit, then new here, which of late has been abused ad nauseam. It was no longer in its prime—hardly capable, perhaps, of being produced mezzo forte or piano; for which reason he had adopted a style of extreme contrast betwixt soft and loud, which many ears were unable, for a long period, to relish. After a time these vehemences (in themselves vicious) were forgotten for the sake of the transcendent qualities by which they were accompanied, though in the last years of his reign they were exaggerated into the alternation of a scarcely audible whisper and a shout....[12]

In *Il pirata*, composed by Bellini for Rubini, Giuseppe Morino replicates this basic approach to dynamics, alternating soft phrases with loud, making his performance one of the more individualistic since De Lucia and Gigli. (Morino, however, does not use rubato as expressively as either one and is not so extreme in style as De Lucia.)

Pirata, the opera of Bellini's Scala debut, made his reputation. In 1826 Donizetti, Saverio Mercadante, Giovanni Pacini and scores of other composers were under Rossini's spell. Pacini wrote in *Le mie memorie artistiche*,

> Everyone followed the same school, the same veins, as a consequence they were imitators…of the great star. But, good God! What else was to be done but imitate Rossini if there was no other means by which to sustain oneself.[13]

Bellini's individuality of soul made him the alternative. Rossini matches Bellini's affective qualities only on occasion, such as at the end of *Tancredi*. On the whole, Bellini is more intimate, personal and impassioned if less brilliant.

Nearly all other Bellini performers today miss his spirit entirely, but in a 1987 *Pirata* from Macerata, Morino captures the pathos, for example, in the touching Act I duet and the haunting Act I finale. Some other highlights include Morino's hushed mezza-voce singing in much of Act II, the longing and heartbreak of his pleading ("Ah! sentimi") and the rapt beginning to the trio.[14]

Morino lacks Rubini's top-of-the-head voice placement and attendant tonal qualities, and his voice is a little short for someone undertaking a Rubini role: Rubini sang the last-act tenor scena in D, Morino sings it in the published key of C. Rubini went up to G in performance, whereas Morino only ventures to E—a limitation for ornamentation as well as for interpolations at climaxes. Despite this his ornamentation is lovely and skillful.

His embellishment of Donizetti's *Maria di Rohan* in a 1988 performance from Martina Franca is much less persuasive.[15] For instance, he several times resorts to interpolating high notes abruptly, without preparing them by rewriting the vocal line higher, so that they come as a shock and seem grafted on rather than integral to the expression. Donizetti, who typically composed with specific voices in mind, crafted the tenor part for the robust baritonal tenor Carlo Guasco. When other singers took over parts, the composer characteristically went to pains to adapt them and, for a Morino-like tenor, would have relocated the tessitura upward, which is what the tenor himself or his coaches should have done.[a]

For a high tenor Morino's voice has a remarkable degree of fullness through the middle and bottom, to the point that it is slightly spread in pitch. He sings an accurate quick ascending scale. His rhythm is good, he punctuates with apt pauses, and his turns are particularly graceful, with consonances shortened, dissonances emphasized. He at once has two seemingly antithetical qualities: pellucid diction and excellent legato. And he has a soulful mezza voce. His notes with the most personality, from middle voice B-flat to high B-flat, have an elegiac, mournful, plaintive quality—I've never known a voice to stay in my ear so vividly months after I heard it once.

But as his voice ascends it becomes white and doesn't gain in power or ring—it lacks climax. He doesn't capture the characters' heroic qualities and is not compelling in expressing bitterness, rage or hate. He's lovely but not exciting. Evidently he has no trill. Sometimes, as in much of the *Rohan* and in a 1989 Carnegie Hall *Pirata*, he has a conspicuous fast vibrato, alien to American taste but again reminiscent of Rubini (see the vibrato chapter, in vol. 1). He sometimes interrupts phrases with breaths and has a tendency toward "last syllableitis"—prolongation or accentuation of the last syllable of a phrase. (Many singers mar their phrasing by accentuating and holding on to a syllable set to the resolution of an appoggiatura, even where that syllable is on a weak beat that resolves a dissonance. This mislocates the phrase's climax, inappropriately transferring it from a point of structural tension (the appoggiatura) to one of structural repose (the resolution). In addition to throwing music out of kilter, mislocating accentuations to resolutions of appoggiaturas often causes Italian to be stressed incorrectly: *amoRE* instead of *aMOre*.) His intonation is not really secure although it is

---

[a] For a related discussion see my "Singers Who Changed Singing, from 1775 to Callas and Sutherland," in *Opera Fanatic* magazine, Issue 3, available at BelCantoSociety.org.)

Giuseppe Morino as Gualtiero in the Macerata Pirata

better here, in the Macerata *Pirata*, than on his Nuova Era aria CD or in the Carnegie *Pirata*.

In short Morino has major shortcomings—more than enough to make it easy to dismiss him. Maybe they will cause him to pall for me over time. But for now, for the sake of his good points, I'd sooner hear him than anyone else who has come along in years. Like tenors before Donzelli and Duprez, Matteuzzi and Morino emphasize head voice over chest voice.

Magda Olivero as Violetta in Traviata

OLIVERO ATTACKS DEL MONACO'S TECHNIQUE

The following interview is from the outtakes of the film Opera Fanatic: Stefan and the Divas *(shot in October 1996):*

SZ: Did you sing often with Corelli and Del Monaco?

Magda Olivero: Yes.

SZ: Can you compare the two?

MO: (firmly) No. They were diametrically opposite. Corelli always was striving to be able to sing better and to acquire a technique—he studied with Lauri-Volpi. Del Monaco had a technique *all his own*. When Del Monaco and I sang *Francesca da Rimini* together at La Scala [in 1959] he explained his whole technique to me. When he finished I said, "My dear Del Monaco, if I had to put into practice all the things you've told me I'd stop singing right away and just disappear." The technique was so complicated: you push the larynx down, then you push this up, then you do that—in short, it made my head spin just to hear everything he did.

SZ: Both Corelli and Del Monaco studied with a certain Arturo Melocchi—

MO: Yes.

SZ: —who taught a technique based on lowering the larynx. Corelli, however, later modified the technique. He moved the larynx around.

To sing piano he positioned the larynx relatively high, to sing forte, he positioned it at the base of the neck. For me it was incredible that anyone would try this—and that he would get it to work!

MO: Yes, indeed.

SZ: If you had to choose between the two, which would you pick?

MO: Well—Corelli was able to sing those long piano phrases—Del Monaco, no. We recorded *Francesca* excerpts together [1969]. Francesca has a beautiful phrase, "Paolo, datemi pace," marked "piano," and then Paolo enters with "Inghirlandata di violette," which also should be sung softly, delicately. Instead, Del Monaco was terrible—he *bellowed* the phrase! [She imitates him and laughs.] When he listened to the playback he exclaimed, "I can't believe it! After that soft poetic phrase I come in and what do I sound like—a boxer punching with his fists!" He recorded the phrase again, but the second attempt more or less was the same because he was incapable of singing piano. He was furious with himself because he wanted to. He tried everything, but his technique would not permit him to sing softly since it totally was based on the muscles.

Conductor Vincenzo Bellezza and part of the cast of Fanciulla, *including Olivero, Lauri-Volpi and Giangiacomo Guelfi. Teatro dell'Opera, Rome, 1957*

Rehearsals for Francesca da Rimini, *with Gianandrea Gavazzeni, Olivero and Del Monaco, La Scala, 1959*

Corelli as Raul in Gli Ugonotti

DIFFERENT SINGING TECHNIQUES

Even if Del Monaco couldn't sing piano for the *Francesca da Rimini* recording there are many examples of him doing so. As previously mentioned, however, he found it risky for the voice.

Del Monaco's and Corelli's techniques are of the so-called "mechanistic" variety and are bound to shock any singer with a traditional technique. At least from 1773, when Giacomo David began to use top-of-the-head voice placement, most opera singers have relied on sensations to monitor their voice production. Most such techniques involve voice placement. By "placing" in a certain way a singer learns to expect vibrations and sounds characteristic of that placement. For the singer it's as though the sensations—ultimately, his placement—excite his coordination. It's as though his body and organs of phonation adapt themselves as a result of his placement (and the pitch, dynamic level, vowel and tone color he is aiming for). According to this view, for any singer, voice placement and the condition of his organs of phonation determine voice quality. So the singer with a sensation-governed technique ends up striving to experience and re-experience particular sensations, and the more attuned he becomes to those sensations the more secure his technique.

Compared to Pina's explanation of Corelli's technique, placement talk may seem lacking in lucidity. Yet sensation-governed singing can be taught easily, for the sensations can become manifest after little study. (I can get a singer to experience placement in one to two hours.) There are or have been many different sensation-governed techniques, however.

Luigi Lablache and Mario as Dr. Dulcamara and Nemorino in L'elisir d'amore. *(Mario, a nobleman, was known by the one name only.) He was renowned above all for elegiac singing and for communicating romance.*

In the twentieth century most who relied on sensations placed in the mask. At Juilliard and other American conservatories in the early 60s "mask placement," depending on the teacher, referred to placement at the bridge of the nose or on the forehead (Lauri-Volpi's placement is of this kind). This placement dates at least as far back as Luigi Lablache's *Lablache's Method of Singing*, published in French, Italian, English, Swedish and Russian in many editions from 1841 onward. (Lablache, creator of Giorgio in *Puritani* and Don Pasquale, was the most famous bass of the period; for a biography see Clarissa Lablache Cheer's *The Great Lablache*.[1]) But many singers have defined mask placement differently.

Jan Peerce told me in 1977 that he placed on the lower teeth. At the time he was studying with Alex Lorber. My girlfriend in those days, Judy Nitzsche, was one of Peerce's accompanists and one of Lorber's studio accompanists. She told me that Lorber spoke of lower-teeth placement with all his pupils.

Martinelli, as already mentioned, placed on the upper teeth.

Bianca Berini told me on the "Opera Fanatic" radio program in 1984 that she placed alongside the nostrils. As we have seen Kraus placed in the area beside his nose, just above the nostrils.

Simionato told me in 1996 that she placed in the cheeks. Olivero told me, also in 1996, that she aimed her breath into little receptacles in the cheeks. I interpret that to mean that she places there. (Both interviews were for the *Opera Fanatic* film.)

Corelli told me in 1991 that some of the teachers he studied with other than Melocchi advocated placement in the middle of the forehead; to show me he put his index finger on what is now thought of as the principal pressure point there.

Of the ninety-nine celebrity singers I have interviewed, all except Schipa, Corelli, Hines and Marcella Pobbe relied on some form of mask placement (as Hines had done when he studied with Samuel Margolis).

Not all placement singers placed or place in the mask, however. In the early nineteenth century, some, Rubini among them, placed at the top of the head, at a point between the ears but higher up, in the area of the sphenoidal sinus, where a baby's skull comes together.[2]

Rubini's locus of breath support was the area of the pubic hair, where he felt a simultaneous contraction and expansion. (In the language of today's voice teachers his inspiratory muscles opposed his expiratory muscles.[3])

At Juilliard in the early 60s they taught one to pull in at the diaphragm—which is what Simionato and Olivero each do. Others push out at the diaphragm, as did a fabulous tenor, the late Giovanni Consiglio, for instance.

Changing placement changes the sound. I place at the top of the head. If I switch to bridge-of-the-nose placement the sound becomes less focused (or focuses a little "wider") and less ringing. In any case it's easy for a practiced ear to distinguish if a singer is using mask placement or top-of-the-head placement.

Most singers are doctrinaire about their methods. In 1996 I said to Olivero, "You hold that there is one God, one country and one method of singing."

"Yes, precisely," she said.

My position is different: each of these methods—fixed larynx, floating larynx and placement of one kind or another—has produced some great singers. Still, a singer's choice of technique has a huge impact on what he sounds like and what notes he can hit. (For further thoughts on this subject see "Different Singing Techniques," in *Opera Fanatic* magazine, issue 2, pp. 10–11, where I discuss what I consider the eight fundamentally different singing techniques. The magazine is available at BelCantoSociety.org.) Mechanistic techniques, however, can limit expression. (See "Tenore del Mondo" in vol. 2.)

For better or worse laryngeal methods changed the world's view of what singers, tenors in particular, should sound like, at least in Verdi and verismo. De Lucia, Tamagno and Pertile sang at less than full voice most of the time. To a lesser degree so did Anselmi, Bonci, Schipa, Gigli and many others. As Corelli himself said, when he came on the scene in the early 50s a good mezza voce was expected, but by the time he perfected his mezza voce in the mid-60s no one else sang in mezza voce anymore. After Del Monaco and Corelli nearly everyone sang forte or fortissimo most of the time.

Del Monaco and Corelli by no means were the first singers to change singing by introducing new techniques. I show in vols. 1 and 2 that the revolutions in singing ignited by Giacomo and Giovanni David, Andrea Nozzari, Rubini, Donzelli and Duprez were brought about by changes in technique. The revolutions of the first four of these tenors were obvious because they sang high notes that were beyond the ranges of earlier tenors and because Rubini, in addition, had a different vibrato (see "The Fluctuating Fortunes of Vibrato," in vol. 1). Del Monaco and Corelli, on the other hand, sang the same notes as everyone else. Still, their revolution relegated to the junk heap the sweet tenor singing practiced by Gigli and many tenors before them, along with Gigli's art of chiaroscuro.

Like Duprez and Caruso Del Monaco sacrificed nuance on the altar of power. Corelli tried to have it both ways but was limited by his need to cover all notes above F. The same thing happened with Gigli and Del Monaco as took place with Nourrit and Duprez as well as De Reszke, Tamagno, De Lucia and Caruso: the coarser, more obvious, less nuanced style won out.

In the last few years Vittorio Grigolo has been providing a counterexample to this trend (see below).

Elena Filipova as Elisabetta in Don Carlos, *Vienna State Opera, 1994*

THE RISE AND FALL OF ELENA FILIPOVA

She tells about her meteoric career and why, having studied with Rina Del Monaco, Corelli and Alain Billiard, to resurrect her voice she switched to Hilde Zadek and a technique based on placement.

SZ: Where did you first study singing?

Elena Filipova: At the conservatory in Sofia. I obtained a master's degree with high honors. In *Gymnasium* I received a diploma in oboe. At seventeen I was a soprano soloist in the Mozart *Requiem*.

SZ: Was the technique you studied mechanistic, or was it based on placement?

EF: Both. My teacher had me lower my larynx and at the same time place at the cheek bones and in the middle of the forehead and support below the waist. I took lessons four times a week, studying repertory as well as technique. I prepared the Contessa in *Le nozze di Figaro*, Pamina in *Die Zauberflöte*, Liù in *Turandot*, Micaëla in *Carmen*, Nedda in *Pagliacci* and other parts and sang with orchestra with a maestro from the National Opera.

SZ: How did you get your start?

EF: I auditioned for all the German houses through a government service, the Zentral Bühnen Fernsehen Vermitllung. The opera in

Karlsruhe chose me, and that is where I made my debut, as Marie in *Die verkaufte Braut* in 1981. In 1982 I won first prize in the Karajan competition.

SZ: What happened as a result?

EF: I sang Mozart concert arias in the Kleines Festspielhaus at the Salzburg Festival.

At Karlsruhe I performed many roles, among them Donna Anna in *Don Giovanni*, Micaëla, Pamina, Lauretta in *Gianni Schicchi* and Violetta in *Traviata*.

Giancarlo Del Monaco [one of Mario's sons] was a guest stage director there. In 1986 he wanted me to sing Amelia in *Simon Boccanegra*. I felt the part was too heavy for my voice or that I was too young. He suggested I study with his mother, Rina Del Monaco, which I did in Pesaro for thirty days.

SZ: What did she teach?

EF: She had me vocalize on "oh" for rotundity and "u" [oo] for profundity. She also had me vocalize on "lo-oo," which made the voice heavy. Another reason for those exercises was to lower the larynx. She had me yawn and "drink in air." To achieve brilliance she had me vocalize on "i" [ee].

She also used phrases from the repertory I was preparing, including soft passages such as "e quanta speme" and the end of the "Ave Maria" [*Otello*] and heavy ones such as "Amami Alfredo!" [*Traviata*] and "E son io l'innocente cagion di tanto pianto" [*Otello*]. She emphasized good pronunciation.

SZ: Did she have you do anything in particular with your tongue or soft palate?

EF: She had me sing with the back of my tongue lowered and with the soft palate raised.

SZ: Did she teach support?

EF: Yes, she had me expand my lower ribs in back—my teacher in Bulgaria taught this as well. Rina used to say, "Push down, push down," so that I also supported my voice with my thighs.

Americans who studied with her would lose their voices for a few days, but we Bulgarians have robust voices to begin with and take more readily to singing big. We speak deep in the throat. I had good agility and pianos by nature, and she left them alone. As a result of her teaching I sang with greater volume, body and depth of tone. My voice became heavy enough for Amelia and able to express the part's emotions. I went on to sing it at Karlsruhe in September '86 and had a fantastic triumph. I returned to her in '87 to prepare Desdemona.

SZ: I know that you relocated to Hanover. How did that come to pass?

EF: In 1986 the Intendant of the Niedersächsische Staatsoper, Hans-Peter Lehmann, came to Kalsruhe to direct *Tannhäuser* and heard me sing several roles. He offered me a great contract with suitable repertory and a lot of free time for guest appearances elsewhere.

SZ: Why were you made a Kammersängerin?

EF: The Ministry of Culture for Lower Saxony [of which Hanover is the capital] conferred the title on me for the interpretation of Italian repertoire.

SZ: Did you have a manager?

EF: No one with whom I had an ongoing relationship. But in '93 Zemsky Green offered to represent me. They perhaps were the best-connected agents, and I accepted.

In '93 they had me engaged by the Opera Company of Philadelphia for Tatiana in *Eugene Onegin* and arranged further American engagements with Philadelphia for the *Trovatore* Leonora, Baltimore Opera for Nedda, Opera Pacific for *Butterfly* and *Manon Lescaut* and Seattle Opera for *Butterfly*.

SZ: Where else did Zemsky Green arrange for you to sing?

EF: The Teatro dell'Opera di Roma, Deutsche Oper Berlin, Zurich, Sydney, France, Mexico, Brazil. My repertory ranged from Donna Anna to Aïda, Butterfly, Mimì, Tosca, Amelia in *Ballo*, Maddalena in *Chénier*, Minnie in *Fanciulla*, Desdemona, Francesca da Rimini, Lady Macbeth.

Through Zemsky Green I made a great deal of money, and they were very good to me. However, we did have a disagreement. They kept pushing me into dramatic repertory and wouldn't seek engagements for me for lyric roles. Their roster was full of lyric sopranos whom they were able to market successfully. Dramatic sopranos were paid better. By selling me for dramatic repertory they were able to cast more roles and make more money.

SZ: When did you study with Corelli?

EF: In 1996, when I was about to do *Don Carlos* at the Vienna State Opera.

SZ: What did he advocate?

EF: Singing with the larynx low. He said nothing about pronunciation and contributed very little apart from some coaching in *Don Carlos*. [Corelli was reluctant to interfere with a singer's technique before an engagement.—SZ]

SZ: How did your relationship with Zemsky Green progress?

Filipova and Martinucci in Manon Lescaut, *Teatro dell'Opera di Roma, 1994*

EF: They wanted me to sing Lady Macbeth at the Bavarian State Opera. I objected that the part was too heavy. But the Intendant, Peter Jonas, wanted me to do it. I had had a big success opening the Bavarian Festival with *Aïda*. He liked my temperament. I had an expensive lifestyle and so, reluctantly, I agreed to go ahead. I replaced Julia Varady and had only a month from the first solfeggio to the first stage rehearsal.

SZ: How did you prepare vocally?

EF: Rina having died in 1991, in 1996 I had begun to study with Alain Billiard, who had been a pupil of Marcello Del Monaco. I invited Billiard to come to Munich from Italy to help me with *Macbeth*.

SZ: Describe Billiard's teaching.

EF: He too strove to make my voice heavier and had me vocalize on "o" and "u." Rina had had me sing piano and coloratura, but Billiard focused only on making my sound more dramatic. He had me repeat the heaviest phrases from *Chénier*, *Macbeth* and *Tosca*.

SZ: What was the result?

EF: My sound became very dramatic but lost flexibility and freshness. I no longer sang piano well, and I lost my high E-flat and had to force my other high notes. Zemsky Green said my sound had become "hard."

SZ: What transpired at the *Macbeth*?

EF: The production was by Harry Kupfer. He costumed singers as Nazis. Hitler and Stalin were onscreen. Kupfer was booed. The entire cast was booed at the end of Act I.

SZ: What thoughts went through your mind?

Filipova as Minnie in Fanciulla, *Canadian Opera Company, Toronto, 2001*

EF: I wished a hole in the ground would open and swallow me. Nothing like that ever had happened to me. But after the first act we understood the booing probably would continue, so we were prepared for it.

SZ: Where were you yourself booed?

EF: At the end of the "Sleepwalking Scene." The set was very dangerous. Paolo Gavanelli [the Macbeth] had been injured in rehearsal, had gone to the hospital and had to sing while using a cane. [In the second performance a chorister fell twelve feet, and the performance was suspended.] During the "Sleepwalking Scene" I was barefoot. I cut my foot and was bleeding. The music culminates in a high D-flat, sung softly and inwardly as the character is walking offstage. As I was about to sing the D-flat I walked past a stagehand who had a cellphone and was cursing. It was not my best D-flat.

SZ: What was the upshot?

EF: Newspapers and magazines had a feast! Before I had the opera world at my feet. Afterwards it treated me as a pariah.

SZ: Did you get enough engagements to make a living?

EF: I fulfilled pre-existing contracts successfully, but Zemsky Green offered me nothing new. Instead—without telling me—they stopped soliciting work for me and moved on to other sopranos. I had made a lot of money but hadn't saved it. Because they still encouraged me to think they were representing me I depended on them and was ruined financially.

SZ: Did your voice recover from Billiard's teaching?

EF: Yes, in 2001 I went to Hilde Zadek. [She had sung at the Vienna State Opera, Covent Garden and the Met after the war.—SZ] She made it possible for me to sing with ease again by having me sing lightly, including exercises requiring control and pianissimos, using a placement-based technique. She reintroduced me to my head resonance. My E-flat came back and so did my vocal bloom. She also restored my confidence. Too bad I didn't work with her sooner!

I can sing Pamina and Violetta again!

SZ: You also can sing Lady Macbeth, Aïda and Gioconda without having to manufacture a dark sound.

Where did she have you place?

EF: She had me place vowels between the eyes and at the same time feel my voice at the highest point on the head. For high notes she had me place more and more at the highest point on the head.

SZ: Did she teach a breathing technique?

EF: She had me make the sound "FT," to get the diaphragm to flex in and out. Rina worked from the waist down almost entirely, Hilde from the waist up.

SZ: Billiard evidently exaggerated singing heavily with the larynx low, but you had great success when you used Rina's less extreme version of the technique.

EF: I wouldn't have gotten in trouble if I had stayed with Rina's technique and sung lighter parts as well as heavy ones.

SZ: What are the two techniques, Zadek's and Rina's, each best suited for?

EF: Zadek's is best for brilliant music, Rina's for verismo—for singing with more body. Today I mix the two methods by using each of their exercises.

SZ: What are you doing today?

Elena Filipova in 2010

EF: Performing on cruise ships, giving recitals and teaching. I'm a professor at Privatuniversität Wien-Konservatorium [in Vienna].

SZ: What have you recorded?

EF: In 1993 I recorded the Verdi *Requiem* with Sergiu Celibidache, live, with the Munich Philharmonic. It was released on EMI in 2002. In 1994 I recorded Zandonai's *Francesca da Rimini*, live, at the Bregenz Festival, for Koch-Schwann [in its review *Gramophone* said she is in the league of Olivero, Gencer and Raina Kabaivanska[1]]. And in 1996 I recorded the Verdi *Requiem* for Naxos, while in 1998 I recorded duets from *Manon Lescaut* for *Boiko Svetanov Portrait*, for Arte Nova Voices. In 2011 I appeared in the film *The Audience*, aka *Das Publikum*, thanks to you.

SZ: Your singing—your recent singing, above all—moved me, so what choice did I have?

Although Elena Filipova's voice made a complete recovery her experience with Billiard illustrates Corelli's view that, with most teachers, lowering the larynx leads to a poor result.

In 2000, at Alan Green's insistence, Filipova flew to New York for a week of lessons with his voice-teacher wife, Cathy Green, but afterwards didn't continue with her. Without telling Filipova the management effectively dropped her.

Ten years later tenor Christopher Bengochea found himself in the same position after he didn't return for a second lesson. Seeing the handwriting on the wall he switched managements.

Filipova on the other hand feels awkward about promoting herself. She didn't have to struggle to make a big career; everything was handed to her. When that stopped she felt lost, and she made no real effort to find another management.

Elena and I lived together in 2006. We noticed that when we cried out as we came we each lowered our larynxes; she sounded like a heavy mezzo, I—the World's Highest Tenor—like a heavy baritone.

If you're trying to figure out how to utter a sound with your larynx lowered, you might replicate our example.

On the subject of sex and singing, here's something to try: record your singing. Then give cunnilingus. Then record your singing again. See if it has additional body, heft, ring and core—additional pharyngeal resonance. In my experience you get some of the benefits of lowering your larynx without having to become a mechanist. Sticking your tongue in and out of your mouth doesn't have the same effect, nor does licking your finger, say—I don't know why. Instead of making fun of me, try cunnilingus. If you're not a singer, be charitable and pretend you never read this. Cecilia Gasdia allegedly claimed giving fellatio had the same effect, something I never tried. I don't know if it was the licking she found helpful or depressing the back of the tongue.

Courtesy Universal Classics & Jazz. Photographer Jean Marc Lubrano

"When I performed blood clots came out of me! I felt the sound in my chest and teeth. But up high, where you need the mask, I couldn't find my sensations. Above high A I couldn't feel the sound at all, on account of the swelling.... Thank God I had the courage to continue to sing with an instrument that no longer was responding and to endure the nastiest and most malicious criticisms."—Roberto Alagna

ROBERTO ALAGNA ON SOMETIMES USING MASK PLACEMENT, SOMETIMES A LOWERED-LARYNX TECHNIQUE

He Tells of His Battle to Keep Singing Notwithstanding a Tumor Behind an Eye.

Roberto Alagna: As you know I've been singing for many years, beginning with pop music that I performed for my family. At seventeen I sang professionally in Parisian cabarets while studying opera singing daily. At twenty I took my first steps as a tenor, performing five operas in a week—*Traviata, Rigoletto, Roméo et Juliette, Trovatore* and *Carmen*—performing my part complete, onstage, in public, to piano accompaniment but without ensembles or chorus. At that time this tour de force seemed normal to me in view of the fact that I had acquired some stamina singing from midnight to 6 in the morning. Thus you can see that singing always was second nature for me. After that I began my big career singing in all the most important theaters with passion, generosity, sincerity and love.

SZ: Did your singing begin to change at a certain point?

RA: In 2006 I began to feel a strange physical fatigue. I had problems with glucose in the blood. My immune system was weakened, and my blood-platelet count became too low. My voice lost its vibrations and became duller and duller, my breath shorter and shorter. For the first time my body let me down.

In 2007 doctors finally discovered a benign tumor behind my right eye. In June of that year they removed the tumor, which was damaging my sinuses.

SZ: Did you have laser surgery?

RA: No, the doctor used a scalpel. He told me to wait six weeks before singing, but I sang right away because I didn't want to forget my voice's position [placement]. When I performed blood clots came out of me! I felt the sound in my chest and teeth. But up high, where you need the mask, I couldn't find my sensations. Above high A I couldn't feel the sound at all, on account of the swelling.

When you're young the mucous membranes are humid, but when you're old they become hard. That's what I had after the operation. After three years the mucous membranes finally are reconstituting themselves, and only now am I feeling again the sensations I was accustomed to when I sang. Thank God I had the courage to continue to sing with an instrument that no longer was responding and to endure the nastiest and most malicious criticisms.

Today things are going much better, and I'm very happy. I have the luck to continue to do that which I love most in the world—sing! Dear Stefan, I don't wish to complain. I've been very lucky. I've had much more than I ever hoped for or imagined. A voice is a gift of nature. It's a sacred thing.

SZ: Your explanation is helpful because some opera fanatics have written on the Internet that your voice has lost sweetness and bloom. Now they'll have to reconsider their judgements.

RA: I think these opera fanatics speak of me and my vocal state without knowing my story and perhaps without knowing me. I am aware that a kind of legend has grown up around me.

Many people should have the honesty to look a little deeper before expressing an unfavorable opinion. In twenty-eight years I canceled only twice for vocal reasons. The first time was a Met *Bohème* in '96. I was so unhappy that I sang for more than three hours in my room. I had an allergy and didn't dare sing for the public. I realize I was stupid. The second time was during a *Cyrano* in France in 2006, when I quit after the first act because of tracheitis but sang the remaining performances, beginning two days later.

Apart from these two cancelations I've always sung, even when sick, tired, with blood-sugar problems, torn ligaments in my ankle, problems in my private life, etc. The day after they removed the tumor I made a record and a week later performed the world premiere of my brother's opera in Paris, followed by *Trovatore* in Orange and *Marius et Fanny* [by Vladimir Cosma] in Marseille, not even stopping for a vacation.

The truth is that after the booing episode at La Scala many said what they wanted to, "Roberto finally has destroyed himself!" They wrote me off, so they no longer were interested in knowing what I was doing.

It's true that when you never cancel you can have evenings that are less good. It's also true, as I've already remarked, that the tumor caused me problems. But where are these horrible performances and evenings when I was unlistenable? When did I crack?

SZ: Have you used the same technique throughout your career?

RA: I always sing with the same technique but never in the same way. Singing should be born of the moment, not premeditated.

When I speak of sensations it's because my technique is based on resonance. Sound is very important to me. I always seek a sound high in the mask, behind the nose and between the eyes—right where I had the tumor, which impeded the voice not only from ringing [*squillare*] but also from covering the sound. If this resonance point is clean, humid and not congested my voice sounds easily. It's vibrant, and the sound covers easily and naturally. The breath span increases, and the voice floats. The sensation is of an incredible well being.

It's not important if you are a tenor, baritone or bass; according to me you always must seek a clear, youthful sound. This in my view is the real purpose of singing technique.

SZ: Do you use a breathing method?

RA: You must not think too much about breathing. Otherwise you can't breathe. Breathing is natural, and we must rediscover this naturalness. It is the first thing we do at life's beginning and the last thing we do at its end. Support from the diaphragm comes automatically if, as we attack a note, we put ourselves into a beatific state—smiling within ourselves, happy, with a positive attitude. This for me is the basis for correct breathing.

SZ: What is your opinion about methods based on lowering the larynx?

RA: When the mucous membrane isn't functioning well and is congested or damaged you can try to use lowering the larynx. It helps—but it also is a little dangerous. The sound can go into the throat, in back, so that it can't resound in the mask. You need to be very vigilant.

For me a voice is healthy when the sound is light but broad, spacious, ringing and never open in the area of the *passaggio*—E, F, F-sharp, G.

SZ: To which records do you listen?

RA: Before being a singer I am an opera fanatic. I adore the human voice. I love interesting vocal colors—unique sounds—not only in tenors but also in baritones and basses.

I don't vocalize but instead listen to singers. I prepare to sing *Aïda* by listening to Björling, on account of his lightness. To prepare for *Elisir* I listen to Corelli. To sing *Lucia* I listen to Del Monaco. If I'm going to sing an Italian opera I listen to Gedda. If I'm going to sing

Courtesy Universal Classics & Jazz. Photographer Jean Marc Lubrano

"I'm an autodidact. I learned from listening, from asking myself, "What are they doing in the half second before the sound— 'How are they breathing and placing their voices?' I sing along with Gigli and record myself. That's how I learned to sing.

"I listen every day. There's always something to discover. Great singers all have something that transcends the human."—Roberto Alagna

a heavy opera and listen to Del Monaco my voice becomes too heavy. If I have to sing a light opera and listen to a light tenor it becomes too light. If I have to sing *Don Carlos* in French I warm up by singing the Italian version. If I have to sing it in Italian I warm up by singing the French version. The French version makes me sing less open. The Italian version makes me sing rounder. French lowers your larynx because it's more in the throat, and it helps your voice "canalize"—become more focused.

The tenor voice never should go to extremes—too light, too high, etc. To sing a light part I warm up in the baritone range. To sing *Carmen* I warm up on *Sonnambula*. You need to find the right balance. It's important to return to tones that are soft in texture when you sing dramatic parts, so that the tone can float. Vickers told me that to sing Canio he warmed up on Almaviva.

I always use the same technique but never the same colors. For *Sonnambula* I use lighter colors, for *Norma* darker ones.

SZ: Do you do anything in particular with your mouth or lips?

RA: I use my lips to color and keep my mouth soft, without opening it too much. If you're congested you need to open your mouth wider.

SZ: What is your opinion about smiling while singing, in the manner of Lauri-Volpi and De Lucia?

RA: Luis Mariano only sang happy things because his technique was based on smiling. But Gigli and Björling, in view of the shape of their faces, didn't smile. I never open the sides of my mouth in singing.

SZ: Do you manipulate your tongue or your palate?

RA: No, I don't. My singing is closer to speech.

SZ: Why did you choose to focus your voice behind the eyes?

RA: My voice sounds most youthful there.

SZ: Have you yourself used a lowered-larynx method?

RA: Yes, I did, for a year or two. It makes the voice heavier and broader. But Del Monaco, who used the method successfully, kept his sound high and in the mask. Corelli didn't support. [He would disagree strongly.—SZ] If your nature is to have the voice resonate high you can use this technique. Otherwise you become too heavy and end up wobbling. For the CD *Roberto Alagna Live at the Salle Gaveau*[1] I used the lowered-larynx technique. It's dangerous. It makes the voice less youthful. A tenor needs a youthful sound.

Before the War nobody used such a technique, not even Rosvaenge, not even Merli. He goes up into the mask on high notes. [Corelli, who took some lessons from Merli, said he used a laryngeal method.—SZ] Actually there is an early example of someone who used it, Guillaume Ibos, the original French Werther. He must have been the first to sing that way. You can find a couple of his records on YouTube. [His "Pourquoi me réveiller" is far more Romantic in its treatment of tempo than anyone's since—De Lucia's included. Notice the lengthened dissonances. Ibos's version is a key to unlocking further expressive potential in the role.—SZ]

It's good to be able to lower your larynx, so you can do a mix. But don't be obliged to lower it. It should lower by itself—as does Björling's. At the same time he's placing in the mask. You know that because he hardly opens his mouth.

SZ: In 1984 I interviewed Björling's son Lars Björling, himself a tenor, on "Opera Fanatic." He told me that although he himself placed in the mask, his father did not—that he sang farther back in the head.

RA: No, Björling sang in the mask. [Alagna may be assuming Björling used the same technique he himself does.]

SZ: Your singing fifteen years ago seems to me to be more open than your singing now. Do you agree?

RA: Fifteen years ago my voice was more open because I kept my larynx down. I was focusing the sound forward. It never was in back.

SZ: Bergonzi told me in a 2002 interview that the difference between his singing of *Bohème* and *Trovatore* was the degree to which he covered. Rodolfo, he explained, is a lighter role, so he covers less, but Manrico is more dramatic, so he covers more. To illustrate the point he demonstrated the openings of "Che gelida manina" and "Ah! sì, ben mio" with a marked difference in the degree of covering. What do you think of his position?

RA: If you sing dramatic repertoire you do need to cover more. On a recording Bergonzi sings "Celeste Aïda" with the Fs almost open. I agree the entire voice should be covered to make the sound noble. With my placement the voice covers by itself even in *voix mixte* or in falsetto.

SZ: How did you learn to sing?

RA: I'm an autodidact. I learned from listening, from asking myself, "What are they doing in the half second before the sound—how are they breathing and placing their voices? Nicolai Gedda is interesting. He swells himself up with air and opens his mouth wide. His voice was throaty; that's why he opened his mouth. He exploits his sinus cavities to the maximum. No one else had his high notes.

It's easier to imitate a constructed voice like Corelli's. Pavarotti is more difficult because he had a special voice. He gave me spinal chills [*brividi*]. Kraus can be imitated. Del Monaco is easy to imitate—but you can ruin yourself. Tagliavini imitated Gigli. Young Vickers was different. Later, like Corelli, he constructed a different voice. You can't imitate Björling without his morphology. But you can imitate his position [what singers today call his "setup," the placement of his voice—SZ]. I don't imagine anyone can imitate me.

SZ: Which singer influenced you the most?

RA: I sing along with Gigli and record myself. That's how I learned to sing.

SZ: Can your singing be compared to that of some tenor from the past? If so, what are the similarities and differences?

RA: I'm really glad you asked that question. No one ever put it to me before. Paul Franz may be compared to Georges Thill. You can compare every tenor to past tenors—except for me. Our sounds come from our languages. Corsican singers can be compared to one another because they grow up speaking Italian and French. My mother tongue is Sicilian, but I was brought up in France. No other singer has or had that background. That makes me unclassifiable—and this disturbs people.

SZ: What is your position regarding the *voix mixte*?

RA: You need to have it. You need to have all sounds available—even falsetto.

You can do *voix mixte* with a lowered larynx. In François Bazin's *Maître Pathelin*, in the aria "Je pense à vous quand je m'éveille,"[2] I sing a high D-flat in *voix mixte* but with a lowered larynx—like some of Corelli's B-flats. Just that one note. In *La Damnation de Faust* I sang a high C-sharp with my larynx down just for that one note, to retain the color I had been using and not shift gears. I do the E-flat in the duet with the soprano in *Lucia* that way.

Today few heavy tenors do *voix mixte*. Kaufmann uses it, Gedda too—but with a lowered larynx. You lower your larynx when your mucus isn't working well. If it is you don't need to. Today, with Spring allergies I would lower my larynx and sing with my mouth wide open. Your mucus determines what you need to do.

Technique is makeup. It hides the problems you have from day to day as you age. Singers often sing piano to hide their problems.

André D'Arkor is the king of the *voix mixte*. But in World War II he lost his voice because his mucus wasn't flowing properly.

SZ: What are some differences between Escalaïs, David Devries and French singers of today?

RA: Escalaïs focused his tone without lowering his larynx. Today all tenors want to sound like baritones—not bright. He instead was like Tamagno and Antonio Paoli.
    Devries was a French imitation of Gigli in that he used *falsettone*. His singing was elegant, soft and beautiful, like McCormack, Kozlovsky and early Tagliavini.

SZ: What is your opinion about Gigli's mezza voce? Was it really falsetto or *voix mixte*?

RA: Gigli's mezza voce is not *falsettone* but light chest. It's like yogurt with the fat removed. The last note of his "Je crois entendre encore" is falsetto.

SZ: What about his "Là ci darem la mano," where he sings the part of Zerlina in the film *Solo per te*[3]?

RA: Even that isn't falsetto. Bonisolli does the same thing in Domenico Scarlatti's *La dirindina*.
    We're habituated to a certain sound. Every time singing has taken a step forward it was because someone broke all the rules.

SZ: Yes, that is the underlying thesis of the book I am writing. It was the case with Rubini, Duprez, Caruso, Del Monaco and Corelli.

RA: Also Pavarotti. He had a big voice but sang like a *tenore di grazia*, with a soft texture. Gianni Raimondi had the same volume of voice as Pavarotti but sang more like a spinto, whereas Pavarotti sang like Luigi Alva but with a big volume. Kraus sang more like a spinto.

SZ: I need to ask you something banal.

"Singing is my life. I don't sing for money, fame or glory but because it's something essential for me—my therapy. But I'm no prostitute—even if I do something stupid!"—Roberto Alagna

Courtesy Universal Classics & Jazz . Photographer Jean Marc Lubrano

RA: Go ahead.

SZ: Please discuss your La Scala booing episode.

RA: It was in December 2006, during my health problem. My big success with my Luis Mariano program [*C'est magnifique! Songs of Luis Mariano*[4]] offended certain people. Moreover they didn't want the new regime at La Scala to have a success. La Scala made a mistake continuing the performance with my understudy [Antonello Palombi]. You can't judge a singer by an aria. [Alagna was booed after "Celeste Aïda" and walked offstage.] I could have gone into a coma because of my glycemia. La Scala should have held up the performance for a short time. I would have taken sugar for my glycemia and asked the public, "Signori e signore, shall we continue"?

Where did I crack? Never! Go find one! I never paid a claque. Singing is my life. I don't sing for money, fame or glory but because it's something essential for me—my therapy. But I'm no prostitute—even if I do something stupid!

La Scala canceled my contract. Now they call me, but I feel they betrayed me.

SZ: On September 26, 2011, two days before the opening of a new production of *Faust* at L'Opéra de la Bastille, you had differences with conductor Alain Lombard, and the company replaced him with Alain Altinoglu. What happened?

RA: Something unfortunate. I think Lombard a fine conductor, but he insisted on cuts that interfered with my conception of the role, and his tempos weren't good for me. Because of traffic I came late to rehearsal twice, and this upset him. The second time I only was seven-minutes late. But he already had dismissed the other performers because he didn't think I was going to appear, he said.

I've been singing Faust for twenty-eight years, but he so disturbed my conception of the role that I felt insecure in it. I explained to the administration that I had to withdraw from the performances, but they persuaded me to remain.

SZ: Did they promise you a different conductor?

RA: Yes. But the episode made me depressed.

SZ: I had heard that you and Angela [Gheorghiu] were separated, so I was surprised when she answered the phone.

RA: We're together and happy in our private life. We never divorced. After twenty years of career, pressures build up. That's true still more for a couple. It's easier if one thinks only of one's own singing, not one's mate's. Couples have crises, but great loves return. The press exaggerated. We separated our careers. Angela wanted to record with others. [In January 2013 she filed for divorce. Alagna married soprano Alexandra Kurzak, and the couple had a baby girl, Malena. They now live in Poland.]

SZ: What is your opinion about Corelli?

RA: He's an inspiration because of the pathos he communicates, the freedom of his sound and its rotundity—it's soft in texture yet powerful. He has a beautiful musical instinct. His musicianship is subtle. He feels phrases deep within himself.

Tucker was a phenomenon—his attacks and how he stole breaths! The sound always was dramatic but bright. No one speaks of Araiza anymore, but he had an outstanding technique with wonderful facility.

I listen every day. There's always something to discover. Great singers all have something that transcends the human.

Singers are full of doubts. No singer feels secure. They all have fear—tenors above all. They easily lose their nerve.

Why does a singer crack? Mucus on the cords. It's like sweat—you can't control it.

SZ: Is booing ever justified?

RA: No, never. Why insult singers for what has gone wrong?

SZ: Not even for stage directors?

RA: That's different. You're booing what he has done. But I think it neither elegant nor civilized.

Making a career has become more difficult because of the Internet.

Bill Schuman

BILL SCHUMAN

For More Than 100 Years No Other Voice Teacher Has Had as Many Students Appearing with Major Companies (possibly excepting Marcello Del Monaco).

We Discuss His Hybrid Technique.

SZ: With whom did you study?

Bill Schuman: Luisa Verna Franceschi. She taught Eugene Conley, Michael Molese, Richard Stillwell, Martha Lipton, Frances Yeend, Mario Lanza, George London, Winifred Heidt and Zinka and studied with Paul Bleiden, an assistant of Giovanni Battista Lamperti. [Some of these singers studied with other teachers as well.—SZ] Luisa Tetrazzini sent her to Melocchi. Florence Foster Jenkins presented her at the Monday Musical Concerts. She was the great niece of Lillian Nordica—and one of Mussolini's mistresses and Ronald Reagan's speech therapist. My technique basically is Luisa's, but I also studied with Vera Rózsa, who taught Kiri Te Kanawa and Ileana Cotrubas. I observed Margeret Harshaw teach for two weeks. She had studied with Anna Eugénie Schoen-René, a pupil of Pauline Viardot. Zinka sent her niece to study with me.

SZ: Who are some others you've taught?

BS: Aprile [Millo], for eight or ten years, after Rita Patanè returned to Italy, Marcello Giordani, who came to me in '93, Alessandra Marc, from about 1998 to 2003, including when she sang *Turandot* at the Met, Stuart Neill, Robert Brubaker, Eglise Gutiérrez, Rachelle Durkin, Lisette Oropesa, Nancy Fabiola-Herrera, Angela Meade, Stephen Costello, Ailyn Pérez, James Valenti, Michael Fabiano, Michael Bolton, Burak Birgili, Carl Tanner, Indra Thomas, Latonia Moore, Olivia Stapp, Stephen Dickson, Kallen Esperian, Melanie Diener, Mariusz Kwiecień, Wendy Bryn Harmer, Bryan Hymel and at the end of his career Jerry Hadley.

SZ: To my ear your students seem to be lowering their larynxes somewhat. Am I correct?

BS: Yes.

SZ: How does what they do compare to Jonas Kaufmann?

BS: They don't have an imposed darkness, unlike Kaufmann. His results from an extremely low laryngeal position. Instead they use a floated lowered larynx but never a forced or depressed one. As you inhale the larynx should rest. In teaching I don't mention lowering the larynx but use exercises to bring it lower. In actuality the larynx tilts backward.

SZ: What are these exercises?

BS: I use a variety of them—they are different for each throat. They help singers use the tongue and larynx separately. You don't want to tell a singer to lower his larynx and cause him to experience tension in the throat.

SZ: Do you teach anything in particular with regard to the tongue?

BS: It should be relaxed, touching the lower teeth. The back of the tongue should not be depressed. If they push the tongue muscle down it locks the larynx.

SZ: Ponselle claims that Caruso told her he "kept a little stretch in the back of the throat to keep it open, open in the back and relaxed. It feels like a square, but only on the high notes.... The palate is high and the back of the tongue flat. This [makes] the square." Do you agree or disagree with that approach?

BS: Yes, I believe in the Caruso box. That's how I always was told he described it. But there must be caution not to depress the tongue in the back as you open the space.

SZ: The mouth?

BS: Everyone's different. They have to learn to use their lips, which need to be relaxed.

SZ: Why do Valenti and your other singers spread their mouths wide on high notes?

BS: I have them sing with oval mouths—mouths shaped like hockey rinks—until high B-flat. Then I have them open their mouths sideways. Above B-flat Marcello shows a little bit of his upper teeth. On high C his mouth really is open. Opening the mouth sideways results in more chest resonance, which is in vogue today. Vertical mouths result in more head resonance.

SZ: The more I open my mouth sideways on high C, the more I get an open sound. Is that true of your tenors?

BS: YES. YES. You have *very* easy top notes, so you can sing them in many different positions. You're very lucky in that. Many tenors only can find those notes (actually vibrate the pitch) in one position.

SZ: First I learned to sing high notes. Then for the sake of expression I learned how to color and inflect them.
   What is your view of mask placement?

BS: In the middle voice singers need it.

SZ: How do you teach it?

BS: By having them hum with the position of the "n." I think of the mask as a raccoon-like space.

SZ: Where do you have them place in the mask?

BS: On low notes, at the mustache, then at the eyes. I have them aim their voices into the upper cheeks but not at the nose.

SZ: And the palate?

BS: Lifting the palate creates the sensation of opening space and causes the sound to go up in back.

SZ: Yawning?

BS: I teach the beginning of the yawn. People take it too far.

SZ: What about the jaw?

BS: It should feel unhinged—the back molars feel like they're opened up. The jaw should be released and without tension. It should be tilted slightly back, not jutted forward.

SZ: Covering?

BS: There's no set rule about where to cover. When singers are young their sounds are more open. Singers should be able to go in and out of covering from E to G. In general you need the option to cover or to sing open.

It's dangerous to force a tenor to cover too low. When someone's been taught to cover too low, it's a mess to try to fix it because the muscles fight you. I develop singers from an open position. The most natural tenors sing open when they're young. If you introduce head resonance gradually the voice will start to cover on its own.

SZ: What is the problem if a singer covers low—apart from circumscribed expression? Consider Neil Shicoff. When he recorded *Carmen* he covered throughout his range.[1] Rolando Villazón often does the same thing, for example on the CD *Cielo e Mar* [see p. 286]. Del Monaco sometimes covered in the middle voice, as did Gigli.

BS: Covering is like a damper peddle. It suppresses *squillo* (ring or ping) and causes singers to lose easy access to their tops. Gigli covered only because he wanted that color. Stephen [Costello] lost access on top when he started to cover Fs. We had to work to undo that. Ramón Vargas lost his ease on top from covering. Even Pavarotti began to transpose because he covered.

SZ: If a tenor is singing high notes open why make him cover?

BS: I don't—unless he's extremely open.

SZ: On the one hand Valenti told me, "I think of protecting the voice around E-flat, turning [covering] at E, F and F-sharp. By G/A-flat the process is complete," and Giordani and Costello said they also cover. On the other hand Fabiano contends that he is opposed to covering and doesn't do it.[2] How do you reconcile their positions?

BS: Through certain exercises I try to achieve a covered tone. You can achieve the tonal æsthetic without ever mentioning "cover." I haven't used the term "covering" with Fabiano very much at all, because it induces a dark, throaty sound from him. When he thinks to keep a good high palate, a good vowel and a slightly narrow focus to the sound, his voice turns over [covers] very easily. Fabiano is covering his voice, but he never employs the thought of covering. He has achieved the effect by other thoughts.

I actually prefer a mixed production as my preferred sound. Some voices travel up the scale rather easily, and others require a *lot* of assistance. Both Marcello and Stephen can open or cover at will. I'm very proud of that. It really depends on what they are singing. Right now Stephen and I are working on the *Anna Bolena* score for the Met opening, and part of the work we're doing is determining where to open certain phrases but cover others. It's actually very interesting how a phrase can be made much easier by adjusting the covering of a note or two.

SZ: Bergonzi told me in a 2002 interview that the difference between his singing of *Bohème* and *Trovatore* was the degree to which he covered. Rodolfo, he explained, is a lighter role, so he covers less, but Manrico is more dramatic, so he covers more. To illustrate the point he demonstrated the openings of "Che gelida manina" and "Ah! sì, ben mio" with a marked difference in the degree of covering. What do you think of his position?

BS: I disagree with it. The issue is shading more than covering. You do have to sing Verdi less open than Puccini and cover more in the *passaggio*.

SZ: Why is that?

BS: The color of the music. Also Verdi's music has a different line. The line guides you. Puccini jumps over the *passaggio*. So does Faust, but Roméo lies more in the *passaggio*.

Incidentally young singers shouldn't sing a lot of Mozart. Bellini and Donizetti are better for tenors. Mozart is too confining and instrumental. You have to learn to let your voice out. [Jerome Hines takes the same position about singing Mozart, during the March 3, 1990 interview with Corelli; see belcantosociety.org.—SZ]

SZ: What about breathing?

Giordani and Schuman

BS: I'm against pushing out. The lower abdominal muscles should come in and up. You need to apply pressure underneath the diaphragm. That affects breath pressure.

I don't want to give the impression that I treat all voices alike. If a voice is bright I add darkness. If a voice is very dark I add brightness.

SZ: How do you do those things?

BS: With bright voices you have the singer sing "aw" instead of "ah." With dark voices you add the "a" sound as in "man." You make the rest of the scale sound like the singer's best note. The most beautiful tone is the chiaroscuro—dark and light at the same time. You sculpt a voice.

SZ: Giordani and Costello don't sing softly often. Why is that?

BS: I build from the full voice. Marcello sings "E lucevan le stelle" piano. His breadth of repertory, from *Aïda* to *Puritani*, is beyond everyone else's today and reminds one of tenors of the past. He sang high Ds in *Pirata*—even if we repositioned them. The way they are written is awkward. [I disagree.—SZ]

255

My sopranos are famous for their pianos. Their roles require that. Male roles typically don't. My job is to create singers with healthy voices and let the singers decide what to do artistically. Stephen sings "Danny Boy" in mezza voce.

SZ: On his CD of arias on Naxos Giordani's voice sounds a little tired.[3]

BS: He's become a multi-million dollar corporation, performing one night here, the next night there. I on the other hand favor not speaking the day of a performance or the day afterwards. I can't get him to rest his voice for a week or ten days. At the least he's always got people around him and talks non-stop. Also, that CD was made under trying conditions. The best takes got lost!

SZ: My understanding is that when he came to you he was in vocal difficulty.

BS: Yes, he studied with Maria Gentile [a soprano who also taught Salvatore Fisichella—SZ]. Then he worked with a larynx depressor by the name of Mario Carta, who distended Marcello's pharyngeal cavity. Next he studied with Bergonzi, who had him over-darkening and over-covering. The sound was foggy, and his top was limited.

SZ: How did you overcome the problems?

BS: If I had known how bad they were I wouldn't have gotten involved. The voice was in serious crisis. His range stopped at high B-flat. I worked to get the voice back to what it was like on a tape of him from when he was 22. Then the voice was beautiful, clear, even. I had to teach him cordal closure—his cords weren't coming together except on three notes—and to get him to breathe lower.

SZ: To judge from clips on YouTube Costello's pitch sometimes sags.

BS: Pitch is not usually a Costello problem. His former manager, Neil Funkhouser, removed his best clips from YouTube. The ones there were posted by amateurs. It's tough to make a career today because you can't afford to give a bad performance.

SZ: What was he like when he came to you?

BS: When he auditioned at AVA [The Academy of Vocal Arts], which is where I teach as well as at the Hotel Ansonia, in New York, the other voice teachers wanted to reject him because he had a terrible *caprino* [goat-like vibrato]. They said he had nothing going for him and never could sing professionally. I saw the possibilities and so did Christofer Macatsoris, our music director, who had worked with Serafin.

SZ: How did you eliminate the vibrato?

BS: I got rid of the tension in his larynx and throat.

SZ: How did you do that?

BS: His throat was tight. I used Melocchi exercises to isolate muscles in his throat and teach them to relax and let go. Even then he had a real singer's guts: he'd go for a note even if he couldn't hit it.

SZ: Fabiano can sound glorious in the middle, but his top sometimes doesn't provide a climax.

BS: He's a young spinto and is growing into his top notes. His C is good, but his B-flat and B aren't secure and lack the color of the lower voice. You can't force color on high notes. He spreads on top. When he's 31 or 32 you'll hear the complete voice. He by the way has a gorgeous mezza voce.

SZ: Hadley famously switched voice teachers from Tommy LoMonaco to you. What happened?

Voice teacher Giovanni Battista Lamperti. According to his assistant William Earl Brown, Lamperti, although married, was homosexual, so he moved from Milan to Dresden, where he felt more comfortable. His absence changed the course of singing in Italy. Among other things top-of-the-head placement fell by the wayside, and covering became nearly ubiquitous among men.

BS: LoMonaco studied with Stanley and taught a technique that involved a lot of artificial darkening—over darkening—and extreme lowering of the larynx. Jerry was loyal to LoMonaco and stayed with him many years. Eventually he left him because he had lost his top. He told me, "I was destroyed by LoMonaco." He studied with me the last four years of his life. [Hadley committed suicide in 2007.]

SZ: What did you do to try to repair Hadley's voice?

BS: Methods descended from Douglas Stanley, such as LoMonaco's, make space in the pharyngeal cavity. You can't get to your head voice that way. Our skull and face are resonating chambers. The throat—the pharyngeal cavity and larynx—are passageways, not resonating chambers. He had to relearn how to get his pharyngeal cavity to relax so his larynx was free to float. When he was able to use his head voice again his top returned.

SZ: Adherents of LoMonaco use a lot of physiological terminology to support their contentions.

BS: Science confuses people. It can help a teacher diagnose a problem but is of no use with regard to actual singing. [Shades of Santley on García; see p. 167.] Singing is an art, not a science.

I don't know any great singers who were taught by Stanley or his disciples. Linda Roark-Strummer studied with Tommy LoMonaco. I never thought her anything special. Another one of his students, Craig Sirianni, had a disaster at La Scala. Where is he singing now? Hildegard Behrens worked with Jerry LoMonaco [Tommy's brother]. She was a marvelous artist but not an outstanding vocalist.

Melocchi, however, helped singers cope with the demands of verismo. But you need someone with a bel canto background to avoid damaging them. I'm one of the only teachers to combine Lamperti and Melocchi.

SZ: A voice teacher called Neil Semer invokes Lamperti's name to legitimize a technique of his devising involving chakras, no less.

BS: What's Semer's lineage?

SZ: I don't know, but when I spoke with him on or about March 15, 2003 he gave me to understand he had read *Vocal Wisdom* and done a fantasia on it.

BS: He hasn't produced any top-echelon singers. The majority of his successful students sing in minor German houses.

SZ: Stanley disciple Cornelius Reid published a book called *Bel Canto*,[3] in which he quotes out of context a number of old masters—Francesco Lamperti among them—in an attempt to show that they supported his, Reid's, technique.

BS: Voice teachers at the highest level get the same level of vocal talent to study with them. Reid produced no one or at least no major singer.

SZ: The Lamperti tradition in which I am steeped (that of *Vocal Wisdom*) can be reduced to pelvically based breathing, such that one presses in and out *concurrently* in the area of the pelvis, without pumping air. As a result of pelvic breath support the voice takes only the air it needs.

At the same time the technique involves placement at the top of the head, between the ears but higher, where a baby's skull comes together, in the area of the sphenoidal sinus. Larynx, palate, tongue, mouth and lips are left to adjust themselves as a consequence of one's placement.

BS: I concur that that is Lamperti's position.

SZ: Singers who use the technique don't cover or have *passaggio* or high-note problems. Why did you head in a different direction?

BS: We've accepted the Del Monaco sound and sacrificed sweetness for power. Luciano did that.

SZ: What elements of your teaching come from Lamperti?

BS: Lamperti went for the freest, most unmanipulated sound. For top notes my students all go up into the head.

SZ: But you also teach mask placement.

BS: Yes, but only to about C. By D or E-flat I want a lot of head resonance. You lift the palate higher and direct the tonal beam into it. The thought makes the adjustment. Sense memory is crucial—you hold on to sensations. Non-singers shouldn't teach voice. They can't know about placement. Placement is the result of correct throat function. Voices that keep mask placement all the way up sacrifice ease of top—Tebaldi, for example.

SZ: I find it easy to identify a Lamperti pupil or a Strongin pupil [she was the assistant of Lamperti's assistant William Earl Brown] because of characteristic sound qualities. The same is true of students of Melocchi or the Del Monaco brothers—their sound has a characteristic brassiness. Is there a Schuman sound?

BS: No, there'll never be a Schuman sound because each student is different.

Singing is the most beautiful thing anyone can do. It expresses the soul and is a gift from God. Vickers told me it's the greatest blessing—the greatest joy—and the greatest curse because you have to make a sacrifice: you can't have sex before singing. I believe it and tell it to all my tenors. It takes something away from top notes. They all try to prove me wrong but end up conceding that I'm not. Women's voices, however, aren't affected by it.

SZ: It's my understanding from Corelli that Melocchi had his pupils sing with fully lowered larynxes, but you have your pupils lower their larynxes only part of the way and then float them.

BS: I adopted Luisa's approach. The floating larynx comes from her. She taught me Melocchi's exercises. Some are to build the voice. Others are therapeutic.

Melocchi is an option for a voice trained in bel canto. For a Rossini voice I might not add Melocchi.

SZ: When did Luisa study with Melocchi?

BS: In the 20s and 30s, at the same time as Del Monaco.

SZ: Before Corelli—so he may not have coined the term "floating larynx."
   To what extent is Corelli an influence on today's tenors?

BS: When tenors get together they listen to Corelli. He's more of an influence on those 30 and younger than on those 30 to 45. The older ones listen to Del Monaco. In the practice room the younger ones sing along with Corelli's recordings to try to emulate his ease of emission and figure out what he did to access those high notes.

SZ: Corelli told me he used to sing along with recordings of Lauri-Volpi and others to learn from them.

BS: Singers should study the great ones who came before them.

Three of Schuman's Most Prominent Tenor Pupils

Marcello Giordani

SZ: Many singers have been influenced by the teaching of Arturo Melocchi, Mario and Marcello Del Monaco and Franco Corelli. For better or worse, depending on one's point of view, their teachings, based on lowering the larynx, have changed singing. What are the advantages and disadvantages of this kind of technique?

Marcello Giordani: I don't know what are the pros or cons of this or that technique. But in my opinion the larynx always must remain in its physiological position, that is to say, relaxed.

SZ: When you sing do you do anything in particular with your mouth, tongue or soft palate?

MG: Once it has been determined that vowels do not change and remain the same in all registers it is easier to make the tongue and its appendages assume the most natural physiological position: mouth in the vertical position, relaxed tongue—I always think of the tongue's tip as being near the lower dental arch—high palate, almost in a yawning position.

SZ: Please clarify how you can yawn without having the larynx lowered.

MG: The two positions aren't contradictory. Try to yawn, and you'll see that the larynx returns to its natural position—that is to say, low. But the palate, on the other hand, raises, creating a space with the uvula elevated, giving the voice color and perfect harmonics.

[In short Giordani doesn't sustain the extreme low position of the larynx during the yawn but does sustain the extreme high position of the uvula. When I listen to Giordani I feel that his larynx is lowered but not all the way down. The difference between this approach and Kaufmann's is that during a yawn Kaufmann apparently sustains the low position of the larynx, so that his larynx remains much lower (see p. 284).—SZ]

SZ: Do you use a breathing method?

MG: We should concentrate more on breathing out than breathing in. A slow, careful breathing in enables us not only to shape musical phrases without jerking, abrupt sounds; it also enables us to give the sound manifold colors and shadings, so we can pass from pianissimo to fortissimo and vice versa. Good or bad singing depends on the strength with which we breathe out, on the larynx's opening, on the tension of the soft palate, on the position of the tongue and lips.

It is important to explain what I mean by the term "support" [*appoggio*]. If the singing is unsupported it has no artistic value. But we mustn't confuse support with pushing the voice. After an experience of many years I have come to the following definition: the support is the contact between breath and sound. Without support the sound is flabby and insubstantial. The vowels, when unsupported, seem to be surrounded by a mist and very often are produced with an aspirated "h."

SZ: Were you influenced by another singer, or did you take one as a model?

MG: The model or models who inspired me were those of the old Italian school, beginning with my fellow Sicilian Di Stefano and ending with Pavarotti. I've always been impressed by the sincerity of Di Stefano's interpretations. Di Stefano always conveys fully the expressivity of the Italian language, making it flow into a complete languor that makes you dream. I've always envied the sunny sound of Pavarotti's voice, the joy, melancholy and purity of his singing, the rightness of his emission—never a pushed or unsupported sound. A supreme singer!

Comparisons always are to the detriment of those who come later, but I always try to assume a vocal personality of my own. Nevertheless I try to steal the craft of earlier singers and treasure their "discographic advice." With Pavarotti I always used to discuss the focal point, the correct position for the larynx and correct vowels.

An Email From Stephen Costello:

I have been influenced by many singers. When I first started to sing I was introduced to Fritz Wunderlich. The beauty and passion in his voice really made me love classical voice. I say "classical voice" because the first thing I heard him sing was *Dichterliebe*. I then heard him sing "Granada," and that pushed me over the edge. I really wanted to sing like Fritz!

Then I discovered Jussi Björling. The voice was beautiful and exciting. When studying *Romeo and Juliette* for the first time I listened to his recording from the Met. It was amazing! Also when I am studying an Italian role I will listen to Di Stefano. His vocalism is not the best, but the way he uses the text is an art form in itself.

Costello, Giordani and Schuman backstage at Carnegie Hall, November 9, 2005, after a performance of Guillaume Tell *in which Giordani encored his fourth-act cabaletta and Costello made his professional debut.*

Of course I can't leave out Corelli, but that is just for excitement. His voice is so at ease and free that it is soothing to the throat. I loved to listen to Luciano as well. His voice was so beautiful, especially in bel canto. Sometimes if I listened too long I would cover my Fs, which for my voice does not work—but it did for him. What a voice it was!

Today I listen to Marcello Giordani often. He has been a good friend and mentor to me. We have the same teacher, Bill Schuman, and listening to Marcello is like watching technique in action. He has the best and most consistent top notes in the business. I almost can feel where he is placing the voice in his throat. He has helped me become a better singer.

Michael Fabiano

SZ: Who influenced your singing?

Michael Fabiano: Two people, George Shirley and Bill Schuman. Shirley, my teacher at the University of Michigan, insisted that I not hyper-analyze the pedagogy of singing but sing and make art. He didn't talk about larynx or palate. Instead he had me stand up, take a deep breath and sing. He spoke not about the throat but breathing. He said, "Imagine that there's an inner tube circling your waist and that as you sing the air in the tube releases slowly." He was a singing actor and an acting singer and helped me become one too. We spent hours on how to walk and how to be presentable to 4,000 people. He's rigorous and carries a one-foot baton. When I made a diction error in any language he would slam the baton down on his desk and correct the mistake. He gave me a B-minus the first semester while giving everyone else an A. I was mortified! I had worked so hard so that he would slam the baton twelve times instead of twenty! I studied with him for three years and then went to AVA and worked with Bill Schuman. I began with him at twenty and have been with him for seven years.

Bill reaffirmed what George had said but talks about the body being an air pump. He said to sing without being afraid, that if the sound breaks I should take it in stride. I still have to develop my upper range. When I approach a B-flat I tend to over-open the sound. He has others sing open but asks me to keep the sound more narrow when I approach the top. When I came to him I struggled with range from G on up. My C has come into its own, and I love singing Cs. Four years ago this wasn't so. For me B-flat and B-natural have to be narrow. Bill tells me that my larynx needs to be relaxed and mobile, not raised or depressed, and that I should engage my support rather than rely on extending my mouth and jaw.

SZ: When I mentioned to Bill that I thought Giordani and Costello didn't do enough soft singing he cited you as an example of someone who did.

MF: I'm good at quiet singing. Beginning with my first lesson Shirley had me do a messa di voce [a swelling and a diminishing of the sound]—supported—on every note, as high as I could go. He was insistent that every voice be able to sing fortissimo and pianissimo

Michael Fabiano

in the same phrase. He planted in my mind that quiet singing is necessary. But in singing quietly I struggle with keeping the vowel and the core of the voice the same. I try to achieve this through support. If I lose that the sound goes into the back of my throat, and the core is lost. I work on this every day. Before Bill I couldn't have done it as well. He helped me support better. He demands that my vowels be clear, so that the sound won't get pharyngeal.

SZ: Are there singers on record who influence you and, if so, how?

MF: Corelli is my hero—my man on a white horse with sword in hand. His vocal freedom throughout his range, up to high C, is incredible. Bergonzi's voice is like a silk glove—and yet it's clarion. He helped me realize what legato is. A lot of tenors strive for a big sound, but legato is still more important. He had a golden stream from top to bottom pouring out his mouth—even if it was too dark for my taste. He seldom got into vocal trouble.

Carreras had more heart and fire than anyone else. He spoke to you through the words and was a real communicator. Aragall was

Schuman, Giordani and Valenti, backstage after the Richard Tucker Gala, November 14, 2010, in which Giordani and Valenti had sung. Valenti had won the Tucker award that year.

Many tenors have heads and necks like Schuman's and Giordani's. Valenti is an exception. So was Corelli.

similar. I love Pertile for *squillo* and for his connection to his chest voice all the way up but with head resonance. You can hear in Corelli's singing what he gleaned from him. The other influences are Italian—but I do admire Tucker for his longevity. He had an efficient technique. At the time of his death his voice still was at an optimum level. He was the best Don Alvaro.

SZ: Is there something you do differently because you listened to this or that tenor?

MF: I never copy anyone but use recordings of these tenors in learning music and as reference points.

SZ: When you say the name of an aria I feel I'm not listening to an American but a real Italian.

James Valenti

MF: I lived with relatives in Milan for a while. For twelve years, since age nine, I studied Spanish, but when I went to Italy I absorbed it into Italian. Diction makes clear language. Clear language makes clear vowels.

SZ: Corelli maintained that when one sings with a lowered larynx one sacrifices the purity of vowels, so he felt there was a tension between what he regarded as the best emission and vowel purity.

MF: I don't manipulate my larynx or lower it.

SZ: When you are performing do you think about technique?

MF: No, if I did I wouldn't be living in the moment. The time to think about technique is in the studio. Onstage I serve my muse. I want people to laugh, cry and be touched—not bored because I'm thinking about technique. If I've studied properly my technique will be the basis of the art I present onstage.

SZ: Giordani and Costello told me Pavarotti was among their models. Is he one of yours?

MF: When Pavarotti sings "Veranno a te sull'aure" in a 1972 Met broadcast of *Lucia* with Sutherland there is sun and brightness in the sound, which I try to capture. He doesn't cover or change "ah" to "oh" but uses an open "ah" verging on "aah" as in "man." All voices need sunshine.

Covering for Pavarotti was an option. He doesn't cover high B-flat invariably even if he covers a G. He used covering as an affectation, not a necessity.

Voices shouldn't have a closed off, lidded sound. I strive for a narrow sound, not a beefy or unnecessarily wide one, especially in the upper middle. Covering restricts singers and results in habits that are difficult to break.

James Valenti

JV: I have been influenced most strongly by Pavarotti, because of his technical mastery, beauty of sound and the ease with which he sings, Lanza, because of his incredible charisma and the sex in his sound, Gigli, because of his beauty and the way he uses such a color palate with the words, and of course Corelli, because of his thrilling open-throated singing and dynamic stage presence. I am very partial to warm, Italianate voices. I do appreciate tenors such as Gedda and Björling, but I prefer the Italian sound.

SZ: Unlike some of Bill Schuman's other tenors you seem comfortable singing softly. Why is that?

JV: Mezza voce is one of my gifts. It keeps me out of trouble sometimes—if I feel I'm starting to push I'm not afraid to use it and make many varieties of dynamics and colors. I've always had it, but Bill has helped me expand it and add more core. I like to employ it, particularly in French music. [Not every singer with a good mezza voce was born with it. Ferruccio Tagliavini told me in detail in 1985 how he taught himself to sing in mezza voce—when he began he couldn't.—SZ]

SZ: Are you saying that if you are in vocal trouble you switch to mezza voce?

JV: No, but I can use it in moments to help ease the build-up of pressure in long passages—I can use my soft singing in passages that might give other tenors difficulty. *Butterfly* is fresh in my mind since I had my final dress rehearsal at the Royal Opera yesterday and am opening on Saturday. Toward the end of the "Viene la sera" duet, after the big climatic phrases there is a soft phrase, "ti serro palpitante ahhhhhh vien," on a final G to F, right in the *passaggio*. I can float it quite easily, but I know many have difficulty there. There is some very heavy singing just before that, and there is a build-up of pressure. For some it sometimes is difficult to switch into a softer shade there. But I can use that phrase to relax the throat and help set up the high C coming just after that.

SZ: Do you feel the need to cover?

JV: I think of protecting the voice around E-flat, turning [covering] at E, F and F-sharp. By G/A-flat the process is complete.

SZ: Why do you abruptly spread your mouth on a high note?

JV: To make space and add smile to the sound.

SZ: Are you friendly with Bill's other tenors?

JV: I had a very intense coaching session with Marcello Giordani earlier today [June 11, 2011]. We worked for two hours. He too is performing at the Royal Opera, in *Tosca*. I'm going to see him sing Cavaradossi in a few hours. He's a very kind, gracious man, and I admire his long career and technical prowess. I wanted to get some insight about his thoughts and sensations, particularly about breathing. It was a thrill to stand next to him and feel his breathing and ringing top notes so close to me. Fabiano also is a dear friend and a wonderful young tenor. Bill also teaches fine tenors like Costello and Hymel. We all are friendly and collegial—and we all are scrutinized and attacked all the time by haters. But we all admire and believe in one another and support each other. I know a lot of people are extremely jealous of Bill and his success and the success of his students, but ultimately they can't deny that the guy knows what he's talking about.

SZ: You have the bottom notes of a basso. How did that come to pass?

JV: Well, my range was that of a baritone at the beginning, and I have the physical build of a bass. Many people on meeting me think I'm a bass. I do like rich bottom notes and use a lot of chest resonance in the lower part of my voice. Bill said I have the longest neck and most prominent Adam's apple of any tenor he's ever seen. [My own case is still another counterexample to the claim that physiognomy determines voice type. When I was seventeen a voice teacher sent me to a prominent otolaryngologist called Dr. Friedrich Brodnitz, who contended that my long neck, prominent Adam's apple and the distance between my diaphragm and larynx determined that I was a bass and that if I continued to sing as a tenor I would ruin my voice in two years. At the Hartt School of Music they had me perform the bass role of Farfarello in Prokofiev's *The Love For Three Oranges* although my voice doesn't climax until well above the staff. —SZ]

SZ: Bill mentioned that you're studying with Virginia Zeani. I interviewed her twice in '86, on the radio, as well as in '07. She told me she believes in covering the entire voice as well as in mask placement. How do you reconcile those things with Bill's teachings?

JV: Yes, I work with Ms. Zeani when I'm home in Palm Beach, FL, but Bill is my primary teacher for technique. I coach repertory with her. She is an incredible resource and is very helpful with style and interpretation. She sang with so many legendary tenors, including

Gigli, and studied with Pertile. Incredible! She really believes in my talent. I talk a little about technique with her. She helped me prepare a role debut this past season, Maurizio in *Adriana*. There are audio clips on my web site, jamesvalenti.com/media_audio.htm.

SZ: Does it matter that she isn't a tenor?

JV: Both my first teacher, Augusto Paglialunga, and Bill are tenors. The tenor voice is very strange and unique, and I prefer to work technique with tenors since I believe they can illustrate better the feelings, sensations and imagery. I think the sensations are quite different for men and women. Ms. Zeani does speak a lot about mask placement and closing the mouth. Sometimes as a result of attempting her sensations I end up singing above the core of my instrument and get tight while trying to place the voice so high, and my larynx feels like it's coming up very high. The sensation doesn't work for me. I feel that the sound isn't connected to the body and the entire instrument. Still I understand what she's getting at. I believe mask resonance is a result, but it doesn't work if I try to begin by placing it there. Bill's sensations are lower: the position in the throat, the box feeling at the back of the mouth and as you ascend a small, intense, condensed feeling deep in the throat. Also opening the mouth in a vertical way and adding some smile once you have the proper feeling deep in the throat.

SZ: Bill speaks of the sound "going up in back" for high notes. Do you feel your voice at the top of the head?

JV: Yes, I do have the sensation of the sound going up in back and out the top. But one shouldn't think of placing the sound at the top of the head. The feeling has to be lower, deeper, and head resonance is a result. And of course I always pump air and try to find the proper balance of breath pressure. Did you listen to the *Adriana* excerpts?

SZ: Yes, you seem to be singing far forward in the mask.

JV: There are moments when I do think frontal placement.

SZ: Is your placement Schuman's or Zeani's?

JV: I suppose it's my own.

Update, August 12, 2012: James Valenti told me via email, "I don't work with Zeani any longer. Her technical ideas were really messing me up. I'm still studying with Bill." Valenti wouldn't be specific about the problems he felt Zeani's precepts had caused him.

I learned from another Schuman student, baritone Jeffrey Hoos, that at the end of 2012 Schuman had dismissed Valenti from his studio because Valenti was taking lessons from Arthur Levy. I emailed Valenti on February 27, 2013:

Dear James,

One of Bill Schuman's students mentioned that you no longer are with Bill but have switched to Arthur Levy.

My assumption [based on the singing of other Levy students] is that you now are singing with a lower larynx. I wonder, what are the tradeoffs?

Here's what I would expect:

Your sound has become more hefty and robust, more *squillante* [ringing], more suited to stentorian utterances on the order of "Sacerdo te, io resto a te" [*Aïda*].

But I also would expect:

  less bloom (*smalto*)
  less ability to sing in mezza voce
  less control of dynamics

less ease of emission
less ability to sing legato
less ability to color
less vocal stamina
less ability to sing high

I would be very grateful if you would fill me in. Are my assumptions correct? What motivated you to make the change? And above all, what do you find to be the tradeoffs?

With every good wish,

Stefan

He replied on February 28, 2013:

> Your assumptions are inaccurate. I am singing with more core of sound, more connection to my body and therefore have more power, more ease, more security and more stamina. The top is freer and has more bloom and ring. The *passaggio* is deeper [in pitch] and sets the throat up well so that I don't get lifted [?], then the top is more easily accessible. I feel the voice has more warmth and color. I still have retained the ability to sing mezzo [*sic*] voce, I just have to always stay true to my voice and not get lifted. Stay on my core of my sound.
>
> I don't think any one teacher has ALL the information one needs. We need to seek out the information, and the quest for a healthy, working vocal technique that suits one's instrument never ends. I am continuing on my journey and I'm happy with where I am. The results speak for themselves. I hope you enjoy my recent *Tosca*, *Carmen* and final scene from *Lucia* in which I'm employing my newer fuller singing.
>
> I wish you well with your book,
>
> James

Bill Schuman commented by email on February 28, 2013:

> I sadly did dismiss James as a pupil right before the end of the year. I am very proud of what we accomplished together as teacher and pupil. I took a young, wild tenor and took him to winning some of the biggest prizes in the opera world, and watched him triumph in many of the greatest opera houses of the world. I love his voice, the color and musicality. I only wish him the very best.
>
> But when one is taking other advice and deciding they want to follow it, it becomes impossible for me to stand by and take the blame for the results. Trust me, I get blamed for enough already!!!!! haha. I have so many successful and wonderful students that I need to focus on the ones who trust me and what I have to offer. There are many schools of singing out there, and singers can find some success in all of them. I know how hard the road of a singer is, and I wish them all well. When one falls by the wayside I truly feel sad. I have great hope that James will not end up as another statistic of the depressed-laryngeal school of singing.
>
> All my best, Bill

Valenti has many clips on YouTube. In those from November 2012 onward, after he switched methods, he sounds like a different singer. I hope you'll make comparisons and determine your preferences.

Virginia Zeani

From a telephone interview, August 23, 2013:

Tenors aren't always intelligent—to find an intelligent one is a miracle! Valenti has a beautiful voice but isn't an intelligent tenor. [I disagree.] He took only three or four lessons with me. His parents came with him. He doesn't do vocalises. His breathing technique wasn't what I wanted. I never speak about the larynx and don't think

Zeani in her signature role, Violetta in Traviata. Although the photo may be posed, from the look of her face you can sense that she is placing well down in the mask, including the cheeks. Notice her bared teeth and hint of a smile.

The Metropolitan Opera Archives, photographer Louis Mélançon

about where the larynx is. But I do believe in relaxing the jaw. Bill Schuman is a great teacher.

Update from an email chain in late October 2017:

SZ: Why did Fabiano leave?

Bill Schuman: He didn't leave. I dismissed him. His *Opera News* article stated the truth. He didn't want it in print but they wanted to make it clear as did I. His jealousy of other singers (not only tenors) and his emotional problems were too much for me. I wish him only the very best. I don't like the direction his voice is taking. I don't feel guilty for it, just sad.

SZ: With whom is he studying now, and what is happening to his voice?

BS: I believe he is studying with Shicoff now. When I have heard him sing, I am hearing a voice in distress as it ascends into the top. He is pushing the sound forward and losing the head resonance that he was finally finding. So the result is throaty and nasal. At least to my ears.

SZ: I agree that is no way to produce high notes. My experience was that high notes entered me through the top of my head and took possession of my head, throat and sometimes even my chest. I didn't make this happen. Instead I allowed it to happen.

Shicoff's high notes always were hit or miss. That said Fabiano sustained a ringing high C in the 2017 *Traviata* telecast.

BS: Fabiano was the second tenor I dismissed in the last five years. I dismissed Valenti first. Then Fabiano. And this summer I had to dismiss Costello. It was a very difficult decision but a correct one. I am very proud of my work with all three, but the time had come to say goodbye.

I am very happy and proud to be the teacher of Bryan Hymel!!!!! And many other wonderful young tenors and even some old timers still hanging on!!!!

SZ: You considered Costello your most promising student. What led you to dismiss him? With whom is he studying now, and what is happening to his voice?

BS: I have no idea if he is studying with anyone. He is singing beautifully and would be wise not to change things. I wish him nothing but the best in his career and life. Things just became unbearable, and it was the correct time to end my teaching relationship with him. I still feel that his voice is one of unique beauty, and I hope he maintains it.

On November 11, 2017, Michael Fabiano emailed:

> Dear Stefan
> I have nothing but respect and admiration for Bill.
> Thanks and all best to you
>
> Michael

On November 13, 2017 Stephen Costello emailed:

> Stefan,
> Would love to answer all of your questions, but in a rehearsal at the moment. But briefly, yes I no longer work with Bill Schuman. Bill was very upset with me because I got married this summer. He is very controlling about his students' personal lives. I honestly believe that is none of his business. A teacher should teach, not tell you who you can and cannot date, let alone marry. Also, he speaks in a very negative way about a lot of people in this business. He may tell a different story, but I have emails that show the truth. He makes his own reality sometimes. Yes I am studying with someone else and would love to share it. Talk soon.
>
> Stephen Costello

Neither Fabiano nor Costello responded to emails requesting further information.

Jonas Kaufmann: In German opera he feels the words. In Italian opera he doesn't and is gutteral.

FOUR LOWERED-LARYNX TENORS

Jonas Kaufmann: The New Corelli?

During the course of drooling over Kaufmann in the booklet to *Jonas Kaufmann: Romantic Arias*[1] Roger Pines quotes him as saying, "I love moving from one style to another—I never get bored! I always need a challenge, both vocally and interpretively." How self-indulgent! The question should not be which styles do I enjoy singing but which styles can I serve best?

With rare exceptions Italian and French operas are served best by native speakers. Consider Jan Peerce, Richard Tucker, James McCracken and Jon Vickers. To me they sound like outsiders in Italian repertory. All have temperament. But their interpretations are compromised by faulty Italian. (None of them could hold a conversation in that language.) Not only do they have accents and inappropriate consonants, but their colorations and emphases are unidiomatic. I even feel this way about Björling, his gorgeous voice notwithstanding. (Still, his is the greatest "Ah! sì, ben mio," in the 1939 *Trovatore*; this "Ah! sì, ben mio" is available as a free sample at belcantosociety.org)

Kaufmann too can be fervid, but he is as unidiomatic as any of them. Not one vowel sounds as if uttered by an Italian. That's because he sacrifices purity of vowels to the exigencies of his lowered-larynx voice production, even if now and again, seemingly forgetting his technique, seemingly at random, he lets a bright vowel slip through. He's guttural—far more so than any Italian singer, even Giacomini. It's as if he were introducing the umlauted "o" sound, as in "*Götterdämmerung*," into Italian. At forte he doesn't sing a true "ah" but mixes it with "eh." As a result his Italian sounds as weird and distorted as McCracken's. Worse, his darkened, throaty vowels make his colorations "off" and his singing monotonous.

A few foreign singers do serve Italian opera well: Callas comes to mind. She differs from Italian singers in that her "oo" vowel is exaggerated, her consonants are heavier, and in the middle register she almost has no vibrato. But her feeling for coloring saves her. Similarly Gencer, from Turkey, succeeds although her voice likewise doesn't sound Italian. But then she spoke the language impeccably. Spanish-speaking singers come close, Carreras in particular. So can Slavs, Elena Filipova being an example.

I heard Kaufmann interviewed on the RAI radio program "La barcaccia." He speaks Italian well. (Pines quotes him as bragging, "People say, 'Your parents probably run a pizzeria'!") But in the Italian selections on *Romantic Arias* he often gives little sign of feeling the words. His singing lacks the warmth and subtle shifts in color and emphasis that result from doing so.

For the past eighty years the Met has cast few Italian or French singers. As result I am unenthusiastic about nearly all its performances of Italian and French opera. They may be impressive, but they don't really satisfy. German opera is harmed less when sung by non-native speakers, and German audiences are more likely to take them to their bosoms. (That Italy and France have produced few world-class singers in the last half century is a reason for opera's decline.)

I hate glottal stops (hard or rigid offsets). Caruso makes them sometimes. So does Corelli. In "Celeste Aïda" even McCormack makes them. Kaufmann makes them maybe more often than any other famous singer—even in soft passages—to the point that I wince.

His intonation is spotty. He doesn't italicize by opening his tone, in the manner of Gigli. He sounds throaty and ungainly in such lyric pieces as "Parmi veder le lagrime" from *Rigoletto*. And his singing is full of random accentuations—he'll accentuate any note, heedless of its place in the harmonic structure. His "Io la vidi e il suo sorriso" from *Don Carlo* is particularly bad in this regard. Ordinarily I don't object to vibrato, but Kaufmann's sometimes

Jonas Kaufmann

obscures the pitch. To be sure his *voix mixte* on the high C of "Salut! demeure" from *Faust*[2] is a throwback to pre-war French tenors.

In German repertory Kaufman's big middle voice is a big asset, and he feels the words. In "Durch die Wälder" from *Der Freischütz*[3] he momentarily is thrilling. As Lohengrin he creates a hush with his pianissimo. He's better in this role in part because he feels it more, in part because the music permits him to sing much of it at volume levels less than forte. On May 14, 2011 Kaufmann sang Siegmund in a Met matinee broadcast of *Die Walküre*. The role was a departure for him because of the baritonal tessitura and the required power and heft. In Act I he sounded like a thin-voiced baritone and was somewhat underpowered. Sometimes his *passaggio* was muffled, including on the first "Wälsc!" Although he sang note by note rather than with phrasing he did make us feel the words. In Act II he hit his stride, singing with majesty and a wonderful legato, and was thrilling in the confrontation with Hunding.

Still, when he sings Italian repertory not enough happens emotionally. Certainly he is no substitute for Corelli. Corelli was proud of having modulated his sound to capture Faust (see "Tenore del mondo," in vol. 2), whereas on a December 10, 2011 Met matinee broadcast Kaufmann sang it with a tone like that he used for Siegmund. The story of the opera of course turns on Faust's transformation from an old man into a young one. When the moment came Kaufmann's voice remained the same. It lacked the melting, seductive lyricism, the romance, freshness, sweetness, liquidity and spin of tone and ease of emission called for by much of the part and failed to contrast with the lower male voices. However secure and accomplished his singing—including a spectacular diminuendo on "Je t'aime"—his voice production precludes him from capturing these essential aspects. Think of what the many Gounod-period French Fausts who recorded a hundred years ago sounded like.

On YouTube one can find examples of Kaufmann's singing prior to 1995. (See, for example, *Jonas Kaufmann, The Tenor*.) Then his voice was bright and focused like a laser beam. Now it's dark and spread. Recordings with Kaufmann from before 1995 show that until then he used mask placement. Compare his "Rêve" from *Manon* from 1993 and 2008 and you'll hear the difference a change in technique can make. In 1993 he is placing in the mask and his larynx is lowered. In the 1993 recording he isn't guttural and sounds like a tenor. In the 2008 one he sounds like he does today.

Beginning in 1995 Kaufmann studied with an American baritone living in Germany, Michael Rhodes, a pupil of Giuseppe De Luca. Rhodes says that De Luca taught him to maintain the position of a yawn while singing.[4] If you try yawning while touching your larynx you'll find it lowers. Indeed, Corelli practiced yawning. On online newsgroups some have called Kaufmann Corelli's heir. Well, in

José Cura as Turiddu in Cavalleria rusticana. *He too lowers his larynx.*

terms of technique he's a fellow traveler. With his approach there is no difficulty making diminuendos or singing softly, as repeatedly evidenced in his recordings. To me he sounds like a throatier Rosvaenge. But Kaufmann doesn't have his ease on top.

In *Jonas Kaufmann: Verismo Arias*[5] Kaufmann has fabulous control over dynamics (as good as Pertile's) allied to a long breath span: he sings phrases in one breath that everybody else takes in two.

Still, try comparing any of Kaufmann's many recordings or videos of "E lucevan le stelle" to Corelli's from the Parma *Tosca* (listen to the free sample at belcantosociety.org), and you'll find that Corelli has more warmth, personality and passion. That Kaufmann makes a Corelli-like diminuendo on "disciogliea dai veli!" in the middle of the aria suggests that he may listen to him.

José Cura

Compared to Cura even Del Monaco seems effeminate. At his best he is exciting in a tough, masculine way—tenor as strongman—as in a *Cavalleria* from 1996 on YouTube, in which, however, his "Addio alla madre" sags in pitch. One does not expect that from an orchestra conductor, which Cura is. I attribute it to inadequate breath support. As is typical of mechanists, in lyrical passages, such as an aria from Puccini's *Edgar* from 2000, he can sound throaty and labored.

Unlike so many others, for Cura the basic musical entity is not the note but the phrase—he binds the notes together into expressive units with a destination. Sometimes he indulges in extreme rubatos that usually are convincing. Often he rushes, presumably to move the music forward.

YouTube videos reveal his voice to have become constricted and woofy in the *passaggio* and to have lost focus, for example, in clips of the *Traviata* "Brindisi" from 2007 and 2008, from *Edgar* from 2008 and *Tosca* from 2009. Nevertheless he is moving in a "Niun mi tema," from Hungary in 2008.

Rolando Villazón

On the CD *Cielo e Mar*,[1] recorded in March 2007, Villazón sings arias from *Gioconda, Adriana, Il giuramento* (Saverio Mercadante), *Mefistofele, Maristella* (Salvatore Pietri), *Fosca* (Antônio Carlos Gomes), *Simon Boccanegra, Poliuto* (Donizetti), *Il figliuol prodigo* (Ponchielli) and *Luisa Miller*. He has the dramatic temperament to do justice to the music, but left to its own devices his voice isn't heavy enough. To make it meet the music's demands he lowers his larynx and covers. The tone that results is thickened and more steely.

Corelli, sometimes, and Del Monaco did the same thing. But their voices lent themselves more readily to this approach—and, unlike Villazón, Corelli floated his larynx. Villazón has to exert himself to sound robust and, like Del Monaco, once he has gone down that path he is unable to retreat and sings throughout in the same manner.

Sometimes, as in "Cielo e mar," which is rhapsodic and toward the end full of romance and sexual excitement, he sounds labored and ungainly. At other times, as in the *Fosca* and *Boccanegra* selections, he manages to extract all the passion, and the result is thrilling. But

Rolando Villazón

the tradeoff is that there's almost no chiaroscuro, and in the two *Mefistofele* arias he sounds beefy and musclebound. As with Del Monaco, who is more clarion, one comes to miss caress, lyrical beauty and an unconstricted sound. But Villazón's objective is to maximize ring and resonance to better enable himself to plumb emotional depths. He is more complex emotionally than Del Monaco, and his legato is better. Some of his Fs at the top of the staff are nasal and labored, however, and he frequently makes glottal attacks on "ah" and "eh" at the beginnings of phrases, which disrupts any feeling of upbeat. Above the staff in the *Boccanegra* aria he sings "Pietàw," within the staff he sings "Pietàh." Nevertheless because the album makes his viscera audible and they pack a wallop this is his best solo CD. Nothing recorded thus far in this century shows Del Monaco's influence more clearly than this.

In *Rolando Villazón: Italian Opera Arias*[2] from 2004 he shows himself to be a musician first, a tenor second: he is sensitive to harmonies—apart from protracting consonances at phrase endings unduly. Like his fellow Mexicans Araiza and Vargas he uses almost no portamento, sings 16ths and other short notes loudly enough so that they don't drop out of the vocal line and sets forward rhythms clearly and unambiguously. Like them he uses rubato sparingly and eases in and out of tempo gracefully. His legato is excellent, his dynamic variety minimal. Again like them, because of the relative lack of portamento, rubato and dynamic variety his treatment of nineteenth-century repertory seems unRomantic. He seems to be as proficient as Cura but without the musical eccentricities. A conductor could obtain a good result with Villazón with minimal rehearsal. But on this CD his singing lacks inwardness, temperament and depth of feeling and is monochromatic as well as without bloom. He darkens vowels in the *passaggio*, which he covers heavily. The feelings in my throat while listening tell me his was not feeling well when the recording was made, and it is less successful vocally than his others.

Villazón sings the opening of the *Arlesiana* aria mezzo piano and the *Il duca d'Alba* aria with no hush. He doesn't feel "Tombe degli avi miei" deeply and doesn't inflect or italicize the words. He attacks the high B with a *coup de glotte* (glottal stroke). He articulates the *fioriture* in the "Donna è mobile" cadenza well—he clearly sounds every note without calling attention to the separations between them. His "E lucevan le stelle" is well-proportioned musically but understated emotionally.

The album *Viva Villazón!*[3] consists of a CD compendium drawn from his previous recordings plus a DVD of a November 11, 2005 concert in Prague. He is engaging to watch—warm, ebullient, brimming with personality—puts a smile on your face and takes the audience by storm. What he does *not* do is infuse words with much meaning. His jaw drops on high notes, in back as well as in front. You see his larynx move. His middle voice is quite open.

In *Rolando Villazón: Opera Recital,*[4] recorded in September 2005, he is playful, ironic and feelingful in "Il était une fois à la cour d'Eisenach"—like Kraus, who, however, doesn't cover and interpolates a high C. But then Villazón also doesn't interpolate the high B first inserted by Gigli in the *Arlesiana* aria or the high B-flat in the one from *Duca d'Alba*. He captures the breathlessness of Hoffmann's "Allons! Courage et confiance" despite covering heavily. In "Recondita armonia" he covers even in the middle voice, but what distinguishes his version from just about everyone else's is that the notes have destinations—through the use of crescendos he moves them ahead toward chord changes. In "Addio alla madre" he also covers throughout but sings one of his most substantial high B-flats. But where's the heartbreak? Covering throughout makes his voice sound too old in "Amor ti vieta," and his high A is flat.

Most singers lag behind the beat at least some of the time as a result of putting consonants on the beat instead of vowels. Like Callas and Gencer Villazón is among the select few who do not do this—except when he sings in German, in "Ach so Fromm" (the original of "M'appari"). This suggests that at least that aspect of his musicianship is intuitive and that the language disrupted his intuitions. Were it intellectual he would have disciplined himself to insert the consonants at the ends of preceding beats. Despite the covering he sounds sweet for a tenor singing in German. But his high B-flat is flat. Didn't they do a retake? In "Jungfrau Maria" from Flotow's *Alessandro Stradella* Villazón's tone is too covered to have bloom or sound youthful. Why did he do it? His account of Lenski's aria is disfigured by glottal attacks, and he covers very heavily above the staff. His rendition is not inward enough and lacks sufficient pathos. In "Di rigori armato il seno" covering leads him to turn "ah" into the German vowel sound "eu" above the staff. His top has a wide vibrato.

His "Ma se m'è forza perderti" from *Ballo* is the pick of the litter because it is deeply felt and affecting. Astonishingly he opens his tone a tiny bit momentarily on the "Ah" of "Ah, lo segnato!" The effect is exciting. Still, he makes some glottal attacks. On the other hand "Com' è gentil" from *Don Pasquale* is a huge disappointment—covered to the point of being labored, too old and mature sounding. The unornamented repeat becomes a bore, and the high B is flat. "Spirto gentil" from *Favorita* is taken at a fast clip, with singing that is neither limpid nor fresh. The C is flat. In "La fleur que tu m'avais jetée" he has some nice mezzo pianos near the end, followed by a loud high B-flat, heavily covered. In "Je crois entendre encore," on the one hand he conveys the highly elusive lilt of the 6/8 meter and sings in one breath phrases nearly everyone else takes in two. On the other he sings the high Bs in a *voix mixte*, introduced so abruptly that the transition is jarring and disrupts the legato. The second one and a couple of the As are flat. Because of covering he sounds middle aged, and he fails to capture the dream-like feeling. Even had he done so it would have been marred by his glottal attacks. Pavarotti in his performances of *Ernani* sang an alternate aria Verdi composed, "Odo il voto," to stunning effect. Villazón's version, covered so heavily that some of the "ah" vowels are distorted, fails to efface that memory.

In a 2008 DVD of *Don Carlo*[5] he's appealing but not thrilling. His voice doesn't peal forth or satisfy you on a visceral level the way Corelli's does. Also he lacks Corelli's longing and yearning. He trills beautifully and more than on his earlier recordings is able to sing piano above the staff. His voice gives no hint of the health problem to come.

Unfortunately I have had no opportunity to hear him since his comeback.

Walter Fraccaro

Gianfranco Cecchele studied with Marcello Del Monaco but around 1970 modified his technique. In an exchange of emails with me in October and November 2011 unfortunately neither Gianfranco nor his son, Lorenzo, were able to explain what the changes consisted of. From listening to Gianfranco's singing I think he made the technique *more* mechanistic. In any event he is able to teach it since the moment I heard Fraccaro I knew he only could be a Cecchele pupil—the emissions sound the same, and my throat feels the same when I listen to each of them. In 2011 Fraccaro sang heavy Verdi and Puccini all over Italy, in San Francisco and Tokyo.

Walter Fraccaro

Vladimir Galouzine: He switches back and forth between lowering his larynx and placing in the mask.

MASK-LARYNX-HYBRID TENORS

Vladimir Galouzine

In YouTube clips from *Pagliacci, Pique Dame, Luisa Miller* and *Otello* Galouzine uses a lowered-larynx technique, and the throaty sound becomes monotonous. But there are clips where he sings with rather extreme mask placement—the "Nessun dorma" with a red costume, for example. There also is a "Non piangere Liù" where he uses mask placement for the more lyrical sections in the middle voice and then lowers his larynx for the high notes. In addition there are two clips of "Celeste Aïda," one with mask placement, the other with a lowered larynx.

When he sings in the mask he makes you feel his temperament more and is able to sing with pathos. The clips illustrate the effect of voice production on timbre—and why understanding technique is essential to understanding why a singer sounds as he does. (If he switched to top-of-the-head placement he would sound like still another tenor.)

Piotr Beczala

Beczala switches betwewen mask placement and lowering his larynx. On every high note he aims his voice at the cheekbones, bares his upper teeth, drops his lower jaw in back and raises his soft palate, probably through yawning. He keeps his middle voice bright but covers heavily from F-sharp on up.

Above high B-flat his voice loses substance and sometimes is constricted. In general he's monochromatic. Mostly he just vocalizes, not unpleasantly, with insufficient involvement and contrast and no spark. His phrase endings sometimes have glottal stops. He lacks inwardness, pathos, caress, delicacy of feeling, grace, romance, brio and panache. He doesn't bring words alive. His intonation sometimes is sour, often sharp. He sings loudly most of the time, with inadequate variety of dynamics. He lets one opportunity for expression after another go for naught. He's cold, impersonal, stolid. I have to pinch myself to pay attention when he's singing.

In a *Rigoletto*[1] he mostly kept his larynx low until "La donna è mobile," after which he switched to mask placement. When his larynx was lowered he used a lot of glottal attacks and glottal offsets. (The former ruin any feeling of upbeat, the later any feeling of repose.) And he sounded labored, throaty and bloomless and frequently sang sharp. When he placed in the mask these faults vanished, and his top was free. Indeed, he held the high B with which the role concludes a long time, with a hint of diminuendo.

MASK-PLACEMENT TENORS WHO DON'T COVER

Vittorio Grigolo

I'm eager to replay Grigolo's CD, *The Italian Tenor*.[1] He feels the music and the words—and makes you feel them too. No syllable, no note is perfunctory. He sings with a kaleidoscope of colors and a full dynamic range. His phrases typically have soft moments, build to loud ones and then taper. He is able to create a hush. He has a youthful, fresh sound—not one like a middle-aged man. He is a lover both tender and passionate. In the aria from Puccini's *Le villi* his voice exudes pathos, fear and, in the *Luisa Miller* aria, anguish.

He has a sense of measure—a feeling for proportion and balance with regard to how long to make notes. Still, if he made resolutions of dissonances a little shorter they would provide a greater feeling of repose.

He is like Pertile in that he often sings pianissimo, piano or mezzo forte rather than full voice and in general reserves forte singing for climaxes. As with Pertile his voice is at its most appealing at less than full volume. (Pertile's voice is more substantial.) In his sensitivity to words and music Grigolo evokes Schipa and Anselmi. Schipa, however, has a defter touch with regard to rubato and uses more of it—Grigolo uses hardly any—and Anselmi is more elegiac. A comparison is Vinson Cole. They each have similar control over gradations of dynamics.

Grigolo's voice is a little white above the staff—the result of singing piano so much? He sings closed all the time; he doesn't cover. (In the *Rigoletto* from Mantua he covers some passages in "Parmi veder le lagrime," before and including the high B-flat.) His cries of "All'armi!" in "Tutto parea sorridere" from Verdi's *Il corsaro* would have more impact sung open. (At the end of "E lucevan le stelle" he sings "amato" and "tanto" slightly open.) In "E lucevan le stelle" he "lives" the recitative. In the opening of "Ah! sì, ben mio" Grigolo sculpts the phrase "avrò più l'alma intrepida, il braccio avrò più forte" better than anyone else (with the exception of Björling in the 1939 *Trovatore* recording—listen to the free sample at belcantosociety.org—who is as good): he makes one continuous crescendo to the high A-flat on "brac-" and one continuous diminuendo after it to the middle-voice A-flat on "for-." (An alternative would be to head the entire phrase toward "for-," so that it would climax there.) Nearly everyone else's version is blighted by inadvertent or misplaced accentuations arising because of one note or another being stronger in the voice or because the singer doesn't make the 16th notes loud enough to sustain the crescendo or because he isn't aware of the hierarchy of notes in the harmonic structure of the phrase. Grigolo trills in "Ah, sì, ben mio" and has good *note minute* in the "Pira." Both his legato and his breath span are superb.

Particularly in "Una furtiva lagrima" Grigolo creates an urgent intimacy that sets him apart. You feel he's singing to you. Also, he has more tenderness than others. In the middle voice he has some flicker vibrato. In "Se il mio nome" (*Barbiere*) he has good agility and velocity. He is able to let his voice fade away to nothing. His intonation is uncommonly good. He has solid breath support. In "Tutto parea sorridere" and "Se il mio nome" he subordinates ornamentation, both written and added, to melody by singing the ornamentation with less emphasis and making it softer. And in Schubert's "Ave Maria" he even sings with rubato. Above high A his voice sometimes turns a little white ("Chi son?" and "la speranza" in *Bohème*, or "l'amerò" at the end of the *Traviata* cabaletta). Also, it lacks punch, a real climax—something Pavarotti provides in abundance. Grigolo is endearing but not exciting. He has a boyish charm laced with charisma.

Vittoro Grigolo. He is evocative of Schipa. He places in the mask, which Schipa did not do, and seldom covers.

In part there are technical reasons for his accomplishments. He uses a lot of head voice and doesn't try to carry up chest voice, unlike most in the last sixty years. He's not a mechanist but uses placement (his is in the mask but not crammed far forward), so the sound isn't thick, coarse or labored. There's nothing manipulated about his singing. He's completely free of the influence of Del Monaco.

I'm amazed that such a singer could come out of today's Italy! Perhaps the explanation is that, like Di Stefano, who also doesn't cover, his pop singing seemingly informs his opera singing, so perhaps he should be thought of as his successor—they each create intimacy and make you feel they are singing to you.

Juan Diego Flórez: He places in the mask and doesn't cover. But he simplifies and transposes Sonnambula.

© Decca / Josef Gallauer

Beyond all that there is Grigolo's beauty of soul. To judge from his records and videos (I haven't heard him live) he's the loveliest Italian tenor since Gigli (who had much more oomph and a far greater variety of sonorities) and Schipa (who didn't).

From the recording I don't get the impression that his voice is voluminous. Because it lacks *squillo* (ring or ping) it is not exciting inherently. Still, his sonority on top is more pleasing than Flórez's. He has still more art and heart than voice. He lacks the ecstasy of the high note—something Corelli and Pavarotti had at their peaks—a state in which the high note takes possession of the singer's head and throat and drives the audience into a frenzy.

Grigolo's significance is that he is bucking the trend to sing Verdi and Puccini with less youthfulness, sweetness and nuance.

Giuseppe Filianoti

I'm mainly familiar with Filianoti from his *Dom Sébastien Roi de Portugal* recording.[2] He begins with his voice sweet and fresh, the tones true in pitch, not darkened, not covered but closed, his placement far forward in the mask, in the manner of Kraus. Unlike Kraus Filianoti sometimes sounds constricted in the *passaggio* and sometimes goes flat on high notes.

Filianoti lacks *slancio* and is much given to ending phrases with a glottal stop. He is erratic within the recording, which according to the album's booklet was taken from more than one performance. As the opera progresses he begins to sound labored and throaty like a mechanist. At moments he breaks out into a vibrato. Are these problems the result of his voice being too light for the part, inadequate technique, problematical health? It's hard to be sure.

Juan Diego Flórez's Strengths and Weaknesses

Juan Diego Flórez's strengths include not only the ability to articulate fiorituras at rapid tempos but also the musicianship to organize them so that dissonances (which are important harmonically) are emphasized and consonances (which are subordinate harmonically) are deemphasized. Not only does he sing descending scales well but ascending ones too. He doesn't need to have recourse to covering, has clear diction and a long breath span, also for a light tenor a considerable amount of volume around G in the low middle voice.

He uses mask placement and is entirely free of Del Monaco's and Corelli's influences.

In the booklet to *Juan Diego Flórez: Bel Canto Spectacular*[3] Roger Pines declares, "For the past decade the Peruvian tenor has earned ecstatic critical and public response internationally for a technical prowess and an authoritative style that must surely equal what the public would have heard from the greatest tenors more than one hundred and fifty years ago." Not so. Flórez's weaknesses include lack of vocal range for the music he sings: his range, which extends to high D, is a fourth shorter than Rubini's (he ascended to G above high C^4), a minor-sixth shorter than Giovanni David's (by one account he went up to B-flat above high C^5). Flórez's high notes from B-flat on up don't climax—instead of gaining volume or *squillo* (ring or ping) they thin out and don't add excitement. He lacks the ability to color notes above the staff or imbue them with feeling. He is unable to sing softly above the staff, in mezza voce or *voix mixte*, with whisper-quiet pianissimos, so that he cannot provide enough chiaroscuro of color and dynamics. His dynamic curves are too restricted—there's not enough range of volume between loud and soft—so that as a result melodies are less expressive. He often doesn't ornament or under-ornaments repeated passages. His ornaments typically don't widen the melodic curve, nor do they make the music more active rhythmically through the introduction of divisions. As a result repeated passages often sound redundant. (Suppose the basic rhythmic unit of a movement is an eighth note. With a division it becomes a sixteenth note, say, so the music becomes twice as active.)

Consider Flórez in his *cheval de bataille*, "Pour mon âme" from Donizetti's *Fille*. The part of the aria with the high Cs consists of a theme that is repeated three times. In accordance with the dictates of the style each repetition should be embroidered. Ideally the decorations of each repetition should widen the melodic curve by ranging higher. The idea is that once high C has been sung it becomes passe as a climax point. Once high D has been heard it too is old hat, etc. Like Pavarotti before him Flórez sings the piece as written, so that it lacks the variety and brilliance it could have. And he encores it the same way! He lacks sufficient range to enable him to do justice to the style.

Consider him in "Nel furor delle tempeste..." from *Pirata*, from his Rubini CD.[6] He sings the repeat softer and more tenderly. Without ornamentation and higher notes that's not enough to keep it from sounding anti-climactic.

Consider him in "Di mia patria o bel soggiorno" from Donizetti's *Marin Faliero*, written for Rubini. He throws in an interpolation here and there but does not ornament systematically. More, he lacks ease aloft. The high notes should sound like part of the melodic curve, not show the singer at his limit. Also, he doesn't do enough soft singing.

The same could be said for Flórez's rendition of "All'udir del padre afflitto" from Bellini's *Bianca e Fernando*. (Bellini originally composed the music for Giovanni David under the title *Bianca e Gernando* and later revised it for Rubini.) Here Flórez's emotional limitations come into play: He can muster neither the pathos nor the loathing called for by the part. His temperament is too bland.

The part of Elvino in *La sonnambula*, also written for Rubini, is beyond Flórez, both technically and emotionally. He fails to convey the sublime aspects of the score as well as much of its rage. Throughout, he is superficial.[7]

In "Prendi: l'anel ti dono" he is too loud and not intimate, tender, caressing, loving. He doesn't sing in mezza voce or create a hush and doesn't float any of the notes above the staff. To accommodate the music to his voice he sings it in the traditional, transposed keys, a whole step lower than the original.

He also sings "Son geloso del zefiro errante" a whole-tone lower. To avoid having to sing high pianissimo, as called for in the score, he is stentorian where he should be tender. He omits the "Ah! costante" section, with its high tessitura and chromatic run up to a high D (high C in the transposed version), meant to be sung in *voix mixte* or at least mezza voce. He doesn't contrast loud passages with soft. The tenor and soprano parts are in sixths—including the passage where the score specifies fifteen trills. Flórez omits nearly all of them, the higher ones in particular, leaving the Amina, Natalie Dessay, to trill by herself. Although he does trill within the staff elsewhere, his technique plainly won't enable him to do so above it. The last section of the duet in particular should be an effusion of tender love. The feeling eludes him completely.

He sings "Tutto è sciolto" a whole tone lower and interrupts phrases with extra breaths. He sings "Ah! perché non posso odiarti" a major third lower and doesn't capture Elvino's bitterness. (That bitterness motivates him to try to marry Lisa instead and explains his relief when he understands Amina wasn't unfaithful after all.) Part of the problem is that in the lower key, B-flat major, Elvino has a mamby-pamby personality bordering on the insipid, whereas in the higher key, D-major, the interpreter has the potential to reveal the heroic side of the character's personality.

At the the end of "Lisa mendace anch'essa!" instead of simplifying the passage with a chain of four ascending trills Flórez simply omits it. In short he can't do justice to music written for Rubini, not technically and not emotionally.

Flórez's Arturo in *I puritani*[8] is fraught with problems similar to those of his Elvino. He sings with an all-purpose sweet sound that doesn't convey intensity of feeling, fire, inwardness or yearning and isn't deeply touching. He doesn't have enough passion, urgency or emotional tension. He has many small lapses of intonation and makes any number of random or misplaced accentuations. More, although he does sing three high Ds he replaces the F, E-flat and two D-flats of "Credeasi, misera" with lower notes.

There is a myth that the music is meant to be sung with D-flat at its climax, that Bellini inserted the F after Rubini surprised him by singing it by mistake. "Since you're able to sing it I'll write it in for you," Bellini is supposed to have said. Not so. Rubini had been performing Fs for years. By *Puritani*, according to Bellini, Rubini's tessitura actually had descended a half step, so he wrote a comparatively low-lying part for him.[9] Although it has high notes much of it centers around E at the top of the staff. The music of "Credeasi, misera" is structured to build to the F. If it isn't sung the melody doesn't develop properly, and the act doesn't climax. The D-flat makes no sense harmonically and jars the music so that the singer never can sound right. In comparison with the Fs, say, in "Ascolta, o padre" in *Bianca e Fernando*, that Bellini composed for Giovanni David, this one is easy to sing because the voice is doubled by the first violins, which carry it aloft.

Flórez sings the two written high Ds in "Vieni fra queste braccia" and interpolates another one at the opera's end. Apart from that one interpolation and the simplifications mentioned above he sings *Puritani* as written. Rubini on the other hand, according to contemporary accounts, decorated lavishly.[10]

Alfredo Kraus insisted in our interview that the basic vowel for all tenors is "i" ("ee"). Well, Flórez plainly is an "ah" tenor: to accommodate a D-flat in "Credeasi, misera" and the three Ds he replaces the written vowels with "ah."

The performers make structure-destroying cuts to the music yet curiously include a duet, "Ah! sento, o mio bell'angelo," that Bellini himself cut after the premiere. (According to me it is located implausibly from an architectural standpoint, with joins and transitions that are too abrupt; it is less inspired than the rest of the score and makes the measures afterward seem too short to balance it and conclude the opera.) The reason to buy this *Puritani*, however, is that the performers do include a plaintive trio in Act I for Arturo, Enrichetta and Riccardo, "Se il destin a te m'invola," which Bellini also cut after the opening night, striking it through lightly. The tessitura for the tenor is high, and Flórez makes heavy weather of some high Bs. An oddity is that the booklet for the DVD claims the performance includes the Act III duet "Da quel dì che ti mirai," but it does not. Both pieces are among the composer's most haunting.

For *Puritani* to succeed the performers need to be touching, but the ones here are not. In addition to Flórez they include Nino Machaidze, Gabriele Viviani, Ildebrando D'Arcangelo, with the Orchestra e Coro del Teatro Comunale di Bologna, Michele Mariotti, conductor.

Flórez's interpretations not only of Bellini but also of Rossini suffer because he is deficient at expressing love and hate. He lacks variety of tone color and feeling and is without inwardness. He doesn't draw you in. One of the most important emotions in Italian opera is pathos, and he offers almost none.

Although Rossini benefits from being sung with personality and heart one can make a favorable impression in it through instrumental-like proficiency as well as phrasing the roulades. On the other hand Bellini sung without personality and heart is lifeless. For that reason I prefer to hear Flórez in Rossini than Bellini (just as I'd prefer to listen to Joan Sutherland in *Semiramide* than *Norma*). In Bellini I'd sooner listen to Morino (when he's in tune) than Flórez. It least he gives you the pathos.

Still, in "O muto asil.... Corriam" from *Guglielmo Tell*[11] Flórez's lack of inwardness, temperament, personality and variety of feeling and tone color are letdowns. It would help if he opened his tone on occasion. Instead he sings everything closed (not covered). He sustains a high C for ten seconds at the end. But his high notes don't thrill—except for one of the other high Cs. The music is exciting, but he isn't.

Lawrence Brownlee and Barry Banks

Seemingly no note gives Brownlee any difficulty in the two octaves from C to C he spans on his CD from 2004 of nineteenth-century songs in Italian,[12] yet the recital as a whole is less than the sum of its parts. In fast songs such as "Me voglio fa 'na casa" (which the album says was composed by Donizetti although in actuality it only is attributed to him) and Rossini's "La danza" Brownlee isn't warm or ebullient enough. And in soulful material, with some exceptions he fails to offer sufficient pathos, yearning, tenderness, caress, in-

Lawrence Brownlee

wardness, urgency, *slancio*, desperation or personality. The key missing ingredient, I suspect, is love for the material. He sings it both because it fits his voice and because it fits together into a balanced program, with contrast between slow and fast selections, also with pieces in 6/8 coming after those in 4/4, not because he is obsessed by or cherishes it.

Nor does he compensate for these shortcomings with musicianship. He does little shaping of phrases. Upbeats don't move ahead to downbeats. Weak measures don't balance with strong ones. Lilt eludes him. And compound meters don't flow well. He'll slight a dissonance (a moment of harmonic tension) and overemphasize its resolution (a moment of harmonic relaxation). However, his legato is really good, his intonation excellent.

He doesn't give much evidence of involvement with words and colors them only on occasion (such as "Spazzacamin," which he sings open and without vibrato, like a street urchin, in the Verdi song "Lo spazzacamino"). In short he under-interprets. His diction, however, is clear (even if he does sound American).

Brownlee's bottom doesn't lose resonance, and his voice is full throughout the two octaves. At times his mask placement makes him nasal. His tone above the staff on "ah" is darker than within it; at moments he almost sounds like he's covering. In "Lo spazzacamin" he trills on high A three times. True, the trills wander a little in pitch, but in the context of today's "bel-canto tenors" that he even attempts them is a marvel.

The music to Donizetti's "L'amor funesto" says the composer dedicated it to Napoleone Moriani (who was known as "il tenore della bella morte," the tenor of the beautiful death, on account of his exquisite manner of expiring in such operas as *Lucia*). But the album instead lists him as the poet who wrote the words. Presumably the misinformation was provided by the artists—an indication of their lack of involvement with the subject matter. No wonder they left insufficiently realized some of Donizetti's markings with regard to interpretation!

By 2008, when Brownlee recorded *Italiana*,[13] his emission had changed. His placement is much less far forward in the mask, and there is little trace of nasality. And his voice above the staff matches his voice within it. His vibrato within the staff, however, is more pronounced. He omits all the trills, which suggests he had lost the ability.

In the recognition scene, in the first-act finale, he creates a nice hush.

On a 2009 Met *Cenerentola* DVD[14] Brownlee's top is somewhat white but matches his middle voice better than on his song recital. He smiles slightly on high C. On top notes he fakes the "oo" vowel, mixing it with "oh." His high C is strong enough to provide a real climax (unlike, say, Flórez's). An occasional glottal stop mars his emission, and his fast vibrato is more in evidence. Like others in the cast and even the first clarinetist in this sloppily prepared performance he occasionally lags behind the beat. (The singers have the excuse that they have to get in consonants and are standing some distance away from the orchestra, but I can't imagine what excuse the clarinetist would have.)

Flórez sometimes organizes notes into phrases by imparting some stress (even if not enough) to appoggiaturas and shortening their resolutions (so that an eighth note becomes a dotted sixteenth), and he sometimes subordinates notes that are less important harmonically and moves phrases ahead. Brownlee, by contrast, often just sings the notes. But he does have better intonation.

In watching the DVD of Rossini's *Armida*[15] from 2010 I found myself looking forward to Brownlee's high Cs because they peal forth and provide glorious climaxes, for example, in the Act III trio. The part has a baritone tessitura but with forays to high D. The singer has to keep his throat poised to sing high notes yet have enough resonance available for the low ones so they'll sound. After a tenor has sung a good number of high Cs and a couple of Ds his low notes tend to dry up. Brownlee manages to avoid the problem, presumably by keeping his throat relaxed. His pianissimo high D-flat, sung in *voix mixte*, has a pleasing sonority—unlike his forte high Ds, which sound pinched. One in Act I, on the word "sì," seems to be in a different register, verging on falsetto. In general the color of Flórez's Ds match that of his Cs better. The highest Brownlee sings without appearing to change register is D-flat.

It's noteworthy that Brownlee, like Flórez, not only can sing Lindoro in *Italiana*, a high-lying role, but also Ramiro in *Cenerentola*, a low-lying part with top notes. That Brownlee also can sing Rinaldo in *Armida*, which is still more low-lying, is all the more remarkable. (Rossini tailored the part to the capabilities of Andrea Nozzari.)

Brownlee's mezza voce is lovely, yet he often isn't tender enough. He excels at low-lying busywork. But on occasion his vibrato is so active as to compete with the rhythm of the sixteenth notes. On high notes he does have less of it, however. Most irritatingly he tends to over-extend the last syllable of a phrase to such a degree as to mislocate the phrase's climax. In any case in *Armida* he is put in the shade by Renée Fleming's charisma, and when they sing together he fails to match her sensitivity to phrase shape and structure. (In "D'amor al dolce impero" she even manages to be sensual while dispatching the surpassingly difficult theme and variations, and in crying for vengeance in her scene at the end she gives a spinal chill.)

The opera has roles for six tenors. One of them, Barry Banks, does sing with expressive downbeats at phrase endings—his appoggiaturas and resolutions seem like one unit, with tension and relaxation balanced. He trills although they are not in tune. He organizes fiorituras so as to emphasize harmonically important notes; however, they sometimes are out of tune. Some of his high Cs are a little white and flat when forte. To sing them he bares his upper teeth. He places in the mask. His breath support seems lacking. He has temperament, and he and Brownlee are thrilling in their confrontation.

Another tenor, John Osborn, manages to hit all the notes but with a mechanistic technique that makes him sound labored.

The performance was as fastidiously prepared as that of any Italian opera I've heard at the Met. The score is full of melodic, harmonic and rhythmic invention that repays repeated listening. Unfortunately Mary Zimmerman's production is both inadequate and full of irritating contrivances.

Eric Cutler

On Eric Cutler's CD *Eric Cutler*[16] from 2003 he sings Schumann's *Liederkreis*, Op. 39, with excellent dynamic range and control, including mezza voce, but without the requisite mystery, breathlessness, longing and ecstasy. In "Mondnacht" although he sings softly he fails to create a hush. Alas, he has an American accent.

No such problem mars his treatment of songs by Reynaldo Hahn. His rendition of "À Cloris" is beautifully felt. The most striking aspect of that of "Paysage" and "Le Rossignol des lilas" is his use of *voix mixte* once in each song. Apart from Hugues Cuénod, who was Swiss, I can't think of a non-French singer who manages the effect so

Eric Cutler

idiomatically. Cutler also appears to feel words and music more deeply than in the Schumann.

The CD includes the first version of *Tre sonetti di Petrarca* by Liszt, which he dedicated to Rubini and, to judge from the vocal line, which extends to high D-flat, probably composed for him as well. Rubini and Liszt undertook a joint concert tour in 1842, during which they performed for the King of Holland, whose chamberlain gave them each a jewel-encrusted snuff box. Because Liszt thought Rubini's of greater value he was resentful: "It does not suit me not to be put on the same level as he," he wrote to his mistress Countess Marie d'Agoult, and he gave the snuff box to his secretary.[17] The Rubini-Liszt collaboration came apart in Berlin, and Rubini continued to St. Petersburg on his own, where he was received rapturously.

In the CD's booklet Cutler writes, "As a tenor, I couldn't resist singing [the Petrarch songs]. It's rare and wonderful to have the opportunity to explore the entire vocal range [*sic*] in recital." But in these songs Liszt treats the voice as an instrument, in the sense that the music doesn't demand heart or variety of tone color. The interest is in the harmonies. One has to sing a lot of notes in return for the release of getting in the D-flat, in "Pace non trovo." Cutler scoops the note (slides up to it) in the manner of Corelli. He does interpolate a second one cleanly, in "Benedetto sia 'l giorno." (Pavarotti sang the songs in some recitals in the 1970s, transposing "Pace non trovo" a whole-step lower.) Cutler misses some opportunities for introspection and tenderness suggested by the words.

Cutler is the Arturo in a DVD of a Met performance of *Puritani*[18] from 2007, in an adaptation by Richard Bonynge for Sutherland and Pavarotti from 1976, with the music's structure disfigured by cuts and "Vieni fra queste braccia" lowered a half step. The highest note he sings in the opera is C-sharp. Like Flórez he replaces the F, E-flat and two D-flats of "Credeasi, misera" with lower notes.

Cutler makes some nice chiaroscuros of dynamics near the opening of Act III but lacks the temperament for angry and defiant utterances such as "Or sfido i fulmini, Disprezzo il Fato," "Anime perfide, Sorde a pietà" and "Un solo istante, L'ira frenate, Poscia saziate Di crudeltà" (all in "Credeasi, misera") as well as in the Act I trio. Further, if he expressed more pathos it would be welcome.

His voice sounds somewhat lacking in focus—spread. He muffles the high As of "Ah! tanto amor" (in "Ah! te, o cara"), "Non parlar di lei che adoro" and "Sprezzo, audace" because of covering but sings higher notes open.

From about high B-natural he smiles and bares his upper teeth, and his voice abruptly whitens. I was watching this *Puritani* one night at 11:45 when Ranisha, 8, came wandering in. She had been poisoned against opera so badly that I had thought there was no hope. Somehow she stayed. Periodically I asked if she wanted to go to bed. No. But after "Vieni fra queste braccia" she declared, "One more scream like that and I *am* going to bed." She had a point: those

José Bros

Courtesy Miguel Lerin

high notes are supposed to be cries of ecstasy. But instead Anna Netrebko is strident, Cutler white. Both sound labored.

José Bros

On Bros's 1998 *Sonnambula* CD[19] set he makes the same transpositions as Flórez. For the section with fifteen trills in "Son geloso" he exchanges vocal lines with the soprano, Edita Gruberova, so that he sings the notes she would have sung but an octave lower. This turns Bellini's closely knit sixths into gaping tenths.

Bros's rhythms are sloppy; frequently he blurs the distinction between a pair of even eighth notes and an eighth and a dotted sixteenth. Sometimes his pitch sags, particularly upstairs. Some high

311

notes have a beat. His version of mask placement results in nasality. He sings the repeat of "Tutto, ah! tutto in quest'istante" unornamented but lightly decorates that of "Ah! perché non posso odiarti." To a degree he captures the sweet side of Elvino.

He covers so nearly imperceptibly that I'm tempted to put him into the category of singers who don't cover at all. If you are going to cover, that's the way to do it!

On Bros's 2001 *Puritani* DVD[20] he places far forward in the mask and is slightly nasal. In Act I he makes some effective chiaroscuros of dynamics. He feels words and music in the recitatives more than Flórez and Cutler but is less accurate in pitch and rhythm than Cutler and in Act I sometimes is out of tempo (*squadrato*). His legato is good. He sings "Vieni fra queste braccia" in key but evades the same high notes as Flórez and Cutler in "Credeasi, misera." Still, there and elsewhere he gives the music a nice shape, emphasizing dissonances and deemphasizing consonances. On high C, C-sharp and D he smiles but not as much as Cutler.

He doesn't cover in the *Puritani*.

Joseph Calleja

Calleja has a fresh, sweet sound. He sings closed, with mask placement, and doesn't need to cover (although he does so on a G in *Puritani*). Because of a trace of flicker vibrato his sound evokes many tenors from a hundred years ago. (See the vibrato chapter in vol. 1.) In the booklet to the CD *Joseph Calleja: The Golden Voice* his teacher, Paul Asciak, claims his teacher-to-teacher pedigree includes Pertile and Dino Borgioli.

Calleja's sweetness, however, is one dimensional. His overriding shortcomings are emotional. For his repertory a singer often needs to create a hush, also a feeling of intimacy. Apparently he can't. (He does infuse part of "Je crois entendre encore" with dreaminess but doesn't sustain it.) In such pieces as "Deserto in terra" from *Don Sebastiano*[21] a singer must have fire and *slancio*, (oomph, surge), to which he is a stranger—for comparison listen to the Caruso and

Pavarotti recordings.[22] (His top thins, so even if he did have some oomph in him he couldn't impart it on high notes.) In excerpts from the beginning of *Puritani*, Act III, disfigured by substantial cuts, he fails to sing with pathos and deeply felt, desperate love. His voice is monochromatic—and so is his heart. What a pity that a singer with such a pretty voice should be so superficial!

Musically he is equally bland, evidenced by lack of *Schwung* in "Deserto in terra" and in general a lack of sufficient emphasis. He gives dissonances and consonances more or less the same treatment, so that the music's climaxes have little impact. He doesn't change tone color in response to harmonies. His involvement with words is sporadic. The recording is a sequence of missed opportunities.

His outstanding technical accomplishment is the ability to make diminuendos on high notes, including high C.

He does exactly that on a high C in "Son geloso."[23] But he sings the duet a whole-step down, with out-of-tune half steps, no tenderness and no feeling for the sublime. He omits the "Ah! costante" section. In the passage with fifteen trills he makes an attempt to undertake only a couple of the lowest. Why record a piece on an aria album if you can't sing the notes?

Neither Calleja nor his Amina, Netrebko, has digested the details, and both are sloppy with regard to rhythm and pitch. She apparently doesn't notice that some notes have dots on them. He misconstrues the appoggiaturas in the recitative, inserting anticipations of their resolutions and thereby compromising the pattern of harmonic tension followed by harmonic relaxation. In general they sing with insufficient contrast. This Amina has little reason to reproach Elvino for his jealousy, for he gives in almost immediately, before "Ingrato!"

In his CD recorded in 2003, *Joseph Calleja: Tenor Arias*,[24] his voice is sweeter and more boyish and at moments reminiscent of Björling's first recordings. This is appropriate for Nemorino's "Quanto è bella" but not for most of the rest of the album.

In an April 25, 2011 phone conversation tenor Luis Lima told me, "A problem for every tenor is that people have Corelli and Del Monaco in their ears, and then you come onstage." I admit that when Calleja sings "Ah! la paterna mano" from *Macbeth* and "La dolcissima effigie" from *Adriana* I can't help but measure him against Del Monaco, who programmed the *Macbeth* aria in any number of concerts and made it exciting, and Corelli, who is celebrated for his Maurizio. In the *Macbeth* Calleja makes a diminuendo on the high B-double-flat of "braccia," where Del Monaco and Corelli each have a ringing climax.

Calleja often employs an ultra-quiet mezza voce, which for the most part he turns on and off abruptly, so that there's no transition between it and his full voice. The effect often brings me up short, so wide is the gap in both volume and timbre. (Tagliavini's mezza voce had more body.) In the *Adriana* it's as if a crooner such as Giacomo Rondinella were undertaking the warrior Maurizio. (When Rondinella performed an opera excerpt on TV with Olivero he had the good sense to choose the "Duetto delle ciliegie" from *Fritz*, which he sings quite well.) In contrast with Calleja, Corelli's mezza voce and full voice are of a piece. (I do like that Calleja is able to fade his diminuendos to nothing, so that you don't know if he's still singing.)

In *Joseph Calleja: The Maltese Tenor*,[25] recorded in 2011, Calleja sounds less youthful and sweet. His placement is quite far forward in the mask, and he does some covering just above the staff. In "Sento avvampar" from *Boccanegra* he exudes some suffering and pathos but not enough to do the aria justice. In the one-dimensional "Donna non vidi mai" from *Manon Lescaut* he does sound lovely, however. In general, throughout the CD he offsets a bland and boring singing personality wedded to a pretty voice.

A comparison I can't avoid making is Calleja's *Lucia* tomb scene in his *Tenor Arias* album to any of Gigli's versions, recorded in the mid and late 20s. Calleja is wistful and sentimental where Gigli is desperate, to far greater effect. Listen to the bitterness and sarcasm with which Gigli sings the phrase, "[T]u ridi, esulti accanto al felice consorte!" He communicates the drama as well as the feelings in the words. Calleja does not. Were he himself and those around him so naive as not to anticipate that people would compare him with great

Joseph Calleja: He too places in the mask and doesn't cover. But he simplifies and transposes "Son geloso."

names associated with the warhorse arias? Calleja bears a physical resemblance to Gigli, but if you compare them in the same arias he seems like wallpaper.

The reason to discuss Calleja and the others here is this: Del Monaco and Corelli changed the world's expectations of what tenors should sound like in Verdi and Puccini. Calleja, Filianoti and Grigolo have escaped that influence, restored a youthful sound to singing these composers' music and rescued sweet tenor singing from the junk heap to which Del Monaco and Corelli had consigned it.

MASK-PLACEMENT TENORS WHO DO COVER

Álvarez: He Now Offers Catharsis

To judge from his *The Verdi Tenor*[1] album from 2009 Álvarez's faults come from feeling the music and compelling his voice to express what he feels. He really "gives"—and seemingly rips out his guts and throat to do so.

Consider "Quando le sere al placido" from *Luisa Miller*, both on *The Verdi Tenor* and in a 2008 performance from Parma on YouTube. In both versions a tad more voice would help him realize his interpretations. As matters stand he forces his lyric tenor a bit in the service of expression. Still, his emotional intensity sweeps me away.

A hallmark of the album is its contrasts of dynamics and inflections, for example, in "Di tu se fedele" from *Ballo* and "Quando le sere." In the *Ballo* he covers his tone but momentarily sings open within the staff. He has contrasts of volume and of color. The *Miller* recitative benefits from his interpretation of words plus depth of feeling. He sings the recitatives to "Quando le sere," "O tu che in seno agli angeli" from *Forza* and "Ah! sì, ben mio" from *Trovatore* in a stentorian manner and the arias themselves or at least their beginnings softly. In the latter he omits the first trill but colors the piece compellingly.

In "Ah! la paterna mano" from *Macbeth* his singing is full of shading. In "Niun mi tema" from *Otello* he feels the words, and the piece benefits from his contrasts of dynamics and of volume. Unfortunately for that one selection the producer or Álvarez himself made the

Marcel Álvarez: He places in the mask and abruptly covers in the passaggio *and above. But today he sings with personality and passion.*

decision to use an equalizer to boost the sound in the upper base, to make him sound more hefty. The result seems artificial.

His vocal technique limits his expression by preventing him from carrying through his interpretive impulses. He'll inflect his tone—only to have to abandon the inflection to cover the tone when he gets to the *passaggio* or above. He'll start out brightly—only to have to muffle his sound abruptly. Consider "moRENdo, in "Niun mi tema." "REN" is on a G. Tamagno (the first Otello) sings it closed, but Álvarez's technique compels him to sing it covered, compromising his interpretation.

Grigolo, Flórez, Calleja, Filianoti and company are only the latest examples of tenors who sing in the *passaggio* and above closed rather than covered. If Álvarez did the same he would be able to do some coloring up there. Of course Caruso, Martinelli, Pertile, Del Monaco, Corelli, Pavarotti, and Domingo all covered those notes. But with the exception of Martinelli, sometimes, and Pertile, Álvarez does more shading than the others, so the disjunction between his interpretations when he is singing in the middle voice and when he is singing above is more apparent.

In any case *The Verdi Tenor* warrants repeated listening, unlike Álvarez's earlier CDs, where the singing is on the surface.

I wasn't prepared for his interpretative leap. In October 1996, after shooting wrapped up for *Opera Fanatic*, in Milan, Gencer invited me to the concert to be given by the winner of her competition, Marcelo Álvarez. When I explained I had to be at the wedding of the film's director, Jan Schmidt-Garre, near Venice, she said she would set up a private audition. "You must arrive at 11 am and not one minute early or late." I showed up at the appointed time and was ushered into a fairly small room where, to my astonishment, an orchestra was crammed in. They just had finished rehearsing for the concert. As soon as I was in the room they plunged into one of my warhorses, "Pour mon âme" from *Fille*. When the piece ended, as the orchestra filed out, Gencer asked me what I thought. "He has a handsome voice and a sonorous high C, but he and his coaches are satisfied too easily with regard to details of intonation. Near the beginning there are some half steps, and he made them all too wide." "He's absolutely in tune!" she shot back. "What's more, all the theaters want him. He's just been engaged by Covent Garden!" The three of us had lunch, and he was most genial—not at all stuck up over finally having made it.

Listening to his 1998 CD, *Bel Canto*,[2] I think him oblivious to one opportunity for expression after another—with lots of minor inaccuracies of pitch—and that he is bland and perfunctory.

For example, in the opening of *Puritani*, Act III, beginning "Son salvo!" he fails to capture the contrasting moods: relief, desperation, pathos, exaltation. He is inadequate emotionally and insensitive to words and music. In "Se tanto in ira agli uomini" from *Linda Di Chamounix* he fails to reflect in his singing patterns of tension and relaxation that are in the harmonies. In "Tombe degli avi miei" from *Lucia* he fails to convey the drama in the words or contrast the various moods.

In vol. 1 I quoted Domingo remarking, "The characteristic of Italian tenors is *squillo*, that of Spaniards, velvet. Italian tenors should cultivate *squillo*, Spanish tenors velvet." Well, Álvarez started out with velvet aplenty. But that seemed enough to content him. He let one opportunity for expression after another go unrealized.

On that CD he covers lightly, mainly in the *passaggio* and just above it. Otherwise he sings closed.

When Álvarez began to undertake heavier repertory he made it his general practice to cover heavily throughout his range. (As I mentioned in vol. 1 Bonisolli did the same thing, except on high B and C.) What did Alvarez get in return? An old-sounding, spread voice, without ring or tonal purity. As the years passed he began to sing with more personality and passion—but not enough to compensate for the loss of tonal freshness and focus.

Unmitigated covering limits a singer's tonal palette and is monotonous. As I have pointed out in vols. 1 and 2, Gigli did a great deal of heavy covering. But he engaged not only in chiaroscuro of dynamics but also in chiaroscuro of tone coloring—among other things alternating covered tone with moments of closed tone and open tone. Álvarez is no Gigli.

On his *Tenorissimo*³ compilation Álvarez does put his soul on display but still lacks the *slancio* (oomph, surge) for, say, the "Vieni, o donna" section of "Cielo e mar."

He sings with what Corelli termed "the Spanish "r"—which in Italian sounds too heavily rolled and unduly protracted. In Álvarez's case it disrupts legato.

Álvarez places in the mask—in the cheeks, I think.

Contrary to what one would expect, on *The Verdi Tenor* Álvarez's voice largely seems recovered from the spread tone and other problems from when he was less involved emotionally. Even his intonation is better. This is surprising, because usually the more emotional a singer becomes, the more tone quality and intonation suffer. Still, by pushing his voice Álvarez is singing on his capital, not his interest.

Will he be able to keep it up? I expect not, because his singing sounds too punishing to the throat. But one never can be sure. Simionato told me in a 1996 interview for *Opera Fanatic* that the singing world expected Del Monaco to burn out in a couple of years, "yet look at how long he lasted."

To err on the safe side I'm going to treasure the catharsis Álvarez provides as long as he can continue to offer it.

Aleksandrs Antonenko

In excerpts from *Otello, Carmen* and *Tosca* on YouTube Antonenko lacks inwardness and depth of feeling. His Italian is bad. He plods note by note. His rhythm is poor. He frequently goes sharp by as much as half a tone—his intonation is the worst of any major singer today. He places in the mask.

Ramón Vargas

A remarkably versatile artist, Vargas has a bright top even though in heavy repertory he covers nearly every note. Unlike, say, Corelli he barely opens his mouth. He is a pupil of one of the major influences on opera in Italy in the last half century, the late critic Rodolfo Celletti.

In the "Pira" Vargas has the best *note minute* of anyone except Björling in the 1939 *Trovatore* recording and Grigolo. The piece really benefits from having them sounded properly. Too bad Vargas's Cs are a little flat. Otherwise next to Grigolo he has the best intonation of any tenor here. In a beautifully ornamented "Per la gloria d'adorarvi" from Giovanni Battista Bononcini's *Griselda* Vargas sings some trills in the middle voice. Because he covers much less in the middle voice in this material it reveals the beauty and sweetness of his tone. The same is true in Mexican popular songs—in which he makes you feel the words—and in "Au fond du temple saint" from *Pêcheurs*. In "Granada" he emphasizes the lyricism rather than the *slancio*. The result is lovely if unexciting.[4]

He can be wonderful when he doesn't blunt the freshness and focus of his tone by covering heavily to try to sound more appropriate for heavy repertoire. He lacks drama and charisma. In opera his singing is understated to the point that it is lacking in personality. He doesn't seem engaged or "on," in the manner, say, of Grigolo. In Lensky's aria from *Eugene Onegin* he does sound plaintive for a few moments. In general his great virtue is that he sets forward the music accurately. But because he sings with almost no portamento he makes Verdi and verismo sound unRomantic. The CD with his loveliest singing is perhaps *Ramón Vargas: Rossini, Donizetti*, recorded in 1991, when he was thirty.[5] But in the cabaletta to "Ecco ridente in cielo" from *Barbiere* he aspirates some of the fiorituras albeit lightly. His singing is neither glaringly out of tune nor super clean. The tempo is moderate. It would not be difficult to sing the piece as cleanly without aspirating. Therefore I don't see the justification for it.

The cabaletta is in the key of C. For the final sung note Vargas interpolates a high C—and thereby leaves the piece unresolved. For a piece to be resolved in this style the final tonic needs to be within the octave in which the melody is centered. For a high C to resolve this piece the melody would have to be re-centered an octave higher. But that would call the ostentatious tenors's bluff: he'd have to sing notes above high C. That would be beyond Vargas.

Ramón Vargas: He can be wonderful when he doesn't blunt the freshness and focus of his tone by covering heavily to try to sound more appropriate for heavy repertoire.

To parade his C he should have interpolated it earlier—there are any number of possible places. But why call attention to such a muffled, covered thing?

In "Se il mio nome," also from *Barbiere*, he has good legato and a nice mezza voce but no yearning, and he doesn't caress or inflect the words. He sings the music as written—and as a result it is harmonically bland and boring. It needs the dissonance of added appoggiaturas the way a desert needs rain. His dynamic curve is so limited that phrases are stagnant.

In "Languir per una bella" from *L'Italiana* Vargas adds a cadenza to the cavatina—a departure from the *come-scritto* approach he takes with other Rossini cavatinas. The interpolated cadenza doesn't have enough notes to provide closure. In this aria as often elsewhere his high B-flats are too white to match the rest of his voice.

Listen to him in "Eccomi a voi, miei prodi" from Rossini's *La donna del lago*. It by turns is ravishing and dazzling. I can't get enough of it because of the grace with which he distinguishes melody from ornamentation and organizes substantial numbers of 16th notes into a coherent whole, with every note precisely focused. To be sure the music would have benefitted had he added dissonances in obvious places, in the form of appoggiaturas. The part was written for a principal Rossini creator, Andrea Nozzari, for whom the composer penned not only basso low Gs but also tenor high Ds. Vargas sings some high Cs as well as some basso low A-flats. But would his low notes carry in a theater? (The version on YouTube is lifeless because of compression. You would do well to acquire the CD.)

The second half of the disc is devoted to Donizetti. In works he wrote in the 1830s and 40s the technical demands for tenor aren't extensive compared with Rossini, and the music is full of caressing melodies. But there's a lot of similarity between many of the arias, so less can be more. Apart from "Se tanto in ira agli uomini" from *Linda Di Chamounix*, where Vargas sings with more heart and personality and responds to the music's pathos, he doesn't bring out many of the details in the scores, fails to sweep music forward and ignores even written accentuations. His treatment of the words is no less perfunctory. His chief assets are a sweet tone, accurate intonation and good legato. He foregoes adding ornamentation although it could relieve much of the blandness. His singing is pleasing rather than exciting or moving.

Consider "Tombe degl'avi miei" from *Lucia*. Vargas provides no contrast among the various moods—no bitterness, no heartbreak—as if there never was a Gigli. He provided drama by inflecting open tones—something Vargas never attempts. Vargas's singing is suffused with sadness. Fine. But that's only a beginning.

I had thought Vargas's greatest virtues were accuracy of rhythm and intonation, agility, velocity, a feeling for musical proportion and the ability, when singing 16th notes, to put ornamentation into the background and melody and important dissonances into the foreground. But for many nineteenth- and early twentieth-century Italian and Neapolitan songs, in particular those imbued with the spirit of verismo by the likes of Ernesto De Curtis, personality, word interpretation and heart are paramount, and to such repertory he seemed less than ideally suited. Thus I am astonished that the most successful interpretations on the CD *Ramón Vargas: Canzoni italiane*,[6] recorded live in 1995, are De Curtis's "L'autunno," sung by Di Stefano on his 70th birthday with terrific impact, and Salvatore Cardillo's "Core 'ngrato," a calling card of many of the great Italian tenors of the twentieth century.

In "L'autunno" he seemingly borrows certain open-toned inflections in the middle voice from Di Stefano, which is not surprising, since they share the same pianist, Roberto Negri.

He begins "Core 'ngrato" blandly, with a little tenderness but no desperation. But in the second verse he is seized by a *fuoco sacro* that makes me tremble. His rendition could withstand comparison with anyone's.

The remainder of the recital isn't at such an exalted level, however. "Fenesta che lucive," by an anonymous composer, is based on Elvino's interjections in "Ah! non credea" from *Sonnambula* and requires an inward, plaintive, haunting *fuoco sacro*. This Vargas does not supply. Surprisingly for such a capable musician his musical interpretation is blighted by random accentuations, and he sometimes is behind the beat. (Nobody on records, not even De Lucia or Roberto Murolo, fully succeeds in capturing the song.)

Before recording a song such as Francesco Paolo Tosti's "Ideale" a singer ought to ask himself, "Do I have enough personality and feeling to risk comparison with the competition?" In no way is Vargas in a league with Björling,[7] let alone McCormack,[8] in this music. Their versions are sublime and redolent of caresses and longing. His merely is nicely sung.

Evemero Nardella's "Chiove" is a profound song, if without a real ending, about a real-life woman, a poet, who is dying. To do it justice the interpreter needs to tear out his—and your—guts. Vargas doesn't muster enough intensity of feeling, or suffering or desperation until the final moments.

In the above songs he covers only above the staff and then not invariably, and he sings with dynamic gradations from pianissimo to fortissimo.

Salvatore Licitra: He places in the mask and covers heavily not only in the passaggio *and above but sometimes in the middle. His one feeling is pathos.*

On a CD recorded in 2000, *Ramón Vargas: Verdi Arias*,[9] he darkens his sound—even when he doesn't cover—in an attempt to find an appropriate tone color by adapting his light voice to the heavy repertory. He thereby makes his voice *scuro* with little *chiaro*. His throat is locked into darkening and covering to the point that he sacrifices the possibility of brightening the sound. He also sacrifices spin or flow of tone and sings with almost no vibrato. The result is a sameness of sound that fails to transmit emotions. A singer with a heavier voice, better suited to the repertory, more readily could avoid having recourse to darkening and covering.

His dynamic curves aren't wide enough—there's not enough of a difference in volume between the soft and loud parts of a phrase.

Because he doesn't impel phrases toward their climaxes with crescendos his music making is inert. (Any number of otherwise accomplished singers have this failing.)

He doesn't fill words with meaning or sing with fire.

He doesn't have the ease of high notes of his Rossini album, and even his B-flats sound labored. He places his voice so far forward in the mask that sometimes the sound is nasal.

The only thing he has left to offer is an accurate rendition of the music. Although his intonation is less precise than on the Rossini or song albums, in this he still manages to succeed.

The Verdi album itself is not redundant but contains alternate arias from *Ernani* ("Odo il voto," made familiar by Pavarotti), *Attila* and *Les vêpres siciliennes* as well as unhackneyed ones from *I due Foscari*, *Alzira*, *I masnadieri* and *Jérusalem*. The *Luisa Miller* recitative and aria is the most deeply felt selection on the disc, but in the recitative, perhaps because he is impassioned, he goes sharp.

In the opening of "Ah! sì, ben mio" Vargas molds the phrase "avrò più l'alma intrepida, il braccio avrò più forte" better than anyone else except Grigolo and Björling. Would that Vargas had pondered the phrase structure of the lesser-known selections to the degree that he presumably did that of "Ah! sì, ben mio!"

Salvatore Licitra

The color of Licitra's voice is suitable for Nemorino. But because his sound is voluminous and carries well he performs Don Alvaro in *Forza* and other heavy roles. Gigli began to sing heavy roles with a sweet voice but developed timbres suitable for them. As yet there is no sign that Licitra will follow suit.

His color is lovely, but he never varies it, and it quickly becomes monotonous. The same could be said about his one feeling, pathos. Pathos is required by much of Italian opera, and a singer unable to express it is crippled interpretively. But for many pieces it is inappropriate, including "Cielo e mar" and "Amor ti vieta" (*Fedora*), both of which Licitra has recorded.[10] He even has recorded "Dio mi potevi" from *Otello*"[11] with a lovely, sorrowful beginning but without a soul riven by deep pain and without rage, anguish and a bronze tone color.

He places in the mask, covers heavily not only from the *passaggio* on up but sometimes in the middle, has a heavy vibrato, an excellent dynamic range, a short top, seemingly inadequate breath support and a pronounced tendency to go flat.

I asked Bergonzi about his pupils, including Licitra. He said Licitra was a good example of his teaching but that they hadn't been in contact for some years, that other good examples included Roberto Aronica, Vincenzo La Scola and above all Michele Pertusi.[12]

Bergonzi told me the essence of his technique consists of expanding the diaphragm during inhalation, contracting it during exhalation, placing the voice in the mask at no one spot and covering. The breathing method he describes may sound obvious to non-singers but in fact is anything but, and there is little agreement among singers about the myriad approaches to breathing.[13] (See the Bergonzi chapter.)

As previously noted, Salvatore Licitra died September 5, 2011, age 43.

Johan Botha

Botha is another who sings dramatic repertory with a sweet but strong tenor that he varies little in quality. His intonation can be droopy. He covers notes in the *passaggio* and above. His voice could use more core. Because of lack of temperament his singing fails to sustain interest.

Johan Botha died September 8, 2016.

Summation

From the 1830s until this century singing with a massive darkened tone repeatedly supplanted singing with nuance. Duprez made a hefty-toned paradigm popular at the expense of subtle singing such

Duprez: He provided momentum for the trend to sing with a massive darkened tone. That trend was furthered by Caruso and Del Monaco. Their influence endures.

as Nourrit's. Caruso did the same thing as Duprez, at the expense of subtle singing such as De Lucia's, Tamagno's and Jean de Reszke's. Del Monaco's paradigm replaced those created by Gigli as well as Pertile and Schipa. Corelli to some extent managed to split the difference between Del Monaco on the one hand and Gigli, Pertile and Schipa on the other.

Today Kaufmann, Cura, Villazón, Fraccaro and Valenti continue in Del Monaco's footsteps—even if Kaufmann does make diminuendos and sing softly. Alagna, Galouzine, Beczala, Giordani, Costello and Fabiano combine Del Monaco's approach with older techniques. Grigolo and Calleja make dynamic modulations that harken back to the tenors of eighty years ago. Flórez, Brownlee, Banks, Filianoti, Cutler and Bros uphold the Kraus tradition of uncovered singing together with mask placement. Bergonzi pupils, not discussed herein, Robert Aronica and Celso Albelo, continue with his technique. Álvarez, Antonenko, Botha and Vargas use methods that pre-date Del Monaco.

In short lowered-larynx techniques are used by fewer than half of today's top tenors—even if New York City and the US as a whole are infested with teachers who advocate such mechanistic methods. In any case we are at a crossroads because the lowered-larynx paradigm, which has held sway for sixty years, no longer dominates.

SOURCE NOTES

CONVERSATIONS WITH CARLO BERGONZI (1924–2014)
1. Sinimberghi is the Nemorino on Bel Canto Society DVD D684, a film of *L'elisir d'amore*.
2. This interview is reprinted with minor changes from *Opera Fanatic* magazine, issue 3, 1989, pp. 53–56.
3. The review appeared in several publications, among them *Opera Fanatic* magazine, issue 1, 1986, p. 22f.

THE ORIGINS OF THE LOWERED-LARYNX TECHNIQUE
1. Sir Charles Santley, *Art of Singing and Vocal Declamation* (London: Macmillan and Co., Limited, 1908), p. 24f. I am indebted to Dr. Nardoianni, for providing me with copies of the relevant pages from Santley's book.

JEAN DE RESZKE'S LARYNX-LOWERING
1. Sir Charles Santley, *Art of Singing and Vocal Declamation* (London: Macmillan and Co., Limited, 1908), pp. XIV and 244.
2. Clara Leiser, *Jean de Reszke and the Great Days of Opera*, with a foreword by Amherst Webber (New York: Minton, Balch & Company 1934), quoting Walter Johnstone-Douglas, "Jean de Reszke's Principles of Singing," p. 312.
3. Ibid, p. 314.
4. Ibid, p. 314.
5. Leiser, p. 295 and Johnstone-Douglas in Leiser, op. cit., p. 316.
6. Leiser, pp. 248, 269f and passim. Johnstone-Douglas in Leiser, op. cit., p. 310ff.
7. Johnstone-Douglas in Leiser, op. cit., p. 310.

DID CARUSO USE A LARYNGEAL METHOD?

1. Jerome Hines, *Great Singers on Great Singing* (New York: Doubleday and Company, 1982), p. 253.

SOME LESSONS WITH MELOCCHI

1. In a letter to Rina of December 17, 1953 Melocchi urges her to "cane Mario for singing half voice with a tight throat and his larynx in his mouth, without articulation of the jaw and with his soft palate low." Quoted after Elisabetta Romagnolo, *Mario Del Monaco: Monumentum aere perennius* (Parma: Azzali Editore s.n.c., 2002), p. 35.

SOME DEL MONACO SUCCESSORS

1. Chiara and Giacomini in Concert, VHS video, Bel Canto Society #124.
2. *Aida*, VHS video, Bel Canto Society #694.
3. While Lindroos was alive he was only a name to me. I'm grateful to Torsten Brander for calling his videos to my attention and providing the CD-R. He is the author of *Beniamino Gigli: il tenore di Recanati* (Helsinki: Associazione Beniamino Gigli di Finlandia, 2001). His Lindroos biography, in Finnish, *Peter Lindroos: Suomen Suurin Tenori* (Helsinki: Painopaikka: Oy Nord Print Ab, 2011) is a gorgeous labor of love with many photos, some in color. Would that I read Finnish!)

A CORELLI STUDENT

1. VHS video, Bel Canto Society #120
2. VHS video, Bel Canto Society #85
3. Birgit Nilsson, *La Nilsson: My Life in Opera* (Hanover and London: University Press of New England, 2007), p. 43.

MATTEUZZI AND MORINO: UNAFFECTED BY DEL MONACO AND CORELLI

1. Out of print
2. Out of print
3. *Francisco Araiza: Opera Arias: Rigoletto, Traviata, Bohème, Tosca, Manon, Werther, Onegin, Arlesiana*; Alberto Zedda, conductor English Chamber Orchestra 1 CD Philips
4. Araiza and I discussed aspiration in the first of his two appearances on "Opera Fanatic," January 5, 1991, available from Bel Canto Society as

Digital Download M44, also as part of a *Four Conversations* bundle, Digital Download MSET2, including the March 3, 1990 program, with Corelli, Jerome Hines and Dodi Protero, the May 12, 1990 program, with Corelli, and "Corelli Presents Pertile," March 30, 1991.

5. Pier Francesco Tosi, trans. Johann Ernest Galliard, *Observations on the Florid Song or Sentiments on the Ancient and Modern Singers* (London, 1743), p. 28.
6. Johann Friedrich Agricola, Julianne C. Baird, trans. and annotator, *Introduction to the Art of Singing* (Cambridge: Cambridge University Press, 2006), p. 157.
7. Olivero makes the remarks about Gigli's aspiration in the outtakes of the film *Opera Fanatic: Stefan and the Divas*, shot in October 1996.
8. Olivero's "Sempre libera" is on *Magda Olivero: The Last Verismo Soprano*, VHS video, Bel Canto Society #115.
9. VHS video, Bel Canto Society #674.
10. See the chapter "The Dying Out of the Castrati and Their Traditions and the Decline of Florid Singing," in vol. 2 of this series.
11. Ibid., p. 4.
12. Henry F. Chorley, *Thirty Years' Musical Recollections* (New York: Vienna House, 1972), p. 21. For more on Rubini see "Last of a Breed: Giovanni Battista Rubini ruled as the paragon of virtuoso tenors, king of the high Fs," in vol. 2 of this series.
13. See Stefan Zucker, *Rossini's Rivals: Music by Then-Famous, Now-Obscure, Italian Composers—Vaccai, Valentino Fioravanti, Mercadante, Pacini, Federico Ricci* (New York: Bel Canto Society, 2004), p. 5. This title is a 32-p. booklet bundled with the eponymous CD. The composer biographies—including "Giovanni Pacini: Rossini Thought Him Italy's Best Composer," from which the quote is excerpted—are available free at BelCantoSociety.org.
14. VHS video, Bel Canto Society #639.
15. VHS video, Bel Canto Society #629.

DIFFERENT SINGING TECHNIQUES

1. Clarissa Lablache Cheer, *The Great Lablache: Nineteenth Century Operatic Superstar—His Life and Times* (New Jersey: Xlibris, 2009).
2. See the chapter "The Dying Out of the Castrati and Their Traditions and the Decline of Florid Singing," in vol. 2 of this series.

3. Ibid.

ROBERTO ALAGNA

1. *Roberto Alagna Live at the Salle Gaveau* (January 2001); *Carmen, Cid, Elisir, Juive, Pagliacci, Turandot*, songs; Orchestre des Concerts Lamoureux; Anton Guadagno, conductor 1 CD Deutsche Grammophon D476 739-7
2. *Roberto Alagna: French Arias: Maitre Pathelin, Cid, Les Abencérages* (Luigi Cherubini), *Mireille* (Charles Gounod), *L'Amant Jaloux ou Létendard de Granade* (André Ernest Modeste Grétry), *Juive, Mignon, Africaine, La Damnation de Faust, Iphigénie en Tauride, Pêcheurs, Le Roi d'Ys* (Edouard Lalo), *Joseph* (Étienne Nicolas Méhul), *Samson, Attaque du Moulin* (Alfred Bruneau); Orchestra of the Royal Opera House Covent Garden; Bertrand de Billy, conductor 1 CD EMI
3. *Solo per te* (1938). Italian, new English subtitles. 86m. Gigli, Maria Cebotari, Michael Bohnen, Giulio Neri; Carmine Gallone, dir. *Mefistofele* (2 selections), *Don Giovanni* (2), *Chénier* (3), *Ballo* (2) plus songs. B&W Bel Canto Society VHS #502 out of print
4. *C'est magnifique! Songs of Luis Mariano*, w. Arielle Dombasle, Jean Reno, Elie Semoun; songs by Francis Lopez, Cole Porter, Zambra Gitana, Colette Mansard; Paris Symphony Orchestra; Yvan Cassar, conductor 1 CD Deutsche Grammophon 4775569

BILL SCHUMAN

1. *Carmen*, Norman, Freni, Shicoff, Estes, Jean-Philippe Courtis, François Le Roux, Ghyslaine Raphanel, Jean Rigby, Nicolas Rivenq; Chœur et Maitrise de Radio France, Orchestre National de France; Seiji Ozawa, conductor 1 CD Polygram
2. Emails and phone conversations with Fabiano, July 3, 4 and 5, 2011.
3. *Marcello Giordani: Tenor Arias: Tell, Fille, La Favorite, Pirata* (w. Giovanni Guagliardo), Bellini song, *La fidanzata córsa* (Pacini), *Carmen, Lombardi, Luisa Miller, Trovatore, Cavalleria* (w. Maria Arghiracopulos); Philarmonic Orchestra and Chorus of the Bellini Theatre, Catania; Steven Mercurio, conductor 1 CD Naxos 8.557269
4. Cornelius L. Reid, *Bel Canto: Principles and Practices* (New York: Colman Ross Company, Inc., 1950.)

FOUR LOWERED-LARYNX TENORS

1. *Jonas Kaufmann: Romantic Arias*: *Bohème, Carmen, Tosca, Don Carlo Der Freischütz, Traviata, Manon, Rigoletto, Faust, Die Meistersinger von Nürnberg, Damnation, Werther*; Prague Philiharmonic Orchestra, Jana Sibera, soprano; Marco Armiliato, conductor 1 CD Decca B0010837-02
2. Ibid.
3. Ibid.
4. Mike Silverman, "German Tenor Stars in 'Die Walkuere' at Met" (*The Huffington Post*, April 14, 2011).
5. *Jonas Kaufmann: Verismo Arias*: *Giulietta e Romeo* (Riccardo Zandonai), *Chénier* (3 selections, 1 w. Eva-Maria Westbroek), *Arlesiana, Bohème* (Ruggero Leoncavallo), *Pagliacci, Cavalleria* (2 selections, 1 w. Rosa Feola, 1 w. Cristina Reale), *Mefistofele* (2 selections), *Fedora, Adriana* (2 selections), *Gioconda*, "Ombra di nube" (Don Licinio Refice); Orchestra e coro dell'Accademia Nazionale di Santa Cecilia; Antonio Pappano, conductor 1 CD Decca B0015463-02
6. Rolando Villazón: *Cielo e Mar*: *Gioconda, Adriana* (2 selections), *Il giuramento* (2; Saverio Mercadante), *Mefistofele* (2), *Maristella* (Guseppe Pietri), *Fosca* (Antônio Carlos Gomes), *Boccanegra, Poliuto* (Gaetano Donizetti), *Il figliuol prodigo* (Amilcare Ponchielli), *Luisa Miller*; Coro Sinfonico di Milano Giuseppe Verdi, Orchestra Sinfonica di Milano Giuseppe Verdi; Ruben Jais, chorus master, Danielle Callegari, conductor Recorded March 2007 1 CD Deutsche Grammophon 00289 477 7224
7. *Rolando Villazón: Italian Opera Arias*: *Arlesiana, Duca d'Alba, Elisir, Lucia, Lombardi, Don Carlo, Macbeth, Rigoletto, Traviata, Bohème, Tosca, L'amico Fritz, Nerone* (Mascagni); Münchner Rundfunkorchester; Marcello Viotti Virgin Classics 7243 5 45626 2 4
8. *Viva Villazón! Bohème, Faust, Elisir, Rigoletto, Manon Lescaut, Werther, Eugene Onegin, La tabernera del puerto* (Pablo Sorozábal), *Tosca, Arlesiana, Carmen*, song (Claudio Monteverdi), *Traviata, Cid* (Jules Massenet); Münch-ner Rundfunkorchester; Marcello Viotti; Michel Plasson; Orchestre Philharmonique de Radio France; Evelino Pidò; Orquesta de la Comunidad de Madrid; Plácido Domingo; Le Concert d'Astrée; Emmanuelle Haïm plus Bonus DVD, *Live in Prague: Concert in Municipal House*—November 11. 2005: *Duca d'Alba, Traviata, Carmen, Cid, Ballo, Cavalleria, Lombardi, Fedora*, song (Gioacchino Rossini), *La tabernera del puerto*; Prague Philharmonia;

Marco Zambelli 1 CD plus 1 DVD Linear PCM Stereo Virgin Classics 504762 2 0

9. *Rolando Villazón: Opera Recital*: *Hoffmann* (2), *Tosca, Cavalleria, Fedora, Martha, Alessandro Stradella, Onegin, Der Rosenkavalier, Ballo, Don Pasquale, Favorita, Carmen, Pêcheurs, Ernani*; Bayerischer Rundfunkchor; Münchner Rundfunkorchester; Michel Plasson 1 CD Virgin Classics 0946 3447 01 2 4

10. *Don Carlo* Villazón, Marina Poplavskaya, Simon Keenlyside, Sonia Ganassi, Ferruccio Furlanetto, Eric Halfvarson, Robert Lloyd, Pumeza Matshikiza, Nikola Matišíc, Anita Watson, Alexander d'Andrea, Jacques Imbrailo, Krzysztof Szumanski, Kostas Smoriginas, Daniel Grice, Darren Jeffery, Vuyani Mlinde; Royal Opera House Chorus, Renato Balsadonna, chorus master; Orchestra of the Royal Opera House, Vasko Vassilev, concert master, Antonio Pappano, conductor; Nicholas Hytner, stage director, Bob Crowley, designs, Mark Henderson, lighting designer, Scarlett Mackmin, movement, Terry King, fight director; recorded live June 14 and 17 and July 3, 2008; Robin Lough, film director 2 DVD9s PCM Stereo, DTS 5.1

MASK-LARYNX-HYBRID TENORS

1. *Rigoletto,* February 16, 2003, Diana Damrau, Oksana Volkova, Maria Zifchak, Catherine Choi, Emalie Savoy, Beczala, Alexander Lewis, Zeljko Lucic, Jeff Mattsey, Robert Pomakov, Earle Patriarco, David Crawford, Stefan Kocán; Metropolitan Opera Orchestra and Chorus, Michele Mariotti, conductor; Michael Mayer, production, Christine Jones, sets, Susan Hilferty, costumes, Kevin Adams, lighting, Steven Hoggett, choreography, Matthew Diamond, TV director, Renée Fleming, interviewer.

MASK-PLACEMENT TENORS WHO DON'T COVER

1. *Vittorio Grigolo: The Italian Tenor*: *Luisa Miller, Elisir, Rigoletto, Favorita, Bohème, Gianni Schicchi, Villi, Corsaro* (w. Danilo Rigosa), *Ballo, Manon Lescaut, Tosca, Trovatore*; Coro e orchestra del Teatro Reggio di Parma, Pier Giorgio Morandi, conductor 1 CD Sony 88697752572

2. *Dom Sébastien Roi de Portugal* (Gaetano Donizetti), Vesselina Kasarova, Filianoti, Alastair Miles, Keenlyside, Carmelo Corrado Caruso, Robert Gleadow, John Upperton, Lee Hickenbottom, Andrew Slater, Martyn Hill, Nigel Cliffe, John Bernays; The Royal Opera Chorus, Balsadonna, chorus director, The Orchestra of the Royal Opera House, Mark Elder,

conductor; concert performances recorded live at the Royal Opera House, September 10 and 13, 2005; ballet music recorded at the Casogan Hall, September 11, 2005 3 CDs Opera Rara ORC 33

3. *Juan Diego Flórez: Bel Canto Spectacular*: *La figlia del reggimento*, *Puritani*, *Favorite*, *Elisir*, *Linda Di Chamounix*, *Il viaggio a Reims*, *Lucrezia Borgia*, *Otello* (Rossini), with Netrebko, Domingo, Patrizia Ciofi, Daniella Barcellona, Kwiecień; Cor de la Generalitat Valenciana (Francesc Perales, chorus master), Fernando Piqueras, baritone, Orquesta de la Comunitat Valenciana (Lorin Maazel, musical director), Daniel Oren, conductor 1 CD, Decca B0012445-02, 2008

4. See the chapter "Last of a Breed," in vol. 2 of this series.

5. See the chapter "Heroes on the Rise," in vol. 2 of this series.

6. *Voce d'Italia: Arias for Rubini: Juan Diego Flórez: Pirata* (Bellini), *Elisabetta, regina d'Inghilterra* (Rossini), *Marin Faliero* (Donizetti), *Il turco in Italia* (Rossini), *Bianca e Fernando* (Bellini), *Donna del lago* (Rossini), *Guglielmo Tell* (Rossini); Orchestra e coro dell'Academia Nazionale di Santa Cecilia; Roberto Abbado, conductor 1 CD, Decca B0010302-02

7. *La Sonnambula* Dessay, Flórez, Michele Pertusi, Jennifer Black, Jane Bunnell, Jeremy Galyon, Bernard Fitch; The Metropolitan Opera Chorus, Orchestra and Ballet, Donald Palumbo, chorus master, Evelino Pidò, conductor; Mary Zimmerman, production, Daniel Ostling, sets, Mara Blumenfeld, costumes, T.J. Gerckens, lighting, Daniel Pelzig, choreographer, Barbara Willis Sweete, director, Deborah Voigt, host LPCM and DTS 5.1 audio, 2 DVDs Decca 074 3357

8. *I puritani* Nino Machaidze, Nadia Pirazzini, Flórez, Gianluca Floris, Gabriele Viviani, Ildebrando D'Arcangelo, Ugo Guagliardo; Orchestra e Coro del Teatro Comunale di Bologna, Mariotti, conductor LPCM stereo, DTS 5.1 Surround 2 DVDs Decca B0014859-09

9. See the chapter "The Dying Out of the Castrati and Their Traditions and the Decline of Florid Singing," in vol. 2 of this series.

10. Ibid.

11. *Juan Diego Flórez: Rossini Arias*: *Semiramide*, *Otello*, *Barbiere*, *La gazza ladra*, *L'Italiana in Algeri*, *Zelmira*, *Donna*, *La cenerentola*; Orchestra sinfonica e coro di Milano Giuseppe Verdi; Riccardo Chailly 1 CD Decca 289 470 024-2

12. *Lawrence Brownlee: Schubert, Verdi, Donizetti, Bellini, Verdi—Italian Songs for Tenor and Piano*—Martin Katz, piano Schubert: Vier Canzonen

D688—Non t'accostar all'urna, Bianca che bianca luna, Da quel sembiante appresi, Mio ben ricordati; Verdi: Ad una stella, In solitaria stanza, Il tramonto, Lo spazzacamino, Brindisi, version 1; Donizetti: L'amor funesto, Me voglio fa 'na casa [att. Donizetti]; Bellini: Bella nice, che d'amore, Per pietà, bell'idol mio, Ma rendi pur contento, Torna, vezzosa Fillide, La ricordanza; Rossini: La danza, La lontananza, L'esule, Arietta all'antica dedotta dal "O salutaris Hostia," Mi lagnerò tacendo 1 CD EMI 5 86503 2

13. *L'Italiana in Algeri* Marianna Pizzolato, Ruth Gonzalez, Elsa Giannoulidou, Brownlee, Bruno De Simone, Giulio Mastrototaro, Lorenzo Regazzo; Gianni Fabbrini, harpsichord continuo; Transylvania State Philharmonic Choir, Cluj, Cornel Groza, chorus master, Virtuosi Brunensis, Alberto Zedda, conductor; critical edition by Fondazione Pesaro, edited by Azio Corghi; recorded live at the Kursaal, Bad Wildbad, Germany, July 2, 3 and 5, 2008 2 CDs Naxos 8.660284-85

14. *La cenerentola* Elīna Garanča, Rachelle Durkin, Patricia Risley, Brownlee, Simone Alberghini, John Relyea, Alessandro Corbelli; Robert Myers, recitative accompanist; The Metropolitan Opera Chorus and Orchestra, Donald Palumbo, chorus master, Maurizio Benini, conductor; Cesare Lievi, production, Maurizio Balo, sets and costumes, Gigi Saccomandi, lighting, Daniela Schiavone, choreography, Sharon Thomas, stage direction, Gary Halvorson, director; Thomas Hampson, host May 9, 2009 PCM Stereo, DTS 5.1 2 DVDs Deutsche Grammophon 073 4577

15. *Armida* Fleming, Brownlee, Barry Banks, John Osborn, Kobie van Rensburg, Yeghishe Manucharyan, Keith Miller, Peter Volpe; Teele Ude, Isaac Scranton, Aaron Loux; David Chan, violin solo, Rafael Figueroa, cello solo; The Metropolitan Opera Chorus, Orchestra and Ballet, Palumbo, chorus master, Riccardo Frizza, conductor; Mary Zimmerman, production, Richard Hudson, sets and costumes, Brian MacDevitt, lighting, Graciela Daniels, choreography, Gary Halvorson, director; Deborah Voigt, host May 1, 2010 PCM Stereo, DTS 5.1 Surround 2 DVDs Decca B0015226-09

16. *Eric Cutler*: Robert Schumann; *Liederkreis*, Op. 39; Franz Liszt; Tre sonetti di Petrarca; Reynaldo Hahn; L'Heure exquise, Paysage, Le Rossignol des lilas, À Cloris, Samuel Barber; Despite and Still; Eric Cutler, tenor, Bradley Moore, piano 1 CD EMI 7243 5 85614 2 5

17. Ernest Newman, *The Man Liszt: A Study of the Tragi-Comedy of a Soul Divided Against Itself* (New York: The Taplinger Publishing Co., 1970), p. 110.

18. *I puritani* Netrebko, Maria Zifchak, Cutler, Eduardo Valdes, Franco Vassallo, John Relyea, Valerian Ruminski; Metropolitan Opera Orchestra, Chorus and Ballet, Raymond Hughes, chorus master, Patrick Summers, conductor; Sandro Sequi, production, Ming Cho Li, sets, Peter J. Hall, costumes, Thomas, stage director, Halvorson, director, Fleming, interviewer PCM Stereo, DTS 5.1 2 DVDs Deutsche Grammophon 0734421

19. *La sonnambula* Gruberova, Dawn Kotoski, Gloria Banditelli, Bros, Andreas Mogl, Roberto Scandiuzzi, Tim Hennis; Chor des Bayerischen Rundfunks, Udo Mehrpohl, Einstudierung, Münchner Rundfunkorchester; Viotti, Dirigent 2 CDs Nightingale Classics NC 000041-2

20. *I puritani* Gruberova, Raquel Pierotti, Bros, Carlos Álvarez, Simón Orfila, Konstantin Gorny, Vicenç Esteve Madrid; Orquestra Simfònica i Cor del Gran Teatre del Liceu, William Spaulding, chorus master, Friedrich Haider, conductor DD 5.1, DTS 5.1 LPCM stereo; 1 DVD 5, 1 DVD 9 TDK DVUS-OPIP

21. *Joseph Calleja: The Golden Voice*: *Lombardi, Favorita, Elisir, Sonnambula* (w. Nebtrebko), *Roméo et Juliette, Manon* (w. Tatiana Lisnic), *La Belle Hélène* (Jacques Offenbach), *Werther, Pêcheurs, Si j'etais roi* (Adolphe Adam), *Il duca d'Alba, Don Sebastiano, Puritani, Maristella*; Academy of St. Martin in the Fields; Carlo Rizzi 1 CD Decca 475 6931

22. Ibid.

23. *Joseph Calleja: Tenor Arias*: *Traviata* (w Lydia Easley), *Macbeth, Rigoletto* (3 selections), *Elisir, Lucia* (w Giovanni Battista Parodi), *Adriana, Arlesiana, Butterfly;* Coro di Milano Giuseppe Verdi, Romano Gandolfi, chorus Master, Orchestra Sinfonica di Milano Giuseppe Verdi, Riccardo Chailly, conductor 1 CD Decca 475 250-2

24. Joseph Calleja: *The Maltese Tenor*: *Bohème* (2 selections; one w. Aleksandra Kurzak), *Boccanegra, Hoffmann, Tosca* (2 selections), *Mefistofele* (2 selections), *Faust, Manon Lescaut* (2 selections), *Manon, Luisa Miller, Ballo, Pêcheurs* (2 selections; 1 w. Kurzak); Chœur d'hommes du Grand Théâtre de Genève, Ching-Lien Wu, chorus master; L'Orchestre de la Suisse Romande; Marco Armiliato, conductor 1 CD Decca B0015747-0

MASK-PLACEMENT TENORS WHO DO COVER

1. *Marcelo Álvarez: The Verdi Tenor*: *Aïda, Ballo (2 selections), Luisa Miller, Forza, Trovatore* (w. Annalisa Raspagliosi and Arturo Chacón-Cruz),

Lombardi, Ernani, Don Carlo, Macbeth, Otello; Coro e orchestra Sinfonica di Milano Giuseppe Verdi; Daniel Oren, conductor 1 CD Decca 478 1442

2. *Marcelo Álvarez: Bel Canto: Rigoletto* (3 selections), *Elisir, Duca d'Alba, Puritani* (w. Ying Huang), *Lucia, Linda Di Chamounix, Traviata, Favorita;* Orchestra of Welsh National Opera, Chorus of Welsh National Opera, Gareth Jones, chorus master; Carlo Rizzi, conductor 1 CD Sony Classical SK 60721

3. *Marcelo Álvarez: Tenorissimo: Elisir, Fille, Bohème, Duca d'Alba, La Favorite, Huguenots, Tosca, Gioconda, Marta, Arlesiana, Butterfly, Chénier, Manon Lescaut, Manon* (w. Fleming), a tango, song (w. Salvatore Licitra); Staatskapelle Dresden, Orchestra of the Welsh National Opera, Orchestre Philharmonique de Nice, Orchestra de L'Opera National de Paris, Orchestra Roma Sinfonietta, The City of Prague Orchestra; Viotti, Carlo Rizzi, Mark Elder, Jesus López Cobos, Eugene Kohn, Daniel May, conductors 1 CD Sony Classical 88697597532

4. The selections are on a Vargas recital on YouTube.

5. *Ramón Vargas, Tenor: Rossini, Donizetti: Barbiere* (2), *Italiana, Occasione, Donna del lago, Linda Di Chamounix, Duca d'Alba, Elisir, Anna Bolena, Don Pasquale, Lucia;* English Chamber Orchestra; Viotti, conductor 1 CD Claves

6. *Ramón Vargas, Tenor: Canzoni italiane:* songs by Scarlatti, anonymous, Bellini, Leoncavallo, Tosti (2), Vittorio De Crescenzo, Stanislao Gastaldon, Rodolfo Falvo, Nardella, Ernesto De Curtis, Cardillo plus Mexican encores by Manuel M. Ponce, Tata Nacho, María Grever; Roberto Negri, piano, recorded live at the XXIII Festival Internacional Cervantino, Teatro Juárez, Guanajuato, Mexico 1 CD Laserlight Digital 14 307

7. The Björling recording of Tosti's Ideale I have in mind is from September 24, 1955, *Bjoerling Sings at Carnegie Hall*: Jussi Björling, tenor, Frederick Schauwecker, piano, RCA Victor LM-2003.

8. McCormack recorded Ideale for Odeon, September 7, 1909, with orchestra and an unidentified conductor. The speed of the recording wasn't specified but presumably is 81.00 rpm since the other sixteen recordings he made that day are at that speed. (Seventeen recordings released from one session is extraordinary.) The Matrix number is Lx3157, and the recording was issued on numbers 0236 and 57642. Discographic information was supplied by Joseph Pearce, President of The Vocal Record Collector's Society.

9. *Ramón Vargas: Verdi Arias*: *Ernani, Foscari, Alzira* (w James Anderson), *Attila, Macbeth, Masnadieri* (w Anderson), *Jérusalem, Luisa Miller, Rigoletto, Trovatore* (w Annegher Stumphius and Anderson), *Vêpres, Falstaff;* Männerchor des Bayerische Rundfunks, Münchner Rundfunkorchester; Edoardo Müller, director 1 CD BMG 74321 79603-2
10. Salvatore Licitra: Forbidden Love: *Ernani, Cavalleria* (2 selections), *Arlesiana, Chénier* (2 selections), *Luisa Miller, Don Carlos, Fedora, Gioconda, Mefistofele. Pagliacci, Otello,* song (Rossini); Gandolfi, chorus master; Roberto Rizzi Brignoli, conductor; Warren Jones, piano 1 CD Sony Classical 82876-78852-2
11. Ibid.
12. Bergonzi told me these things in a May 22, 2011 telephone interview.
13. Bergonzi discussed his technique with me in an April 27, 2002 interview at the Mayflower Hotel in New York City.

Franco Corelli
& A Revolution in Singing
Fifty-four Tenors Spanning 200 Years
Volume 1

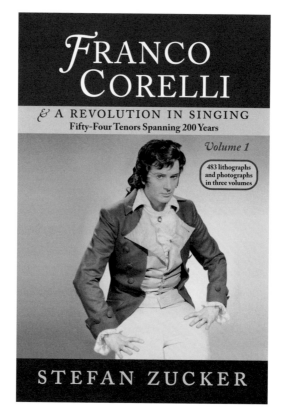

Kirkus Reviews designated *Franco Corelli and a Revolution in Singing: Fifty-Four Tenors Spanning 200 Years*, vol. 1 by Stefan Zucker as among the **100 Best Books of 2015.**

"A thought-provoking read."
—*Library Journal*
"Informative and fascinating."
—*The Record Collector*
"A detailed, passionate analysis."
—*Kirkus Reviews*

***Samples available at
www.belcantosociety.org/store/books/
franco-corelli-and-a-revolution-in-singing:***

The first 14 pages from a chapter

◆

Table of Contents

◆

List of Lithographs and Photographs

◆

From the Jean de Reszke chapter, here are history's three great tenor heartthrobs—Mario, de Reszke and Corelli

◆

Stefan's biography

◆

Video: Stefan discusses Slezak and Schmidt

◆

Video: Stefan interviews Simionato, Pobbe, Gencer and Gavazzi

Franco Corelli
& A Revolution in Singing
Fifty-four Tenors Spanning 200 Years
Volume 2

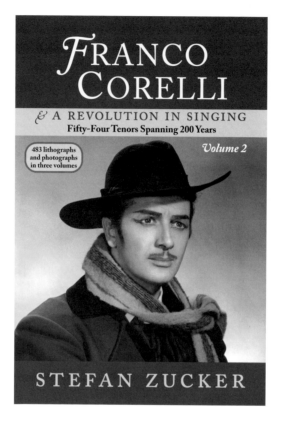

Stefan Zucker on six revolutions that have reshaped singing.

In this volume, in discussions with Stefan, Franco Corelli looks back on his life and career. Here are a few examples:

FC on the "Rome Walkout": Callas was a little sick, and that didn't permit her to sing at her best. Some in the audience heckled her. When she came offstage after Act I she was completely calm, but then she began to stew and announced she was canceling. The management went to her, to push her to continue the performance. She became a lioness and began to scream. She threw some vases and a chair. Little by little she lost her voice. When she left the theater, however, she looked elegant, as if nothing had happened.

SZ: Are you suggesting that she could have continued the performance had she not started to scream?

FC: Absolutely. She was in possession of a fabulous voice and an excellent technique. As late as 1958 she always was able to sing. She could have continued.

FC: There's always rivalry onstage. To go up against Nilsson I had to learn how to put forth 110 percent of the voice that I had. At La Scala in 1964 they screamed "hams" at us because we held high notes so long, trying to outdo each other in *Turandot*. Nilsson was born dominant—her voice was, too.

FC: In the *Faust* recording Ghiaurov screamed and was good only in the laugh. Sutherland hooted. I was the only one who truly sang with a free voice and an expressive top. I threw away some recitatives, though, because I didn't know them well enough.

SZ: Are you able to judge to what extent your pleasing appearance affected your career?

FC: Besides voice, musicality and *physique du rôle* are important. Callas also said that you need a nice *physique du rôle*. If I hadn't had my voice my appearance wouldn't have helped. But if I were a hunchback I would not have had the career that I did.

Some chapters focus on Corelli's personal life and how it intertwined with his singing, including interviews with his wife and two long-term mistresses.

Mrs. Corelli: I was extremely jealous. I didn't have ten fingernails, I had twenty, to scratch out the eyes of women who were after Franco. I gave up my singing career to keep an eye on him. Still, if a man is determined to cheat there's nothing you can do about it.

FC: People assume that in old age I am hearing Verdi and Puccini in my mind's ear. No! The music I am hearing and that keeps me going is the sound of Teresa Zylis-Gara having orgasms. She was my great love, and I think about her all the time.... She was the reason I made so many pretexts to send Loretta [Mrs. Corelli] back to Italy.

FC: Barbieri had paid people not only to applaud her but also to boo me. The man I assaulted had been paid by her!

Loretta's past was the real reason Corelli and Boris Christoff dueled with swords on the stage of the Rome Opera. (They wounded one another.)

Corelli's letters to Lauri-Volpi: some are affecting.

Also included: reviews of three unsatisfactory Corelli biographies and an OK one as well as John Potter's *Tenors*.

Corelli had a no-holds-barred rivalry with Del Monaco, with each trying to block the other's career.

Roberto Bauer (Rudolf Bing's Italian factotum): Franco told La Scala as well that he wouldn't sing anymore in seasons that also include Del Monaco…. He says he knows himself very well and realizes he is capable of socking Del Monaco in the jaw if he ran into him unexpectedly.

A collector's item, the three volumes contain 483 lithographs and photographs, many published for the first time, of tenors from the 1820s to today. For this volume the Metropolitan Opera Archives contributed twenty-one pages of correspondence by Rudolf Bing and others about the Corelli–Del Monaco rivalry, and John Pennino of the Archives provided a chapter comparing the fees the Met paid Corelli, Del Monaco and Callas.

Opera Fanatic

Expressive Singing
◆
How one of Callas's and Meneghini's Closest Friends
Became One of Their Bitterest Enemies
◆
The Corelli-Hines Interviews
◆
Corelli on Guelfi
◆
Stignani
◆
Interviews of Kraus, Ferruccio Tagliavini,
Barbieri and Simionato, Cerquetti, Frazzoni,
Gencer, Olivero and Pobbe

Hitler's Tenor
BENIAMINO GIGLI
His Public Life; His Secret Life; His Singing

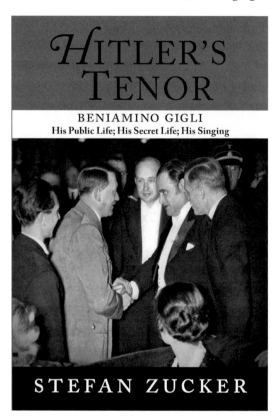

The four biggest stars among twentieth-century Italian tenors were Caruso, Gigli, Corelli and Pavarotti. Gigli had the sweetest voice, but he was a Nazi collaborator. Not only did he write a book, *Confidenze*, praising Fascism, not only did he allege a Jewish conspiracy, not only did he help Mussolini supplant the native culture in Slovenia by singing performances there, not only did he write, "Adolf Hitler and the ministers Goebbels and Goering have honored me with their friendship," but he also collaborated with the Germans after they occupied Rome. He even collaborated after they massacred 335 civilians on March 24, 1944. (The event was Italy's 9/11.) He sang for them, became a go-between, gave them a photo op, helped them create an appearance of normality and an illusion of civilization. After the Allies took Rome in June 1944 Gigli's countrymen singled him out as a collaborator, and the Allies prohibited him from performing. At the end of 1944 a Roman commission held a hearing about his collaboration—and gave him a slap on the wrist. In 1945 he wrote a second book, *La verità sul mio «caso,»* this time to exculpate himself. Although he was able to resume his career his reputation in Italy was soiled. The U.S.S.R. would not let him into any country under its control. The U.S. wouldn't allow him in either until 1955, when he gave farewell concerts.

Why was he a "Nazifascista" and why did he collaborate? He said he was naïve politically. But this contradicts his position in *Confidenze*—and in 1953 he ran for the Italian Senate, so one wonders about his supposed naïvete. He also claimed he was for Italy no matter who was in charge—but that position fails to shed light on his behavior during the Italian civil war of 1943–44.

Gigli's was a religious family, and he was educated by priests. After he became a star he visited the pope on a number of occasions. My thesis is that to understand his actions and inactions one has to consider the role of the Church in Italy and Germany. As will be seen, Gigli followed the Church's lead. (In his personal life, however, he followed that of the Mussolini regime, which exalted male promiscuity, with the Duce himself setting the example. Then he fell under the influence of Padre Pio and was torn asunder by a conflict between the dictates of the heart and those of the Church.)

His personal life was stormy. He had nine children, two of them legitimate, and for twenty-three years maintained two families concurrently. His daughter soprano Rina Gigli discusses his relationships candidly—as well as singing with him for Hitler.

What sets Gigli apart from nearly all other twentieth-century tenors? His singing is full of contrast. Such nineteenth-century holdovers as Fernando De Lucia varied dynamics and tone color as well as rhythm and, sometimes, notes. Most singers since at best have had or have created one sonority of individual character, at one dynamic level. Caruso and those who followed him mostly sang full voice. Pavarotti and company did little varying of dynamics and seldom shaded their tones, using the same color to express both happiness and sadness. Gigli had many sonorities and two basic dynamic levels, loud and soft.

Gigli perfected chiaroscuro like no other singer since the dawn of recording. He achieved chiaroscuro by contrasting loud with soft singing—chiaroscuro of dynamics. But he also contrasted open, closed and covered tones—chiaroscuro of timbre. This last was his great innovation.

The book discusses Gigli's twenty-eight films and hundreds of recordings as well as his rift with The Metropolitan Opera and is full of photos.

INDEX

A

Agricola, Johann Friedrich 206
Alagna, David 237
Alagna, Malena 247
Alagna, Roberto 21, 114, 234–247, 329
Albanese, Licia 88, 130
Altinoglu, Alain 246
Alva, Luigi 244
Álvarez, Marcel 317–321, 330
Andrés, Francisco 150
Anselmi, Filippo 89, 220, 295
Antonenko, Aleksandrs 321, 330
Aragall, Giacomo 51, 53, 134, 267
Araiza, Francisco 152, 201–207, 247, 287
Arlesiana 335
Aronica, Roberto 122, 328
Asciak, Paul 312

B

Banks, Barry 304, 308, 330
Barbieri, Fedora 88
Baruffi, Sandra 124
Battle, Kathleen 83
Baum, Kurt 85, 96, 112–113
Bechi, Gino 86
Beczala, Piotr 293–294, 329
Behrens, Hildegard 88, 259
Bellezza, Vincenzo 215
Bellini, Vincenzo 23, 135, 137, 208–209, 254, 301–304, 311
Bello, Vincenzo 181
Bengochea, Christopher 233
Bergonzi, Carlo 20–21, 116–141, 146, 242, 254, 256, 267, 328
Berini, Bianca 219
Bianchi, Francesco 128

Billiard, Alain 182, 223, 228, 230–231, 233
Bing, Sir Rudolf 41
Bini, Carlo 13–14, 85, 97–98, 98
Birgili, Burak 250
Björling, Jussi 40–41, 65, 67, 86, 238, 240, 241, 242, 264, 270, 281, 296, 313, 322, 325, 327
Björling, Lars 241
Blake, Rockwell 201, 206
Bleiden, Paul 249
Bocelli, Andrea 193
Boeri, Dr. Umberto 123
Bolton, Michael 250
Bonisolli, Franco 244, 320
Bononcini, Giovanni Battista 322
Bonynge, Richard 310
Borgioli, Dino 312
Botha, Johan 328, 330
Brendel, Wolfgang 100
Brodnitz, Dr. Friedrich 272
Bros, José 311–312, 330
Brownlee, Lawrence 304–308, 330
Brown, William Earl 258, 261
Brubaker, Robert 250
Bruscantini, Sesto 159
Budai, Livia 104, 108

C

Caballé, Montserrat 157–158
Callas, Maria 27, 30–31, 39, 80–82, 86, 88, 91, 93, 130, 131, 156, 282, 289
Calleja, Joseph 312–316, 319, 330
Campogalliani, Ettore 123–124
Campora, Giuseppe 79, 92
Cappuccilli, Piero 134

Cardillo, Salvatore 325
Carreras, José 72, 267, 282
Carroli, Silvano 181
Carta, Mario 256
Caruso, Enrico 48, 55–56, 73, 77, 127, 129, 172–173, 198, 202–203, 221, 244, 251, 282, 312, 319, 329, 348, 349
Casciari, Giorgio 123
Cecchele, Gianfranco 181, 189, 290
Cecchele, Lorenzo 290
Cehanovsky, George 138
Celletti, Rodolfo 321
Cestone, Eclesia 130
Cestone, Michele J. 123
Chapin, Schuyler G. 107, 110–111
Cheer, Clarissa Lablache 219
Chéreau, Patrice 78
Chorley, Henry F. 208
Ciaffei, Francesco 170
Ciannella, Giuliano 98, 122, 129
Cole, Vinson 295
Conley, Eugene 249
Connolly, Bob 123
Consiglio, Giovanni 220
Corelli, Franco 20, 29–30, 40–42, 57–58, 70–72, 90–92, 152, 167, 170, 173, 175, 176, 178, 179, 193–199, 207, 213–214, 216–217, 219, 220, 221, 223, 226, 238, 241, 242, 243, 247, 254, 261, 262, 265, 267–268, 270, 282, 284–286, 290, 299, 300, 310, 313–316, 319, 321, 329, 348
Corelli, Loretta 41, 176, 193
Corsaro, Frank 109
Cosma, Vladimir 237
Cossotto, Fiorenza 24

Costello, Stephen 250, 253–257, 264, 264–265, 266, 269, 272, 278–279, 329
Cotogni, Antonio 170
Cotrubas, Ileana 249
Cuénod, Hugues 308
Culshaw, John 74
Cura, José 285–286, 288
Curtis-Verna, Mary 80
Cutler, Eric 308–311, 312, 330

D

d'Agoult, Countess Marie 309
d'Alba, Live in Prague: Concert in Municipal House—November 11. 2005: Duca 335
Dalis, Irene 82, 87–88
Dall'Argine, Simona 178
D'Angelo, Gianna 95
D'Arcangelo, Ildebrando 304
D'Arkor, André 80, 243
David, Giacomo 207, 217, 221
David, Giovanni 207, 221, 300, 301, 303
Davis, Peter G. 88
De Curtis, Ernesto 324, 325
Del Monaco, Giancarlo 224
Del Monaco, Marcello 174, 182, 183, 184, 187, 188, 189, 228, 249, 261, 262
Del Monaco, Mario 20, 43–46, 48, 50–51, 63, 64, 72, 75, 118, 119, 149, 157, 166, 170, 174, 175, 176, 177, 181–189, 195, 199, 202, 213–215, 217, 221, 238, 240, 241, 242, 244, 253, 260, 261, 262, 285, 286, 287, 290, 298, 300, 313, 314, 315–316, 319, 321, 329–331

Del Monaco, Rina 176, 223–225, 228, 231
De Luca, Giuseppe 85, 284
De Lucia, Fernando 77, 118, 209, 220, 221, 240, 241, 325, 329, 349
De Negri, Giovanni Battista 122
De Osma, Marcella 85
de Reszke, Édouard 170
de Reszke, Jean 169, 170, 171, 329
De Sabata 125
Dessay, Natalie 302
Deutekom, Cristina 82–83
Devries, David 244
Dickson, Stephen 250
Diener, Melanie 250
Di Stefano, Giuseppe 20, 264, 298, 325
Domingo, Plácido 29, 35, 72, 85, 114, 116, 129, 195, 319, 320, 335
Dominguez, Oralia 88
Donizetti, Gaetano 135, 209, 254, 286, 300–301, 304, 306, 322, 324
Donzelli, Domenico 167, 211, 221
Duprez, Gilbert 167, 170, 211, 221, 244, 328–329
Durkin, Rachelle 250
Dvorsky, Peter 103, 106

E
Elman 41
Escalaïs, Léon 244
Esperian, Kallen 250
Etienne, Claude François 77, 80, 83–85, 86–89, 92, 96
Everardi, Camillo 167
Ewing, Maria 88

F
Fabiano, Michael 250, 253, 257, 265–270, 271–272, 277–279, 329
Fabiola-Herrera, Nancy 250
Farinelli 101
Fedora 335
Fernandi, Eugenio 87–88
Ferrandina, Ralph 83
Ferraro, Pier Miranda 44–45
Filianoti, Giuseppe 299, 315, 319, 330
Filipova, Elena 114, 176, 180–181, 222–223, 227, 229, 232–233, 282
Filippeschi, Mario 24, 63
Fisichella, Salvatore 256
Fleming, Renée 308
Fleta, Miguel 53
Flórez, Juan Diego 298–304, 306, 307, 310, 311, 312, 319, 330
Ford, Bruce 201
Fraccaro, Walter 290–291, 329
Francardi, Licinio 182
Franceschi, Luisa Verna 249, 261
Franchetti, Alberto 128
Franz, Paul 243
Freni, Mirella 130, 189
Funkhouser, Neil 257

G
Galouzine, Vladimir 292–293, 329
Galvany, Maria 82–83, 88
Ganassi, Sonia 182
García, Manuel II 167, 259
Gasdia, Cecilia 233
Gatti, Daniele 114
Gavanelli, Paolo 230

Gavazzeni, Gianandrea 24, 125, 207, 215
Gedda, Nicolai 39, 80, 238, 242–243, 270
Gencer, Leyla 232, 282, 289, 319
Gentile, Maria 256
Gheorghiu, Angela 246
Ghiaurov, Nicolai 24
Giacomini, Giuseppe 45, 72, 181–183
Gigli, Beniamino 19, 20, 27, 35, 47, 54–55, 61, 70, 118, 119, 127, 129–130, 141, 143, 154, 155, 183, 207, 209, 220–221, 239–253, 270, 273, 282, 288, 299, 314, 314–315, 320, 324, 327–329, 348, 349
Gigli, Rina 349
Giordani, Marcello 249–256, 262–271, 329
Gobbi, Tito 53, 124, 159
Goebbels, Joseph 348
Goering, Hermann 348
Goldberg, Cantor Don 86, 92, 111
Green, Cathy 233
Grigolo, Vittorio 221, 295–299, 315, 319, 322, 327, 330
Grillo, Joanne 102, 106–107
Gruberova, Edita 83, 100, 311
Guasco, Carlo 210
Guelfi, Giangiacomo 215
Gulín, Ángeles 134
Gutiérrez, Eglise 250

H
Hadley, Jerry 250, 257–259
Hall, Sir Peter 109
Handelman, Charlie 111
Harmer, Wendy Bryn 250
Harris, Kenn 96
Harshaw, Margaret 249
Heidt, Winifred 249
Hines, Jerome 28, 40, 152, 173, 219, 254
Hitler, Adolf 348, 349
Hoos, Jeffrey 274
Horne, Marilyn 80
Hymel, Bryan 250, 272, 278

I
Ibos, Guillaume 241

J
Jenkins, Florence Foster 249
Jeritza, Maria 85
Johnstone-Douglas, Walter 169, 170
Jonas, Peter 228
Jones, Gwyneth 84

K
Kabaivanska, Raina 232
Kamioner, Helen 53
Karajan, Herbert von 73, 106–107, 120, 224
Kaufmann, Jonas 243, 250, 263, 280–285, 329
Kerns, Robert 181, 189
Kirsten, Dorothy 130
Kleiber, Carlos 100
Konetzni, Anni 86
Kozlovsky, Ivan 244
Kraus, Alfredo 20, 21, 51, 142–165, 219, 242, 244, 288, 299, 303, 330
Kuhlmann, Kathleen 79
Kupfer, Harry 228
Kurzak, Alexandra 247
Kwiecień, Mariusz 250

L

Lablache, Luigi 218–219
Lamberti, Giorgio Casellato 181
Lamperti, Giovanni Battista 249, 258–261
Lantieri, Rita 181
Lanza, Mario 249, 270
LaRouche, Lyndon 137
La Scola, Vincenzo 123, 134, 328
Lauri-Volpi, Giacomo 24, 45, 85, 155, 170, 194, 199, 213, 215, 219, 240, 262
Lawrence Tibbett 61
Lehmann, Lilli 170
Leiser, Clara 169
Lemeni, Nicola Rossi 146
Levine, James 80–82
Levy, Arthur 274
Licitra, Salvatore 123, 326–328
Ligi, Josella 181
Lima, Luis 313
Limarilli, Gastone 45, 174–176, 181, 183
Lindroos, Peter 181–185
Lipton, Martha 249
Liszt, Franz 309, 310
Llopart, Mercedes 150
Lombard, Alain 246
Lombardo, Bob 83
LoMonaco, Jerome 71, 179, 259
LoMonaco, Thomas 71, 179, 257–259
London, George 249
Lorber, Alex 219
Lugo, Giuseppe 91, 92

M

Macatsoris, Christofer 257
Machaidze, Nino 304
Madrid, Orquesta de la Comunidad de 335
Malaspina, Rita Orlandi 134
Mapleson, Col. Henry 169
Marc, Alessandra 249
Margolis, Samuel 219
Mariani, Gino 77, 84
Mariano, Luis 240, 245
Mario 218
Mariotti, Michele 304
Markoff, Gali 150
Martinelli, Giovanni 43, 319
Martinucci, Nicola 180–183, 227
Mascherini, Enzo 93
Masini, Angelo 77
Masini, Galliano 77, 118–119, 125
Matteuzzi, William 200, 207–208, 211
Mauro, Ermanno 104, 107
McCormack, John 47, 193, 198, 244, 282, 325
McCracken, James 66, 68–70, 80, 103, 108, 281, 282
Meade, Angela 250
Melocchi, Arturo 45, 143, 167, 169, 173, 174–177, 181, 213, 219, 249, 257, 259, 261, 262
Mercadante, Saverio 209, 286
Meredith, Morley 85, 98, 99
Merighi, Giorgio 181
Merli, Francesco 12–13, 45, 52–53, 118–119, 167, 241
Merlini, Arturo 177
Merola, Mario 45
Merrill, Robert 40
Merritt, Chris 57–60, 65, 112, 201
Meyerbeer, Giacomo 24
Miguel Fleta 12, 33, 52
Milano, Stefano 81

Milanov, Zinka 31, 80, 88, 130, 249
Miller, Mayne 83
Millo, Aprile 249
Milnes, Sherrill 85, 96, 97, 112
Miss Manners 100
Mitchell, Leona 79
Molese, Michael 249
Monti, Nicola 201
Moore, Latonia 250
Mori, Angelo 181
Moriani, Napoleone 306
Morino, Giuseppe 207–211, 304
Moscoso, Emilio 189
Moser, Edda 83
Mozart, Wolfgang Amadeus 58, 83, 85, 223, 224, 254
Murgu, Cornelius 181, 189
Murolo, Roberto 325
Mussolini, Benito 249, 348, 349
Muti, Riccardo 58, 59, 207

N

Napoli, Jacopo 128
Nardella, Evemero 325
Nardoianni, Gian Paolo 170
Nave, Maria Luisa 181
Neblett, Carol 106, 108
Negri, Adelaide 76, 81–83, 88, 156, 202
Negri, Roberto 325
Neill, Stuart 250
Netrebko, Anna 311, 313
Nicolai Gedda 39
Nilsson, Birgit 27, 39, 88, 177, 197
Nitzsche, Judy 219
Nordica, Lillian 170, 249
Norman, Jessye 80, 103
Nourrit, Adolphe 221, 329
Nozzari, Andrea 221, 307, 324

O

Olivero, Magda 47, 79, 196, 207, 212–215, 219–220, 232, 314
Oropesa, Lisette 250
Osaben, Fabio 36
Osborne, Conrad L. 154, 179
Osborn, John 308
Ottolini, Luigi 177
Oxilia, Giuseppe 122

P

Pacchierotti, Gaspare 101
Pacini, Giovanni 209
Padre Pio 349
Paglialunga, Augusto 273
Palombi, Antonello 245
Paoli, Antonio 244
Patanè, Rita 249
Pavarotti, Luciano 29, 35, 53–55, 72, 80–81, 116, 129, 155, 203, 242, 244, 253, 260, 264, 269–270, 296, 299, 301, 310, 313, 319, 327, 348, 349
Peerce, Jan 219, 281
Penno, Gino 91
Pérez, Ailyn 250
Pertile, Aureliano 48, 49, 118, 127, 129, 220, 268, 273, 285, 295, 312, 319, 329–330
Pertusi, Michele 122, 328
Petris, Jolanda di Maria 182
Petrov, Ivan Ivanovich 85
Philip, King of Spain 101
Pidò, Evelino 335
Pina, Enrique 192–199, 217
Pines, Roger 281, 300
Pizzetti, Ildebrando 128
Plançon, Pol 170
Plasson, Michel 335

Pobbe, Marcella 219, 343
Poggi, Gianni 96, 103
Ponnelle, Jean-Pierre 105, 108
Ponselle, Rosa 173, 251
Price, Leontyne 28, 40, 88, 93, 111, 135
Prokofiev, Sergei 27, 272
Protero, Dodi 196
Puccini, Giacomo 25, 106, 203, 254, 286, 290, 295, 299, 315

Q
Quilico, Gino 107, 110

R
Raffanti, Dano 129, 202
Raimondi, Gianni 63, 65, 129, 244
Rankin, Nell 88
Rapp, Kenneth 123
Reagan, Ronald 249
Reggiani, Hilde 93
Reid, Cornelius 154, 179, 260
Rhodes, Michael 284
Ricci, Luigi 182
Roark-Strummer, Linda 259
Rocca, Lodovico 128
Rogatchewsky, Joseph 80
Rondinella, Giacomo 314
Rosing, Vladimir 170
Rossini, Gioachino 58, 135, 201–202, 206–207, 207, 209, 261, 304, 307, 322, 323, 324, 327
Rosvaenge, Helge 241, 285
Rota, Nino 128
Rózsa, Vera 249
Rubini, Giovanni Battista 135, 208–210, 219–221, 244, 300–303, 309, 333
Rysanek, Leonie 88

S
Santley, Sir Charles 259
Sayão, Bidú 170
Sbriglia, Giovanni 170
Scarlatti, Domenico 244
Schipa, Tito 72, 118, 120, 127, 129, 203, 219, 220, 295, 299, 329–330
Schmidt-Garre, Jan 319
Schoen-René, Anna Eugénie 249
Schubert, Franz 296
Schuman, Bill 21, 248–262, 265–268, 270, 271, 272–279
Schwarzkopf, Elisabeth 177
Scotto, Renata 76, 77, 79–83, 87–89, 96, 130, 150
Sebàstian, Bruno 181
Segava, Tosiko 125
Sellars, Peter 78–79, 85, 88
Semer, Neil 259
Serafin, Tullio 125, 257
Sereni, Mario 87, 88
Shane, Rita 106
Shicoff, Neil 79–81, 100, 106, 253, 278
Shirley, George 265–266
Siciliani, Francesco 27
Sills, Beverly 83, 106
Simionato, Giulietta 23–24, 88, 186, 219, 220, 321
Sinimberghi, Gino 124
Sirianni, Craig 259
Smirnoff, Dmitri 203
Spaneas, Demetrius 198
Stanley, Dr. Douglas 71–72, 179, 258–260
Stapp, Olivia 250
Stich-Randall, Theresa 111
Stignani, Ebe 91

Stillwell, Richard 249
Stokowski, Leopold 39
Streich, Rita 83
Studer, Cheryl 57, 58, 60, 112
Supervia, Conchita 177
Sutherland, Joan 24, 88, 130, 270, 304, 310

T

Tagliabue, Carlo 91
Tagliavini, Ferruccio 47, 69, 242, 244, 270, 314
Tamagno, Francesco 20, 122, 220, 221, 244, 319, 329
Tanner, Carl 250
Tebaldi, Renata 80, 85–86, 88, 90, 93, 94, 96, 98, 120, 130, 261
Te Kanawa, Kiri 249
Tetrazzini, Luisa 249
Theyard, Harry 105, 108
Thill, Georges 80, 243
Thomas, Indra 250
Tocyska, Stefania 85
Tonini, Antonio 177
Toscanini, Arturo 118
Tosi, Pier Francesco 206
Tosti, Francesco Paolo 325
Tucker, Richard 35, 66–67, 69, 247, 268, 281
Turrini, Roberto 45

V

Valenti, James 250, 250–251, 251, 253, 268–278, 329
van Berge, Joost 58
Vanzo, Alain 155
Varady, Julia 228
Vargas, Ramón 205, 253, 287, 321–327, 330
Verde, Annamarie 123
Verdi, Giuseppe 20, 58–60, 108, 118, 122, 125, 128, 129, 132, 139, 157, 202, 220, 232, 254, 290, 296, 299, 306, 315–327
Verrett, Shirley 106
Viardot, Pauline 249
Vickers, Jon 66–70, 240, 261, 281
Villazón, Rolando 114, 253, 286–290, 329
Viotti, Marcello 335
Visconti, Luchino 27
Viviani, Gabriele 304
Votto, Antonino 27, 125

W

Wagner, Wolfgang 99, 101
Walter, Bruno 118
Webber, Amherst 169
Woitach, Richard 100, 101
Wolf, Rosina 129
Wunderlich, Fritz 264

Y

Yeend, Frances 249

Z

Zadek, Hilde 223, 230–231
Zambòn, Amadeo 181
Zeani, Virginia 146, 272–274, 276–277
Zeritsky 41
Zimmerman, Mary 77, 308
Zucker, Stefan 30, 89, 111, 213, 275, 279